Whoever
saves one life ...

Whoever saves one life ...

The efforts to save Jews in Lithuania between 1941 and 1944

GENOCIDE AND RESISTANCE
RESEARCH CENTRE
OF LITHUANIA

garnelis
Vilnius 2002

UDK 947.45.082:933
Vh-09

This publication was financed by
the Genocide and Resistance Research Centre of Lithuania

Compiled by Dalia Kuodytė and Rimantas Stankevičius
Translated from the Lithuanian by Laima Junevičienė and Aldona Matulytė
English edition edited by Alexander Fortescue
Designed by Albertas Broga

ISBN 9955-428-23-6

Contents

RESCUED PEOPLE WRITING ABOUT THOSE WHO SAVED THEM

THE SEARCH FOR HISTORICAL TRUTH

"All I know is that man is capable of much more than we can imagine, for good and for the worst."

Samuel Bak

When the Nobel Prize winners in literature Wislawa Szymborska, Czeslaw Milosz and Günter Grass visited Vilnius in October 2000, they devoted much attention to the issues of historical memory during their meetings with the public. Tomas Venclova, a professor at Yale University, who was also with them, offered the following definition of memory at one of the meetings: "In a nation, as in man, I would like to see a quiet dignity, responsibility and fearless memory, which includes not only a perception of its offences but also of its own faults and debts".[1]

However, a fearless memory cannot live on offences, faults and debts alone. At the same time it should embrace the goodness done by an individual and the nation: to perceive, admit and present it not as an asset or reminder of somebody else's debts, but as a model for behaviour of a nation or an individual that should be followed and aspired to. Such an extended definition of a fearless memory is useful for looking at the complicated relations between the Lithuanians and the Jews in Lithuania between 1941 and 1944.

From this point of view, a simplified presentation of the extermination of the Jews during the war is unsatisfactory today when the whole responsibility for it is attributed only to the Nazis. As far back as 1946, the statement of the Supreme Committee for the Liberation of Lithuania (VLIK) "On the Issue of the Lithuanians and the Jews" had a separate section "The Page of Disgrace" devoted to the Lithuanians who had killed Jews.[2] Current research being

---

[1] *Kultūros barai*, 2000, No. 11, p. 58.

[2] Ibid., No. 8/9, p. 100.

conducted by the Lithuanian historians Valentinas Brandišauskas, Arūnas Bubnys, Liudas Truska, Alfonsas Eidintas, and data collected by the Commission for the Study of Crimes Committed by the Nazi and Soviet Regimes, and works by foreign historians, give us food for thought about the substantial role that Nazi collaborators played in exterminating the Lithuanian Jews.

The first days of the German invasion of Lithuania were marked by tragedy for the Jews. Around 130,000, out of a population of 209,000 before the war, were killed in the summer and autumn of 1941. According to Alfonsas Eidintas, in a speech to the Seimas (parliament) on 20 September 2001 on the occasion of the 60th anniversary of the beginning of the genocide of the Lithuanian Jews, "material in our archives suggests that by numbers alone local collaborators prevailed in the massacre of the Jews in Lithuania. This means that they killed more than half. This is the Lithuanian aspect of the tragedy of the Jews. We have to be aware of what all Litvaks [Lithuanian Jews] know: that the majority were killed by local police forces, Lithuanians who had become hangmen under the guidance and organisation of the Nazis. The number of those who participated amounted to two or three thousand or even more, and not just several hundred."[3] According to the historian Liudas Truska, "by the beginning of the war there were 6,000 soldiers in Lithuania; 2,000 had been taken to Russia. The Germans put the soldiers who remained in prison camps. A choice was put to them: either they serve in the police battalions or they starve to death in the camps. The majority agreed to serve in the police battalions ..."[4]

However, this is just another simplified version of the relations between the Jews and the Lithuanians during the war, which is often found in books published in New York, London or Jerusalem, in which it is written that the Lithuanians collaborated with the Nazis on a massive scale, and did little to rescue the Jews. This is not adequate today either.

In 1938, Jews who came from Austria had found refuge in Lithuania. They started coming in much larger numbers in 1939, when

---

[3] *Seimo kronika*, 1 October 2001, p. 1,427.

[4] The Days of Memory: International Conference Devoted to the 50th Anniversary of the Destruction of the Vilnius Ghetto, 11–16 October 1993, Vilnius, 1995, p. 477.

Germany had occupied Poland, when from 12,000 to 15,000 people poured into Lithuania and found refuge here (different sources provide different figures). According to Dr Yitzhak Arad:

> Many leaders of Polish Jewry arrived in Vilna with the refugees, including Dr M. Kleinbaum, Chairman of the Zionist Organisation in Poland, Dr Z. Warhaftig, one of the leaders of Mizrachi-Ha-Po'el ha Mizrachi, A. Bialopolski, a Po'alei Zion leader, Menahem Begin, who had been a Betar commander in Poland, S. Millman, a Bund leader, and others.[5]

According to Professor Yehuda Bauer:

> The old liberal people in the Lithuanian government were friendly and understanding. Unlike the Western states, the Lithuanians did not intern refugees, although they were facing a serious threat from the Soviets. Sooner or later, Lithuania would be eaten by Germany or the Soviet Union. Polish and Jewish refugees, as foreigners, had better chances of fleeing abroad.[6]

The Lithuanian state helped the Polish Jews and Polish refugees not only by providing them with shelter but also by issuing them with documents that had international legal authority.

This is evidenced by Moshe Kleinbaum's testimony: "I obtained a Lithuanian sauf conduit which allowed me to embark upon my journey via Riga, Stockholm, Copenhagen, Amsterdam, Brussels and Paris, and from there via Trieste to Palestine." The *New York Times* of 20 September 1994, writing about the Japanese consul Chiune Sugihara in Kaunas, printed a copy of one such document issued by the Lithuanian state (Series A No. 07398 issued to Izaak Levin on 15 July 1940). An example of a transit visa issued by the Lithuanian state can also be found in the book *One More Border* by William Kaplan and Shelley Tanaka.

The number of Jews who made use of transit visas issued in Lithuania is thought to have amounted to several thousand. Dr Arad states: "The number of Jews who left Lithuania during the period of

---

[5] Y. Arad, *Ghetto in Flames*, New York, 1982, p. 17.

[6] Y. Bauer, *A History of the Holocaust*, New York, 1982, p. 283.

Lithuanian and Soviet rule between March 1940 and 1941 has been estimated at 6,500."[7] A special exhibition "Flight and Rescue", held from 4 May 2000 to 21 October 2001 at the United States Holocaust Memorial Museum, testified to the help that the Lithuanian state provided to Polish Jews in 1939. A special display entitled "Temporary haven in Lithuania" said: "In the fall and winter of 1939, an estimated 15,000 Polish Jews found temporary refuge in politically independent Lithuania, most of them in Vilno. The majority belonged to a diverse, educated elite who faced persecution in war-torn Poland for their Jewish cultural, political and religious affiliation." A Lithuanian permit (sauf conduit) Series A No. 08484 issued in Kaunas on 8 July 1940 to the lawyer Zorach Warhaftig was presented as an illustration of this.

The position taken by Lithuania at that time was not limited to granting a safe haven to the refugees and issuing them with permits. According to Dr D. Jasaitis, "when Nazi Germany started persecuting the Jews, the government of Lithuania had protested on several occasions. Three protests were sent: 1) concerning the Nazi decree of 26 April 1938 obliging Jews to register their property; 2) concerning the pogrom on *Kristallnacht* on 8–10 November; 3) concerning Ordinance 385 of 12 November 1938 (Documents on German Foreign Policy (D.G.F.P.) Series D.V., No. 656)."

However, in the summer of 1940, as a result of the Molotov-Ribbentrop Pact, Lithuania lost its statehood and became a part of the USSR. From that time on, a dramatic new period for its citizens, including the Jews, started.

Yves Plasseraud wrote:

Following the Molotov-von-Ribbentrop Pact, in June 1940 the Red Army invaded Lithuania. When the Soviets arrived, they were frequently greeted by local communists and sympathisers; among them was a sizeable proportion of Jews who had previously constituted the bulk of the local revolutionary parties. Furthermore, a number of Litvaks were subsequently associated in one way or another with the Soviet power (including the Political Police, the NKVD administration with its famous director Todes) ... This faith was simply absent for

---

[7] Y. Arad, op. cit., p. 25.

most of their countrymen who did not share their views on internationalism, remembered the exactions of the GPU in 1918, and suspected what the Soviet occupation meant for their country.[8]

On 14–15 June 1941 the deportation of many Lithuanian citizens was carried out, when 30,000 inhabitants (including 5,000 to 6,000 Jews) were deported to western Siberia, Kazakhstan, Altai and Karelia. As a result,

> The Soviet regime, which had always been unpopular, now incurred even greater animosity. Although there were thousands of Jews among those deported, the measures led to an increase in hatred of the Jews, as they constituted a fairly large proportion of those in the local government and the Communist Party. During this period of alarm and fear over further deportations and the growing rancour against the Soviet order and the Jews, the Germans invaded the Soviet Union.[9]

According to many contemporary historians, the cause of the worsened relations between Lithuanians and Jews in 1940–1941 was the fact that the Lithuanians and the Jews were of diametrically opposed geopolitical orientations at that time. After Lithuania had been incorporated into the USSR, the Lithuanians placed their hopes for survival and regaining their statehood on Germany's help. However, the arrival of the Germans meant a deadly threat to the Jews in Lithuania. Such was the background of relations between Lithuanians and Jews when the Germans entered Lithuania.

Could the Jews be saved under such circumstances? If people were rescued, why were they? What was the scale of the rescues? Who participated, and who did they save?

It would seem that the nearly six decades that have passed since these events should be a sufficient period of time to find an answer to these and many other questions. Unfortunately, a lot of time was lost before a detailed investigation into the issue of rescuing Jews began. The introduction to Avraham Tory's book *The Kaunas Ghetto: From Day to Day*, written by Saulius Sužiedėlis, goes as follows:

---

[8] *The Days of Memory*, Yves Plasseraud, p. 350.

[9] Y. Arad, op. cit., p. 27.

"Unfortunately, such a complicated past sometimes makes history assessed in a perfunctory and categorical way, emphasising only one aspect of the issue and without going deeper into the essence of the problem and without trying to present a comprehensive, even if contradictory, view of the time."[10]

Moreover, the historian Lucy S. Dawidowicz states: "The memories of the Jews who went through the Holocaust are often tainted by hatred and feeling. The view of events is often compromised by personal experience."[11] Perhaps the memories of the Lithuanians who lived through the Holocaust and other tragedies can be defined in a similar way. Probably the nationalities of the authors writing on this theme often had a strong influence on their presentation of the issue, the conclusions they made and the emphasis they applied. Of course, in reading the writings of both Jews and Lithuanians, it is important to remember the context and experience, and to take these into account in making assessments.

The time that has passed allows us to look at the issue of rescuing Jews without encouraging prejudice, and with less emotion and more information, and to review what has been written on the subject by Lithuanian émigrés, in the press in occupied Lithuania, and in the work of foreign authors.

***

Material about the issue of rescuing Jews began to be collected and covered in the Lithuanian émigré press right after the war. The first detailed work was the report by Sofija Lukauskaitė-Jasaitienė in Germany, submitted to the VLIK on 15 May 1946, which formed part of the broader report "On the Issue of the Lithuanians and the Jews".[12] The report provided answers to questions as to why it was so difficult to rescue Jews and their children, how to organise an escape, what documents were needed, whether much initiative was shown by the

---

[10] A. Tory, *Kauno getas: diena po dienos*, Vilnius, 2000, p. XXI.

[11] *The Case of the Massacre of the Lithuanian Jews*, p. 659.

[12] *Kultūros barai*, 2000, No. 11, p. 76.

Jews themselves, etc. The author described rescues that she knew about, and mentioned the names of the rescuers: "Of the people I knew in Šiauliai, similar rescue work was carried out by the family of the late lawyer K. Venclauskas, Dr Luinienė, Fr Lapis, Fr Byla, Fr Dzegoraitis, the Jesuits, Dr Prialgauskas, the parish priest at Kužiai Fr Kleiba, the deputy mayor Pauža, H. Kildišius, the agronomist Ibianskis, and J. Sondeckis." The author also stated that "as people rescued not only Jews that they knew but also some who were total strangers to them, many circumstances and cases of rescues have been forgotten. I am also deeply convinced that the number of Lithuanians who rescued Jews from death and gave them help in Šiauliai totalled hundreds, and perhaps even thousands."[13]

The fact that Sofija Lukauskaitė-Jasaitienė was not an outside observer or an engaged assessor of the events that she described add plausibility to her statements. She was an active participant in the work of rescuing Jews in Šiauliai, and her name is mentioned by many authors in their work.

In 1947 and 1948, questionnaires entitled "What do you know about help given to the Jews during the Nazi occupation?" were filled in and collected in Gross Hesep, Rothenburg, Weiden and other displaced persons camps in Germany. Cases of rescuing Jews, and information about their rescuers from all over Lithuania, were recorded in them. A note attached to the questionnaire stated: "This questionnaire must be filled in as precisely and as soon as possible. [...] In case of need, information can be provided by the Board of the Centre of the Lithuanian Union of Former Political Prisoners of the Anti-Nazi Resistance." Up to the present day, 231 questionnaires, some with more and some with less detailed answers about the rescue of Jews, are preserved and stored in the archives of Kent University in the USA. They contain over 500 names of rescuers of Jews, and over 1,200 names of people rescued.

A series of articles entitled "Lithuanians in the Struggle for the Freedom of the Jews" about rescuing Jews, written by Juozas Šalna, was published in the newspaper *Naujienos*, printed in Chicago, in 1948 and 1949. The author discussed the circumstances that formed in Lithuania following the Soviet occupation that were unfavourable

---

[13] Ibid., p. 78.

to rescuing Jews, and declared that, "despite this situation, many Lithuanians from various social groups immediately became involved in the rescue of Jews, saving them from death, and hiding them and standing up for them wherever possible. [...] However, a large number of rescuers stayed in Lithuania, and those who were deported felt it was too early to disclose what they remembered."[14]

The following thought expressed by Juozas Šalna sounds interesting even today:

> The struggle by Lithuanians for the freedom of the Jews constitutes a three-year-long story of heroism. Up to the present day, it has not been objectively revealed. Lithuanians did not take up the cause, and some Jews engaged merely in spreading blame. They remembered just one or two Lithuanians and said a good word about them. They regarded all other Lithuanians as collaborators of the Nazis and, consequently, as murderers of Jews. I hope that the facts that I have presented here will make sober-minded Jews come to their senses, and remember other help that has not been mentioned here and give a correct assessment of the struggle by Lithuanians for the freedom of the Jews. This is of great importance to both Lithuanians and Jews. In the future they will have to meet and cooperate. Those Jews who remained in Lithuania or who return will have to cooperate in re-establishing their common motherland. A deciding word in this matter will rest with the Jews who survived thanks to Lithuanians. Blood shed by Lithuanians in the struggle for the freedom of the Jews, and their sufferings in prisons and concentration camps, cannot be so easily forgotten. They have to put right the lies spread in their writings and books about Lithuanians. They themselves have to make public the consequences of the help provided by Lithuanians on a massive scale. I wish they would do it. The sooner the better.[15]

In the section "All Lithuania Gives Help to Persecuted Jews" Šalna presented lists of people who rescued and who were rescued in small Lithuanian towns and regions. A total of over 500 rescuers and about 1,200 names of rescued Jews was mentioned. Šalna mentioned the names of rescuers of Jews who are well known today

---

[14] J. Šalna, "Lietuvių kova dėl žydų laisvės", *Naujienos*, 28 May 1949, No. 195.
[15] Ibid.

(Ona Šimaitė, Bronius Gotautas, Juozas Stakauskas, Juozas Rutkauskas, and others) and gave a detailed description of the episodes of rescuing Jews that were made public in Lithuania in the book *Soldiers without Weapons* compiled by Sofija Binkienė only a few decades later.[16]

Šalna also gave the names of Lithuanians who were shot dead or suffered in other ways for saving Jews, as well as the names of Jews that were rescued. "Two Lithuanians, young girls, hid and took care of the physician Levinas in Žalioji gatvė in Kaunas. Later the Gestapo found out, and both girls, together with Dr Levinas, were shot." The Jablonskis family, consisting of three people, were arrested in the Old Town of Kaunas for hiding and looking after Jews, and were shot in the place for shooting Jews." "The Germans shot dead Jasaitienė, together with the Jews that she hid in Raseiniai," and so on.

Comparing the data in the questionnaires that were filled out in Germany with the data presented in Juozas Šalna's articles, we can say that most accounts tally.

The subject of rescuing Jews is given much consideration in the articles "Lithuanians – Rescuers of Jews being Exterminated" written by Mykolas Krupavičius.[17] The author wrote about priests he knew personally who saved Jews. He provided a detailed description of the rescue work carried out by Domas Jasaitis and Sofija Jasaitienė in Šiauliai, and provided examples of rescues of Jews in several places in Lithuania. In summarising, Krupavičius drew the conclusion that, "the whole Lithuanian nation with its surviving organisations and institutions, members of the former government, the Catholic Church, the press, political parties and the whole public was opposed to the Nazi policy and practices applied to the Jews, supported them, rescued them and sympathised with them."[18] The author was one of the three people who signed the letter to von Renteln, the German general consul for Lithuania, in 1942, which declared that the Lithuanian nation did not approve of the measures taken by the Germans against the Lithuanian Jews. For this Krupavičius was deported to Germany.

---

[16] S. Binkienė, *Ir be ginklo kariai*, Vilnius, 1967.

[17] See *Tėviškės žiburiai*, 1962, No. 6–10.

[18] Ibid., No. 7.

However, today the conclusions presented in the article appear one-sided. The documents available do not allow us to draw such optimistic conclusions. The decree by the provisional government on 1 August 1941 "Regulations on the Condition of the Jews" and others can hardly be regarded as proof of favour shown to the Jews and opposition to the Nazis. The words of the letter of the bishops of Lithuania written on 14 April 2000 reflect the position of the Catholic Church at that time more accurately:

> We regret that during the Second World War some of the children of the Church lacked love for the persecuted Jews, did not make use of all possible means to protect them, and especially that they lacked the resolution to exert influence over those who collaborated with the Nazis. The memory of the Church is burdened by all manifestations of past anti-Semitism which people devoid of responsibility and Christian love try to instigate even nowadays. We regret that children of the Church, due to human weakness, fear or even personal benefit, did not only accept the crimes committed by the occupying regimes, neglecting their religious, moral and political duties, but also assisted the oppressors.

In volume 35 of the *Lietuvių enciklopedija* published in Boston in 1966, we can find information about rescues of Jews:

> The Lithuanian nation strongly condemned the brutal massacres of Jews and did its utmost to save them. [...] It was impossible to intercede for the Jews in public or to set up committees for rescuing them: many a Lithuanian who addressed German officials by interceding for the Jews was told clearly that a similar fate would befall them. [...] The Lithuanian nation was indignant at the behaviour of the Germans, and many priests, doctors and others, putting their lives at risk, started rescuing Jews individually. The number of Lithuanians who became victims themselves by rescuing Jews is large and impossible to count. Despite the efforts made by Lithuanians in rescuing Jews, often by putting their lives at risk, false accusations are being made today against the Lithuanian nation in the international Jewish press and Bolshevik-occupied Lithuania for murdering Jews in Lithuania. The fact that some Lithuanians rescued Jews at the risk of their own lives is passed over in silence.[19]

---

[19] *Lietuvių enciklopedija*, Boston, 1966, Vol. 35, p. 293.

A new wave of interest in the theme of the rescue of Jews arose in the American-Lithuanian press in 1975.

Jackus Sonda (he is mentioned in the *Encyclopaedia Judaica* and other publications in which lists of rescuers are given) in his article "How a Famous Theatre Critic was Saved" wrote the following:

> There are many Jews who accuse Lithuanians of not rescuing Jews from the extermination carried out by the Nazis, and even of helping them in it. Only one or two examples of rescuing Jews are mentioned in passing. Anyone who is familiar with the situation in Lithuania at that time knows that all Lithuanians are unfairly accused, because the whole nation cannot be responsible for the crimes committed by a small group. If we condemned people in such a sweeping way today the whole German nation would still be in prison for the crimes committed during the war.
>
> The number of Lithuanians who saved Jews from death, or helped them in any other way during the time of the German occupation, is quite high; however, nobody has collected and made public these facts so far because people who made up their minds to rescue Jews, thus putting their lives at risk, are not the kind of people who would boast of their noble and dangerous deeds. However, when the blame is placed on the whole Lithuanian nation, they feel it is their duty to respond.[20]

Other authors also wrote about issues of rescuing Jews: Dr Petras Vileišis ("On the Issue of the Lithuanian Jews"), Stepas Jakubickas ("How Lithuanians Rescued Jews"), Vladas Bakūnas ("Notes from Afar"), K. Gintautas ("We Slept when We were Birched") and others.

Consequently, up till 1977, many facts about rescuing Jews in Lithuania were collected and made public in the American-Lithuanian press, and many thoughts about it were expressed. Following the first attempts to collect data in 1947–1948, material about rescuing Jews was later collected and published, mostly in defence against accusations made in the press that the Lithuanian nation must bear responsibility for the annihilation of the Jews during

---

[20] Dr Domas Jasaitis' archive, American Lithuanian Archives (ALKA), Putnam, Connecticut.

the war. In 1947 a resolution concerning the responsibility of the Lithuanians for the massacre of Jews during the war in Lithuania was passed. It read as follows:

> We, several thousands of rescued Lithuanian Jews who currently reside in the American Zone in Germany, at our first conference, held on 15 April of this year in Munich, passed the following resolution about the guilt of a large part of the Lithuanian nation in exterminating the Jews in Lithuania. The Conference stated that: A. All strata of Lithuanian society (the intelligentsia, officials, farmers, tradesmen, workers and others), together with the Nazis, took an active part in killing Lithuanian Jews, in the provinces in particular; B. A large number of those murderers reside in the American, English or French zones in Germany or Austria, where they are regarded as DPs (displaced people) and make use of assistance provided by UNRRA. The Conference calls on the newly elected Board of the Union to inform the public about the atrocities which large numbers of Lithuanians committed during the time of the German occupation, and about the massacre of their Jewish countrymen in particular.
>
> We, constituting the meagre remaining part of the former 160,000 Lithuanian Jews, have survived those terrible atrocities committed by the Lithuanians against their Jewish neighbours. Each of us can present ample evidence to illustrate the appalling cruelty on the Lithuanian side against their defenceless and helpless Jewish countrymen during the occupation ...[21]

Though it was suggested more than once that the American-Lithuanian press carry out a detailed study about rescuing Jews, this was not done. As has been mentioned, the issue of rescuing Jews was most often raised in defence against accusations that Lithuanians had participated in killing Jews. The editorial of *Tėviškės žiburiai* of 27 May 1976 writes:

> If the Lithuanian Jews take the Lithuanians to court with their accusations, we should not object. Since the Jews have written a lot about the Lithuanians' guilt, and in many different languages, Lithuanians must give their opinion too ... Somehow no institution has undertaken to organise such work ... Though it is late, we should

---

[21] *Mūsų Vytis*, 1992, No. 4, p. 23.

all get to work and prepare a comprehensive study in English and other languages. The facts revealed would show that many accusations against the Lithuanians are ungrounded. There might have been criminals; however, the number of rescuers of Jews was much greater. The Jewish nation itself did not lack criminals either.

Lithuanian immigrants in the USA probably did not know yet at that time that the accusations being made against the Lithuanian nation were not accidental or spontaneous, but constituted part of a well-organised plan. This is proven by a document sent from Vilnius to the Soviet security official O. Netchiporenka in Moscow on 29 July 1980, which read as follows:

Of late in publications in the national press which are distributed abroad (including in the English language), we have systematically published material about participants in criminal formations that have recently come to light, who fled the USSR in 1944, and have recently taken up residence in Western countries, mostly the USA.

All this material was noticed by Jewish society in the West, and was used in the newsletter of the Union of Lithuanian Jews in Israel *Gachalet*, in the information publication of Yad Vashem, and periodicals in Brazil, Canada and the USA, in which the Lithuanians were accused of the mass murder of Jews during the Second World War.

These publications caused a reciprocal reaction among Lithuanian émigrés; they in their turn accused the Jews of committing "serious crimes against the Lithuanian nation during the time of the establishment of Soviet power" (in 1940–1941); it was mainly participation in the deportations of anti-Soviet elements to other regions of the country and common actions taken in cooperation with Moscow to compromise honest immigrants.

On our instruction, an appeal to Jewish families who fell victim during the Second World War will be issued and forwarded to Israel through a reliable person, J.R., who maintains contacts in writing with influential Zionists and journalists in Israel. The appeal will urge the launch of a campaign against the persons mentioned and other participants in criminal groups and their defenders by national organisations of Lithuanian immigrants.[22]

---

[22] «Предложения по активным мероприятиям в связи с попытками консолидации сионистов с литовской националистической эмиграцией», 29 July 1980, 1/3923.

The results of this organised activity were clearly felt. This is shown by the editorial "Concentrating the Defence" published in *Tėviškės žiburiai* issue No. 2 (1405) on 13 January 1977. It reads:

> In 1976 a new propagandist and legal offensive was started in the USA by accusing some people and threatening them with court action and deportation. This action received a sharp response in the international press, television and radio ... The Lithuanians, as a society and a nation, were offended by Dr Dov Levin, director of the Jewish Institute in Jerusalem, who published an accusing article in English in the publication *Journal of Baltic Studies*. The article was reprinted in *Tėviškės žiburiai* and provoked a strong reaction among readers. Summarising the ideas of the readers, it was stated that as long as Lithuania was free, the Jews had had complete political security and cultural freedom. With the collapse of independent Lithuania the freedom and protection of the Jews came to an end; many Jews who were brought up in independence contributed to the burial of independent Lithuania. Nationalist Germany, which ruled Lithuania at that time, was responsible for the extermination of the Jews; only a small number of Lithuanians took part in the action carried out by the German units, and therefore the Lithuanians as a nation cannot take responsibility for it. Many Lithuanians, putting their own lives at risk, rescued Jews; however, Jews pay little attention to this fact.
>
> The necessity for the voice of the Lithuanians to reach world opinion was emphasised. Silence would mean guilt, and an attempt to hide. There is no need to hide. We have to look the world in the face because guilt lies with both parties.

The following thought, full of anger, is found in the pages of this book: "We do not think that we have to make an inventory of our goodness". In fact the accusations have encouraged us "to make an inventory" of our goodness. Thus, in this case the saying "every cloud has a silver lining" could be paraphrased as follows: there was evil (the massacres), one should look for goodness (rescuers). At that time the rescues were important to the American-Lithuanian community, as a counterbalance to the accusations.

As a form of defence against the accusations, it was planned to publish a book about rescuing Jews in Lithuania:

> It has already turned out that the Lithuanian Institute of Investigation, encouraged by the VLIK, agreed to prepare a work in co-operation with Dr Domas Jasaitis (who has written on this theme before). The Reverend

Dr J. Prunskis was asked to prepare the publication about rescuing Lithuanian Jews. The writer and editor A. Baronas has written a book on this issue without waiting for the initiative of political subjects. Bishop V. Brizgys, who lived through the Soviet and Nazi occupations himself, has also written his memoirs, of which he devoted a significant part to the Jewish issue. All these publications are already being translated or will be translated into the English language. Hence, we are on the right track. However, as long as these do not get international publicity, we should remember that publications of this sort must be documentary, of an academic nature rather than propagandist, which, first and foremost, should tell the truth. One serious disadvantage is that the documentation available is mainly in the Lithuanian language. However, the most serious obstacle is that we have no access to the European and American press. It is only with their help that we would be able to refute the accusations of crimes that we did not commit during the Nazi occupation.

Domas Jasaitis was to be one of the authors of the book planned. His publications "The Tragedy of the Jews in Lithuania under the Nazi Occupation", "The Nazi and Communist Genocide in Lithuania" and others contain many facts and thoughts about rescuing Jews, especially in Šiauliai, where he himself was involved in it. In answer to the article "Lithuanians' Past Shameful", published in the *Miami Herald* on 31 May 1972, he wrote:

> In 1939, after Poland had fallen, about 12,000 Jews came to Lithuania Lithuania provided a safe haven to all of them, took care of them and helped those who wanted to go to other countries. The Lithuanians were later unable to curb the violence committed on their land. Severe punishments were imposed for providing any kind of help to the Jews. Many Lithuanians were condemned to death for it. A large number found themselves in concentration camps or were deported to do forced labour in the Reich. Had they not helped the Jews who were driven into ghettos on a massive scale, all of the Jews would have starved to death, because the food ration was designed to starve them. Lithuanians saved thousands of Jewish children, and hid them till the end of the Nazi occupation in 1944.[23]

Judging from the correspondence, the book being prepared was to be written at the end of 1977.

---

[23] Domas Jasaitis' letter to the *Miami Herald*, ALKA, Putnam, Connecticut.

Jasaitis wrote about the work in *Naujienos* in 1977:

The fact that we are denied access to documentary material stored in occupied Lithuania and that it is impossible to contact thousands of people living there who, putting their lives at risk, provided all kinds of help to Jews persecuted by the SS and the Gestapo, makes the work very difficult and sometimes absolutely impossible ... Also, the financial situation of our émigrés cannot compare with that of the Jews ... However, despite these difficulties, the main part of the work has already been done. Factual material is missing for the last part – when, where and how the oppressed Lithuanians rescued Jews being exterminated. Lithuanians, help us to complete this work.[24]

The archive put together by Jasaitis contains a letter written to him on 11 March 1977 by Fr Juozas Prunskis. It records the efforts made to collect material about the rescuers of Jews and accusations against the Lithuanians, as well as the results of these efforts. The priest wrote that he wanted to publish a book in English of statements made by Jews. "Unfortunately, I received only two such statements, which were quite different from what I wanted to receive ... I have addressed Jews rescued by Lithuanians by letter and by telephone who currently reside in the USA, Canada, Mexico and Israel. However, I was greatly disappointed by the results." In another letter, of 8 August the same year, Prunskis wrote:

I have written to the writer Meras, who writes in the Lithuanian press. First, he said that he was very busy with other things. I suggested that he could be paid ten dollars per page of manuscript. By receiving a fee he would be able to give up other work. Unfortunately, [...] he could not make up his mind whether or not to take up this offer. Later, when we received answers from Jews residing in Israel we understood why he avoided having his say. There was pressure from them.

Unfortunately, Jasaitis failed to complete the work he had started; it was brought to an end by his death, on 6 June 1977. The material gathered about the relations between the Lithuanians and the Jews in the pre-war period and during the war was stored for a

---

[24] D. Jasaitis, "Lietuvių ir žydų naikinimas", *Naujienos*, 1977.

long time, until some of it was moved to Lithuania in 1998–2000, and at present it is stored in the archives of the Genocide and Resistance Research Centre. The rest of the material is stored in Putnam and the archive of Kent University, USA.

The situation described in Jasaitis' article is worth remembering: "Secrecy is a major requirement to any successful underground activity, but it is the enemy of history in that it does not usually leave any documented information." This explanation is especially apt for describing the saving of Jews. The slightest breach of secrecy at the time resulted in the death of the rescuer. Letters published in this book of documents testify to this. Vanda Sruogienė wrote: "My husband helped Jews a lot at the time of their persecution by the Nazis, both those he knew and some he did not know. However, I would not now be able to say accurately whom he rescued, or how in such turbulent times we would often keep our underground work secret from each other, as we were both liable to be arrested (he as a famous person in Lithuania, and me as a director of a gymnasium)" [p. 111]. Secrecy was one of the factors which created a contradictory picture. Due to the secrecy, many an episode in the rescue of Jews remains unknown.

This book attempts to bring to light the legacy of Domas Jasaitis, who was a prominent personality, and his work on relations between Lithuanians and Jews, to which he devoted many years. Letters published in the book reveal the dramatic nature of the process of rescuing Jews, the motivation for people's behaviour, and many other things which were not always pleasant. Alongside the noble deeds, modesty and devotion, the letters reveal betrayals, neglect and proof of participation in massacres of Jews.

The original purpose of collecting letters and articles was to illustrate the work in rescuing Jews, and to make certain generalisations. Today each letter or article included in this book and which has not been previously published has an independent value and meaning.

What is valuable is that these letters tell us how difficult it was for people to make up their minds: "I hesitated between fear and courage, between selfishness and moral responsibility [...] in short, between acceptance of the genocide and my duty to humanity" [p. 132].

Letters published in this book are also a gift to the part of the Jewish community which wishes to remember what was good, to see the positive moments in relations between the two nations.

When reading these letters it often becomes clear that the idea to collect data about the rescue of Jews was started too late. "It is a pity that this matter has been delayed. We should have started collecting information right upon our arrival in the USA and to publicise it a long time ago. Now we are in a sad defensive position," wrote Vanda Sruogienė.

The situation is none the easier now, after another quarter century has passed; therefore, Domas Jasaitis' appeal: "Lithuanians, help us to complete this work" is still urgent today.

Jasaitis' appeal was in essence intended for émigré Lithuanians. He could not know then that he would not be able to complete what he had planned to do. By issuing this appeal he expected to receive letters, information about rescuing Jews. Of course, the work could not be completed by the efforts of émigrés alone. Jasaitis understood that very well: important information (what had already been collected and what had not yet been collected) was in Lithuania. It is true that after the war an attempt was made to collect testimonies about rescuing Jews in occupied Lithuania by the Jewish Museum; however, not enough interest was taken in the issue. It was only in 1967 that Sofija Binkienė, one of the Righteous Gentiles, compiled and published the book *Soldiers without Weapons* in which about 400 names of rescuers of Jews and those rescued were mentioned. She writes:

> Though I tried to collect as much material as possible about many people, this is far from everything. Every day I learn about new soldiers without weapons who acted in different corners of our republic. And nobody knows the number of those who will perhaps remain unknown forever: some have died (both the rescuers and the people they took care of), and others have found themselves in foreign countries. Many of them, on the whole, had no chance to tell anyone anywhere about themselves; others thought that they had simply been fulfilling their moral duty.

This is how the situation is described in a very concise and exact manner in Lithuania at that time.

After Binkienė's work was published there was a long pause, which lasted till 1979. Then the article "On Rescuing Lithuanian Jews in the Years of the Nazi Occupation (1941–1945)" by Kazys Rukšėnas appeared in *The Yearbook of Lithuanian History 1978*. Several names of people who rescued Jews were mentioned in the article. Some were the same as in Sofija Binkienė's book. The article contained some very convincing statements such as: "At the beginning of 1942 the chief of the German Security Police and SD wrote the following about the fate of the Jews in Lithuania in his report to Riga: 'The intelligentsia is helping the Lithuanians to change their views. They are already providing help to the Jews'."[25] Rukšėnas also admitted the following:

It is impossible to give the exact number of Lithuanians who rescued Jews during the years of the Nazi occupation and how many Jews were rescued. No exact documentation is available, and naturally there cannot be any. Moreover, since many witnesses have been killed, died or went to live in foreign countries, many cases of rescuing Jews remain unknown altogether. Some modest rescuers of Jews prefer not to publicise it.

The author could not, of course, write that one indispensable condition for being included in the list of rescuers was to be "progressive", that is, to hold communist views or at least to be tolerant of the regime. Many rescuers of Jews who fled to the West could not be listed, because they were not "progressive". They were regarded as "representatives of the bourgeoisie". Many priests, whose number, to the best of our knowledge, totalled 185, could not be put on the list of rescuers. Rescuers who were persecuted and deported to Siberia were also excluded.

Hence, it is quite clear that Sofija Binkienė's book and Kazys Rukšėnas' article were written under conditions of political censorship. Despite the fact that quite a number of names of rescuers were published, the works could not reflect the real situation regarding the rescue of Jews in Lithuania during the war.

In 1990, after independence was re-established in Lithuania, the possibility emerged to turn over new pages in our history, both painful and pleasant, and to interpret them.

---

[25] Central State Archive of the Latvian SSR (f. P-1026, ap. 1, b. 3, l. 265, 275).

The efforts of M. Erenburg to gather information about rescuing Jews at the Vilnius Jewish Museum should be regarded as the realisation of this possibility. In 1992 the Division for the Perpetuation of Rescuing and Memory of the Jews was opened there. Material brought from Šiauliai then formed the basis of the present archive about rescuing Jews. Erenburg received some of the material from L. Libšic who lived in Šiauliai, J. Ronder in Kaunas and E. Jacovskis in Vilnius.

Later the material about rescuers began to be supplemented when letters were sent to the known rescuers and the rescued, and answers received from them. About 400 letters sent out in a year gave results. The award the Cross for Saving People under Threat of Death, established in 1993 in Lithuania, provided an incentive to submit information about rescuing Jews. The award, which was conferred once, and since 1999 twice, a year, increased interest in the subject and helped to reveal many episodes of rescues.

The manuscript of the article "Lithuanians in the Struggle for the Freedom of the Jews" written by Liudvikas Šmulkštys that Romualdas Ozolas received from Dr Kazys Pemkus, brought from the USA and published in the newspaper *Atgimimas*, was a great help in elucidating the issue of rescuing Jews during the war in independent Lithuania. In 1996, Viktorija Sakaitė brought copies of the questionnaires filled out in Germany in 1947–1948. She had obtained them from Jonas Dainauskas, a researcher into relations between the Lithuanians and the Jews in the USA.

Another work about rescuing Jews came from Canada, the book *Lists of A. Gurevičius* published in 1999. It became an additional source in elucidating the scale of the rescue of Jews in Lithuania.

Following several years of work, with the help of sources available in Lithuania and those brought from the USA and Canada, the Vilna Gaon State Jewish Museum researcher Viktorija Sakaitė, and other researchers at the museum, managed to reveal nearly 1,000 cases of rescuing Jews, and the names of the rescuers.

Currently, the number of names on the list of known rescuers totals nearly 3,000.

According to the reminiscences of the artist Samuel Bak, one of those rescued in Vilnius, who currently lives in Weston, USA, in order to survive, ten miracles had to be performed. Nine miracles were not enough. Most of the people who wrote these letters or whose names are on the list of good deeds were performers of those miracles.

***

Reminiscences, books and articles written by Jews who were rescued or managed to save themselves and who now live in different parts of the world contain not only the untold sufferings that they had to endure but also information and thoughts about rescuing Jews. Such information is also found in works written by historians and in encyclopaedias.

In 1949 an article by Joseph L. Lichter appeared in *Laisvė* and *Naujienos*. It was a response to the publications written under the name of Juozas Šalna. The following statement was made in them:

> Information about the small number of Jews who were rescued by individual Lithuanians received the widest coverage in the Jewish press and Jewish public life ... Every Lithuanian who saved a Jew was spoken about with the greatest respect, for he was not only threatened with arrest by the Germans but also denunciation by his Lithuanian neighbours and being handed over to German officials ... The Lithuanians who helped Jews during that dangerous period did so on the basis of humanitarian, political or religious motives. Some of them did it for money ... However, the following fact is very important from a historical point of view: the number of such people was very small.[26]

This statement decided the position of some strata of the Jewish community on the issue of the Jews in Lithuania for a long time, and is still believed.

J. Gar wrote: "To get a more complete view it is necessary to mention people with a clear conscience among the Lithuanians who held out a helping hand to the Jews during the time of the Nazi atrocities, putting their own lives at risk. The number of such Lithuanians is very small."[27]

As far back as 1957, Isaac Kowalski wrote in his book *A Secret Press in Nazi Europe* about the university staff who raised money for the Vilnius ghetto. They were Mykolas Biržiška, Jurgaitis, Antanas

---

[26] *Laisvė*, 27 January 1949.

[27] *Книга о русском еврействе, 1917–1960*, New York, 1968, p. 110.

Žvironas, Levas Karsavinas and Vosylius Sezemanas. The book contains information about the rescuers J. Rutkauskas, Fr Juozas Stakauskas, Vladas Žemaitis and Marija Mikulska.[28]

The chapter "The Woman's Heart" in the book *Their Brothers' Keepers* contains a broad description of Ona Šimaitė's activities in rescuing Jews, and conveys her thoughts expressed during her visit to Israel: "For me, as a Lithuanian, it is a very sad thing to admit that not all of my compatriots, at the time of the Jewish ordeal, showed compassion towards the victims. To my great sorrow, it must be admitted that some elements collaborated in the extermination of the Jews."[29] The nuns of the Benedictine convent, Fr A. Gdowski, Bishop Mečislovas Reinys, Mykolas Krupavičius, Fr Juozas Stakauskas, Marija Mikulska and Vladas Žemaitis are mentioned as rescuers in the book. It provides information about Fr Jonas of Viduklė for the first time who was killed together with 30 Jewish children that he had hidden in the church.[30] In his book *Ghetto in Flames*, Yitzhak Arad, when writing about hiding and rescuing Jews in Vilnius, classifies people according to their attitude towards Jews and the extermination of them. Some helped to rescue Jews, others collaborated with the Germans, and others stood by. The rescuers formed the smallest part. "The third and the smallest group contained anything up to a few hundred people, mostly Poles and several Lithuanians."[31]

A three-volume work published in 1974 in New York in four languages *The Jerusalem of Lithuania* devotes only a few pages to the subject of saving Jews; it carries photographs of Juozas Stakauskas, Marija Mikulska, Ona Šimaitė, Sofija Binkienė, M. Abramovič-Wolska, J. Bartoševič, M. Jurkutaitis, and other people.[32]

Historians also became interested in the subject in Lithuania. On 8–11 April 1974 the Second Yad Vashem International Conference "Rescue Attempts during the Holocaust" was held in Israel. A report "Rescues in Lithuania during the Nazi Occupation" by Sarah

---

[28] I. Kowalski, *A Secret Press in Nazi Europe*, New York, 1957.

[29] P. Friedman, *Their Brothers' Keepers*, New York, 1957, p. 25.

[30] Ibid., p. 21–26.

[31] Y. Arad, op. cit., New York, 1982, p. 132.

[32] *The Jerusalem of Lithuania*, Vol. 2, New York, 1974, p. 470–472.

Neshamit, who was born in Seinai and studied in Kaunas and Vilnius, was included on the agenda of the conference.[33] In her report the help given to the Jews was attributed to the political situation, and the victories and losses of the Nazis in the war, rather than to the human qualities of the rescuers. Attempts were made to answer the question why even in anti-Semitic Poland an underground organisation for rescuing Jews was formed, whereas Lithuania had none. In the opinion of the author of the report, the reason was that Poland was a country simply occupied by the Nazis, whereas the Nazis had been greeted as liberators in Lithuania. After mentioning Juozas Straupis, Juozas Audiejus, Vytautas Žakavičius, Vladas Šleževičius, Bronius Gotautas, Petras Baublys and several other people who saved Jews, the author drew the conclusion that there were only a few Lithuanians who had rescued Jews, and that the number of people they saved was very insignificant. "A few Lithuanians who deserve the title of Righteous Gentile cannot expiate the sins that many of their countrymen committed."[34] And nearly 20 years later, Sarah Neshamit submitted the text of her report to a conference held on 11–14 October 1993 in Vilnius where she stated: "In Israel we respect and worship those Lithuanians who tried to rescue my countrymen who were persecuted and killed during those terrible years of atrocity and helped them in any possible way … It is sad that the number of Righteous Gentiles is relatively small compared to the number of murderers. The majority were absolutely indifferent to the sufferings and deaths of Jews."[35]

The relations between the Lithuanians and the Jews and the circumstances of rescuing Jews in Lithuania is described in the same way in works that appeared later. The book *The Jews of Lithuania: A History of a Remarkable Community 1316–1945* by Masha Greenbaum, published in Jerusalem in 1995, writes: "Only a few Lithuanians were ready to offer comfort and assistance to their Jewish countrymen. The

---

[33] *Rescue Attempts During the Holocaust, Proceedings of the Second Yad Vashem International Historical Conference, Jerusalem*, April 8–11, 1974, Yad Vashem, Jerusalem, 1977.

[34] Ibid., p. 329.

[35] *The Days of Memory*, Sarah Neshamit, p. 428.

names of those Righteous Gentiles are worth our gratitude. They are
Juozas Pranas [?], Bronius Gotautas, Juozas Straupis, Dr E.
Kutorgienė, Ona Šimaitė, Sophia [sic] Binkienė."[36] A former ambassador of Israel
to Lithuania, Oded Ben Hur, expressed a similar opinion. Speaking at
the Seimas on 10 September 1997, he said: "There were Lithuanians
who put their lives at risk to rescue Jews from the Nazis, though their
number, unfortunately, was small."[37] Later, when he visited the Gallery
of Rescuers at the Vilna Gaon State Jewish Museum, the ambassador
was greatly surprised at the number of portraits of rescuers, and did
not say any more in public about the low numbers of rescuers.

One would expect to find more detailed, precise and reliable
information about the rescuers of Jews in the *Encyclopaedia Judaica*
published in Israel in 1971; however, it provides very little data.

> There were among the Lithuanians a few individuals who in the face
> of the Nazis extended a helping hand to the Jews, despite the mortal
> danger to which they thus exposed themselves. In Kovno, those who
> helped the Jews included E. Kutorgienė, P. Mažylis, the writer Sofija
> Čiurlionienė, the priest Paukštys, the nun Ona Brokaitytė, and the
> opera singer Kipras Petrauskas. In Vilna, Ona Šimaitė was of the
> greatest help, while in Šiauliai the daughter of the lawyer Venclauskas,
> the poet Jankus, the priest Lapis, and former mayor Saneckis were
> among those who distinguished themselves in aiding the Jews.[38]

The historian Dov Levin, in his article "Facts Accuse" published
in *Tėviškės žiburiai* on 8 July 1976, wrote about the rescue of Jews in
Lithuania as follows:

> At the most terrible time, in the autumn of 1941, and at the end of the
> war, several hundreds of honest Lithuanians appeared who, despite
> the danger, rescued perhaps as many as several hundred Jews. One
> of these was Ona Šimaitė, whose name has become famous all over
> the world and helped to restore the reputation of the Lithuanian nation
> to some extent in accordance with the words of its national anthem:
> "Let your children follow the paths of honesty only".

---

[36] M. Greenbaum, *The Jews of Lithuania: A History of a Remarkable Community*,
Jerusalem, 1995, p. 378.

[37] Proceedings of the sitting of the Seimas of the Republic of Lithuania of 10
September 1997.

[38] *Encyclopaedia Judaica*, Vol. 11, Jerusalem, 1971, p. 389.

Levin stated in the same article: "From biblical times to the present day, the Jewish nation has created a national memory and has forgotten nothing, who was its enemy and who was its friend." He maintained that Dr J. Robinson and Lev Garfunkel were working on a large book about the fate of Jews in Lithuania during the war. According to Levin, "the book contained facts about what happened in every settlement in Lithuania: the number of Jews killed and the names of those who killed them. And a separate article will say how many people were engaged in rescuing, and who they were."

Unfortunately, in 1994 Professor Sarah Ginaitė, in the book *The Beginning of the Jewish Tragedy in Lithuania*, had to admit the following:

> So far, neither in Lithuania nor anywhere else in the world, has a thorough work been published studying the heroic history of the Lithuanians. It is a civil and moral duty of my countrymen, Jewish historians, sociologists, specialists in political science and witnesses, to provide as exhaustively as possible information about those families ... So let us make haste to do this work, so that humanity and not only barbarity should be used in making clear the relations between the nations, to help to improve relations and overcome misunderstandings and conflicts.[39]

Eight years have passed since the publication of that book; however, no major changes have been seen in this area.

***

The perception of the scale of rescuing and the knowledge of it: is this problem acute only in Lithuania?

In agreeing in essence to the statement made by Saulius Sužiedėlis that no uniform "Jewish", "Lithuanian" or "Western" historiography can be found, we should say that two tendencies can be discerned in studying the literature on rescuing Jews. The first tendency is that many Jewish authors emphasise the small number of rescuers in their work; and the second is that many publications

---

[39] S. Ginaitė, *Žydų tautos tragedijos Lietuvoje pradžia*, Vilnius, 1994, p. 34–35.

by Lithuanian authors point to large numbers. Which are more precise and better substantiated? What is a little and what is a lot, when an individual puts his life and the lives of his family at risk in rescuing others?

The first general statements about the small number of Lithuanian rescuers can be found in the article by Joseph L. Lichter. The report by Sarah Neshamit at the conference in Jerusalem in 1974 allows us to understand better on what the thesis about the small number of Lithuanian rescuers was based. Neshamit drew her conclusions on the basis of information held by Yad Vashem on the Righteous Gentiles.

Since 1963, on the decision of its governing Commission, this title has been conferred on people who rescued Jews, who put their lives and the lives of their families at risk during the war. It is awarded on the basis of information and testimonies filed by Jews who have been rescued. The certificate sent to Domas Jasaitis from Yad Vashem in Jerusalem on 22 March of 1977 wrote that the title of the Righteous Gentile had been conferred on 19 people who lived in Lithuania. Hence, it would appear that Neshamit was right – that the number of Lithuanians who rescued Jews is very small. However, this conclusion is hasty, inexact, and we can be sure today that it is biased and incorrect. It was made without studying thoroughly the situation. We should regard this conclusion as a reproach to historians and politicians who are in a hurry to make biased generalisations, with no reliable data at their disposition, and as a reproach to the rescued themselves who have contributed to these conclusions by their silence.

It is clear that testimonies about rescuing Jews for conferring awards by the State of Israel in the postwar years could have been given by rescued Jews who lived in Israel or in other parts of the free world who were aware of the award, and felt the need to make the story of the rescue public to record the deeds of their rescuers. The combination of such knowledge, will and ability in one person was not common. Jews who found themselves in Israel had the greatest chance, and they constituted the largest part of the people who appealed to Yad Vashem. A statement given by Mykolas Biržiška's daughter (Marija Žymantienė) is published in this collection in which she testifies that the midwife Marija Žakevičienė and her daughter Jadvyga Žakevičiūtė-Jablonskienė brought up a Jewish girl, Salomė (she was later named Dalia) Vilenčikaitė, from the Kaunas ghetto. Due to her, since they were afraid to take her to Germany, Žakevičienė and her daughter Jadvyga stayed in Lithuania in 1944 when all their relatives fled. We find the beginning of this story as far back as 1947 in the questionnaires collected in Germany, later in Juozas Šalna's articles, and in Liudvikas Šmulkštys' article that was published in the newspaper *Atgimimas*. It is only 50 years later that we learn the continuation of it, at the ceremony for conferring the title of Righteous Gentile held in Vilnius on 21 September 2000. Professor Vytautas Landsbergis reported that the rescued Dalia Vilenčikaitė (Jackbo) now lived in Norway. After several attempts she was at last persuaded to write a statement about her rescue. "I asked her to testify. She said that these were sensitive reminiscences and she did not want to speak to journalists about them," said Landsbergis. Only a couple of years ago did Dalia Jackbo come to Lithuania in order to talk about her rescue and to testify about it. Dalia's rescuer, Jadvyga Jablonskienė, who stayed in Lithuania, was arrested and died on 22 December 1948. She became one of the Righteous Gentiles only a short time ago. Jadvyga's mother, Marija Žakevičienė, has not been awarded the title of Righteous Gentile yet.

This shows that many episodes of rescuing Jews will remain unknown simply because the rescued are not always inclined to recall them. This time a person was persuaded to write a testimony. However, how many people are there who have managed to persuade others to give a statement, and how many people were persuaded to give them?

It is difficult to say what the reason is: forgetfulness, a lack of gratitude or an unwillingness to open old wounds. During repeated meetings with the rescued it turned out that some of them found recalling that time unpleasant because it made them go through the suffering again. Therefore, we must understand people who do not want to recall the atrocities of the war together with the goodness that they experienced personally. The rescued people who live in the USA and other countries seem to have taken their time in making use of the possibility:

In the postwar years we often thought about the Žilevičius family who hid us at great risk. However, we did not know how we could send them a message. We fled Lithuania a long time ago, and were afraid that we might get them into trouble by communicating with them. Nevertheless, after Gorbachev had started perestroika, we went to Lithuania, put a notice in a newspaper, and found other members of the Žilevičius family who were alive, and asked them to get in touch with the representatives of the Jewish community in Šiauliai ...

Now that we know that they are alive, on returning home I wrote to Yad Vashem in Israel asking them to recognise them as Righteous Gentiles. The Centre answered me in July 1994.

This is how A. Katz writes about his delayed actions.

Rescued Jews who lived in Lithuania could hardly appeal to Yad Vashem due to the political relations between the USSR and Israel. It was only after the re-establishment of independence that some Jews appealed to Yad Vashem and gave testimonies about their rescuers. Some seem to have absolutely forgotten their rescuers. Therefore, it is not surprising that Fr Juozas Stakauskas, an especially modest person, who, together with the nun Marija Mikulska and the teacher Vladas Žemaitis, saved 12 Jews in the former archive at Šv. Ignoto gatvė 5, wrote in a letter on 6 August 1965 to the Jašunska in Warsaw about the rescued:

Not all of you have such noble qualities. Only Dr Libo and Žirnauskas, whose lives I helped to save, could be put in the category of people such as you. All the others condescended to answer it with silence, including the Jaffes, on account of whom I had, as you know very well, a lot of trouble: the death of old Jaffe, visiting a five-year-old child, and Fira, even while living in Vilnius she never condescended to visit me at home even once, although I asked her to.

Thus, up to 1990, the title of Righteous Gentile had been conferred on 168 citizens of Lithuania; and by the beginning of 2002 the figure stood at 504.

However, even today few are eager to announce the exact information about the Righteous Gentiles, which reveals only in part the scale of the rescue of Jews in Lithuania and other countries. In the summer of 2000, the 1991 figures for the Righteous Gentiles were still on display in the United States Holocaust Memorial Museum, which is visited by hundreds of thousands of visitors. In a decade, their number in Lithuania alone increased significantly. Believing that the display of out-of-date information at such an institution signals disrespect to both the people who rescued Jews and to the truth, one of the authors of this introduction handed a letter to Wesley Fisher, the director of foreign affairs at the United States Holocaust Memorial Museum, at an international conference that was held in Vilnius in October 2000, in which he asked them to update the figures in the exhibition about the Righteous Gentiles.

And the Simon Wiesenthal Multimedia Learning Centre Online 2001 still gives 1993 data: "As of 1993, 200 Lithuanian rescuers had been honoured by Yad Vashem".

***

The issue of the scale of the rescue of Jews during the war is apposite not only when speaking about the relations between the Lithuanians and the Jews. The thesis that the number of people who rescued Jews was small is advocated not only in Europe. A professor of Jewish origin, Peter Novick, clearly says this in his book *The Holocaust in American Life*: "Those who write or speak about the non-Jewish rescuers for purposes other than to emphasise their scarcity, underline that the Jewish audience often treats them with animosity."[40] The book writes that one of the most common complaints that Jews make about Spielberg's film "Schindler's List" is that it destroys the meaning and lesson of the Holocaust because attention is focused on the Christian rescuers.

According to Novick, the very establishment of Yad Vashem is not only to show respect to the Righteous Gentiles, it is also a reproach to others, the non-Righteous Gentiles. There are now 19,141 Righteous Gentiles (as of the beginning of 2002) over an area with a population of 700 million. Commentators often point to the ratio of non-Righteous Gentiles to Righteous Gentiles of non-Jewish origin: nearly a hundred thousand to one. To each Righteous Gentile there were thousands who collaborated, or at least who stood aside and did nothing.

---

[40] P. Novick, *The Holocaust in American Life*, Boston, New York, 1999.

Novick presents his own theory on the possibility of rescuing. According to him, where the conditions of the German occupation were more lenient and where the Jews were better integrated into local society, greater and more effective help was provided. Where the Germans' behaviour was more brutal and where the Jews were not so integrated into local society, less help was given and it was not so successful. By applying this theory, conclusions about rescuing Jews in Lithuania become much more complex than those published so far.

Abraham Foxman was hidden as a young boy in Vilnius. He was later head of the Anti-Defamation League in the USA. "We hidden children have a mission, a mission to proclaim and recognise goodness. For the first fifty years after the Holocaust, survivors bore witness to the evil, brutality and bestiality. Now is the time for us, for our generation to bear witness to goodness."[41]

In looking for the reasons why the issue of rescuing Jews in Lithuania has not been thoroughly studied, and why generalisations were made so hastily, it is worth remembering the idea of Professor Egidijus Aleksandravičius about "victim nations".[42] The idea that some nations keep trying to prove which nation suffered more has been expressed at more than one conference of historians. According to Peter Novick, the Jews are the front-runners in this "olympiad" of suffering. Therefore, when most attention is paid to the study of the suffering endured, little space is left for the study of the rescuing. Furthermore, the help and rescuing have the effect of reducing in a way the suffering endured.

The declaration made in Munich in 1947 concerning the responsibility of the Lithuanian nation for the massacre of the Jews seemed to assume a small number of rescuers. It is clear that after such a statement has been proclaimed it is difficult to speak objectively about rescues of Jews and their scale. Some researchers are still engaged in a competition to count the number of people who shot Jews and the number of people who rescued them: "However, the number of the Righteous Gentiles as compared with the number of

---

[41] M. Gilbert, *Never Again*, p. 103.

[42] E. Aleksandravičius, "Apie atminties archeologiją, kančių kultūrą ir holokausto prisiminimus", *Kauno diena*, 1 August 1998.

murderous, was small. Many people were indifferent to the suffering and death of the Jews."[43]

"The contention that the number of rescuers was greater or at least equivalent to the number of murderers is another preposterous claim that continues to cast its shadow on the relations between the Jews and the Lithuanians."[44]

In many countries where Jews were rescued institutions studying this have been established. Perhaps the data gathered by these institutions reflects the scale of the rescuing better. For example, during the ten years of its existence, the Vilna Gaon State Jewish Museum has accumulated a lot of documentary and substantiated material about nearly 3,000 rescuers of Jews in Lithuania. There are testimonies that have not been studied yet. Therefore, it is an understandable and welcome practice not to be content with the title of Righteous Gentile only in writing about rescuing Jews, but to rely on the latest data from the Jewish Museum. The same must also be said about *The Book of Memory*[45] by S. Ginaitė-Rubinsonienė and the work of Solomonas Atamukas *The Way of the Lithuanian Jews*.[46] These works are to be translated into other languages to serve as sources for researchers who are interested in the issue of rescuing Jews in Lithuania.

Cases of rescuing Jews currently known in Lithuania do not allow us to maintain that there were only "some" or "a few" rescuers, as is claimed in the books. The facts available do not allow us to draw the conclusion that the whole Lithuanian nation participated in rescuing Jews either, as was many a time stated in the American-Lithuanian press.

However, all these considerations and arguments lose their point when we remember the inscription on the certificates granted by Yad Vashem to the Righteous Gentiles: "Whoever saves one life is as though he had saved the entire world."

---

[43] *The Days of Memory*, Sarah Neshamit, p. 428.

[44] *The Days of Memory*, E. Zuroff, p. 400.

[45] S. Ginaitė-Rubinsonienė, *Atminimo knyga (Kauno žydų bendruomenė, 1941–1944 metai)*, Vilnius, 1999.

[46] S. Atamukas, *Lietuvos žydų kelias*, Vilnius, 1998.

***

At the end of this book are lists of people who rescued Jews and became Righteous Gentiles in Lithuania, as well as lists of people who were awarded the Cross for Saving People under Threat of Death by the president of Lithuania.

Letters which describe rescues of Jews in Nazi-occupied Lithuania selected from Dr Domas Jasaitis' personal archive are published here. The letters are addressed to two people, Dr Domas Jasaitis and Fr Juozas Prunskis. They were written mainly in the Seventies, when émigrés had made up their minds to collect material and prepare a book about the crimes committed in Lithuania during the Soviet and Nazi occupations.

The subject of rescuing Jews is not new in Lithuania, this is shown by the publications and institutions mentioned above that have covered the subject. Unfortunately, the information they give is rather perfunctory, since the situation, views, imperatives and motivation of Lithuanian society at the time has not been studied much. Realising that this is an area for future investigation, we present authentic, unabridged letters from people who bore witness to these events and were participants in them. There are also articles written by émigré authors, Domas Jasaitis, Juozas Šalna (Liudvikas Šmulkštys) and others, first published in the Lithuanian émigré press. These are valuable, because as well as presenting facts we find a detailed analysis of the phenomenon in its context, without which it would be difficult to understand and make clear all the aspects under discussion. Furthermore, these publications were practically unknown to a wider circle of readers, and they are worth attention.

This book consists of different parts, related to each other by theme, though they differ in their nature: articles from the émigré press, letters, reminiscences, statements, descriptions of rescues, and a separate chapter for testimonies and reminiscences by the rescued about their rescuers. We cannot say that the number of these testimonies is small because the Jews refused to testify; rather that this is the material found in Jasaitis' archive. Letters written by rescuers and witnesses constitute the greater part of the book. As has already been mentioned, with a few exceptions (for example, the text by Sofija Jasaitienė dated 1946, one of the first known on this theme), the letters were written mainly in the Seventies.

In compiling the book, a territorial rather than a chronological approach was applied; therefore, the letters are classified by the region in which the event being described took place. In many cases it happens that in supplementing and making more exact the circumstances, the names of the same people are mentioned, and so some of these letters duplicate each other. At the same time, there are letters in which several different places in Lithuania are described. In such cases the most important and most accurate description was chosen, and on that basis the letter attributed to one place or another. Letters arranged in this order have no strict framework, they are not divided into sections, but appear to form a general story, which helps to create a common picture for the whole of Lithuania.

This is a collection of translated letters, articles and documents, some of which have been published before in émigré newspapers or journals, and all of which were published in book form in Lithuanian in Vilnius in 2001. Explanatory footnotes have been added to the English edition to clarify issues for readers unfamiliar with Lithuanian history and culture, and to highlight the occasional discrepancies that are inevitable between different versions of the same events written by different people at different times. In order to remain faithful to the originals, names of people have been left as they first appeared, therefore creating a mixture of Lithuanian and English letters and endings. Each item has a short description, with the date and the place where it was written. In some cases it was not possible to establish the date or place of writing. Whether a document is the original, and the way it was written, is also indicated.

In order to avoid duplication, only a portion of the 2001 Lithuanian edition is represented here. The texts themselves have been abridged to the minimum: the exact addresses of the authors and persons mentioned have been taken out, some personal messages that are not related to the book's subject or which repeat themselves have also been omitted. Controversial statements made by the authors of the letters have been left in, leaving space for the reader's own interpretation. Two lists are provided at the end of the book: a list of citizens of Lithuania who have been awarded the title of Righteous Gentile, and a list of the people who have been awarded the Cross for Saving People under Threat of Death, provided by the Vilna Gaon State Jewish Museum.

The compilers of the book are grateful to everybody who has contributed in any way to preserving this important material, and to helping the reader discover it. This includes people from the National Fund (USA), as well as Juozas Rygelis, Sister Paulė Savickaitė, Rasa Razgaitienė, Juozas L. Giedraitis and Dr Kazys Bobelis. We would like to thank the above-mentioned people, and all those who helped us with their valuable advice and who supported us in other ways.

This book is a joint effort, helping to uncover a difficult and barely known chapter of Lithuanian history, but one which is of great significance to the country, and to Europe as a whole.

Rimantas Stankevičius

The Righteous Gentiles

Righteous Gentiles – by country and ethnic origin – 1 January 2002*

Poland	5,632	Switzerland	38
Netherlands	4,464	Moldova	52
France	2,171	Bosnia	34
Ukraine	1,755	Denmark**	17
Belgium	1,322	Bulgaria	15
Hungary	587	Great Britain	13
Slovakia	412	Norway	20
Lithuania	504	Sweden	10
Belarus	497	Macedonia	9
Germany	358	Armenia	6
Italy	295	Slovenia	4
Greece	243	Spain	3
Yugoslavia (Serbia)	113	Estonia	2
Czech Republic	103	Brazil	1
Croatia	91	China	2
Austria	83	Japan	1
Latvia	93	Luxembourg	1
Russia	79	Portugal	1
Romania	48	Turkey	1
Albania	60	USA	1

Total Persons   19,141

---

* These figures are not necessarily an indication of the actual number of Jews saved in each country, but reflect material on rescue operations made available to Yad Vashem.

** The Danish underground requested that all its members who participated in the rescue of the Jewish Community, not be listed individually, but as one group.

Source: http://www.yadvashem.org/righteous/index_righteous.html

THE RESCUERS TELL
THEIR TALE

1. Article by Domas Jasaitis* "The Tragedy of the Jews in Lithuania under the Nazi Occupation"

Chicago, USA: 25 September 1962

The tragedy of the Jews in Lithuania under the Nazi occupation

You reap what you sow.

This law exists not only in agriculture but also in philosophy and sociology. Nietzsche, who applied Darwinism to philosophy, created standards reaching beyond good and evil, and the vision of the overman (*Übermensch*), which shortly gave rise to the theory of superior and inferior races and nations. The advocates of this theory, employing a twisted logic and selecting historical facts that suited them, declared that the Germans were par excellence the superior race, while the Slavs and Jews were inferior.

Nietzsche declared: "God is dead". As a result, men began to appear who managed to usurp and concentrate in their person all the power of the secular and spiritual authorities and all the resulting prerogatives. By using unlimited unrestricted physical and psychological terror, violating divine law and infringing brutally on all principles of humanity, they sometimes pursued completely irrational precepts.

---

* DOMAS JASAITIS (1898–1977), a doctor, was born in the Garliava district, near Kaunas. He studied at Kiev and Berlin universities and worked at the Institut Pasteur in Paris. From 1925 he worked as a therapist in Šiauliai, and was also the founder of the Tuberculosis Dispensary. In 1944 he left Lithuania, and in 1950 emigrated to the USA. He was a regular contributor to the press, both specialist and non-specialist.

*Domas Jasaitis
in his study
in Mount Vernon
(New York)*

Domas Jasaitis and his family in Germany, 1947 (from left): Sofija, Elena, Stasys and Domas

One such historical phenomenon was Adolf Hitler, a writer, prophet and advocate of National Socialism. Some of the key postulates of his ideology were the superiority of the Aryan Germans, anti-Semitism and blind hatred for the Jews. "The Jews are a deadly enemy. The struggle against them is a beacon showing the way to a better era, the salvation of the Aryans" (*Mein Kampf*, 1922).

From 1922 to 1933 the Nazi press, in particular *Der Stuermer* and *Das Schwarze Korps*, insulted the Jews and instigated a campaign of hatred by the German nation against them. From 1933, when Hitler became chancellor of the Reich and later its Führer, pressure on the Jews grew very rapidly. On 15 September 1935, the Law for the Protection of German Blood and Honour was passed; and 14 November saw the issue of rules for the Law on Reich Citizenship. Laws, regulations and rules restricting the Jews' civil rights sprang up like mushrooms. Pogroms, the burning down of synagogues and crippling fines became more and more frequent. These conditions forced many Jews to leave Germany.

In 1934, Himmler proposed to Hitler the idea to move all German Jews to Madagascar. The plan was approved by Poland, which also wanted to send 15,000 Jewish families there (Major Lepecki's Commission). The South African Union showed some interest in the idea and suggested that Jews also be allowed to emigrate to Tanganyika and British Guyana. In December 1938, Hitler sent a financial specialist, Hjalmar Schacht, to London to discuss the funding of the resettlement of the Jews. An English-American syndicate agreed to provide a large loan for this. At the beginning of 1939, Goering appointed Reinhard Heydrich head of the Central Office for Jewish Emigration in Vienna, and, shortly before Germany took Poland, Adolf Eichmann was entrusted with a section of the office in Prague. At that time there was talk about the emigration of Jews to Palestine. The Haavara Treaty was signed, which allowed the transfer of Jewish property from Germany to Palestine. However, the Arabs were firm opponents of this operation. Therefore, Britain, which ruled Palestine as a mandate territory, blocked the treaty. Emigration was negligible. Documents found in archives show that for a long time Hitler did not consider the biological extermination of the Jews. After France was taken in 1940, intensive discussions went on concerning the resettlement of all European Jews in

Madagascar: a "superghetto" for 4,000,000 people was to be set up there. Hitler approved the undertaking on 30 June 1940, and its implementation was entrusted to Himmler, Heydrich and Eichmann. However, the plan was stalled by events.

Representatives of international Jewish organisations, meeting with Eichmann's representative Franz Rademacher in Lisbon, refused to raise funds for the operation, believing that it was only a trap. Pétain's government in France also expressed strong opposition to the plan.

In 1941, Hitler attacked Soviet Russia. The plan suddenly changed. In 1935, Hitler had said: "If the international financiers – the Jewry of Europe and other countries – should again succeed in plunging the world into a war, the result will not be the bolshevisation of the Earth and thus the victory of Jewry, but the annihilation of the Jewish race throughout Europe." He said this for a second time in 1939 in the Reichstag: "Today I will once more be a prophet: if the international Jewish financiers in Europe and other countries should plunge the world into a war, the result will not be the bolshevisation of the Earth and thus the victory of Jewry, but the annihilation of the Jewish race throughout Europe."

The war that broke out speeded up the realisation of Hitler's threat. On 21 September 1939, Heydrich sent the secret PP/II/-228/39 plan for the extermination of the Jews to the commanders of the *Einsatzgruppen*.* The plan was carried out brutally in occupied Poland. It was Heydrich who, after the beginning of the German-Soviet war, sent four (A, B, C and D) Einsatzgruppen to the occupied areas for the extermination of the Jews and other enemies of the Reich. (Concerning their operation, see the report on the activities of Group A below.)

On 31 July 1941, Goering wrote to Heydrich: "I hereby authorise you to undertake all preliminary actions for executing the Final Solution of the Jewish question in the part of Europe under Germany's control. All other government institutions useful in this matter will collaborate with us. I also authorise you to send me as soon as possible a general plan, including organisational, actual and material

---

* Mobile task forces.

measures, necessary for the intended Final Solution of the Jewish question."

Heydrich made a proposal to kill all the Jews in Europe by shooting them. Hitler, Himmler and Goering agreed with this form of the Final Solution.

On 20 January 1942 a special conference took place at the office of the International Criminal Police in Gross Wannsee, a suburb of Berlin. The plan for the Final Solution of the Jewish question was approved there.

At the 22nd annual Nazi (NSDAP) party conference on 23 February 1942, Hitler made the statement for the third time: "Our ideas for a National Socialist and Fascist revolution have defeated great and powerful nations, and my prophecy that this war will not destroy the Aryan race, but that Jewry will be uprooted, is already coming true ..."

In a letter in April 1942, Himmler, SS Führer of the Reich, notified the Reich Security Main Office (RSHA), the Security Police (SD) and the chiefs and the inspector of the concentration camps, of the Führer's decision to implement the Final Solution to the Jewish question without delay. The Final Solution meant biological extermination. The order was secret and known to only 200 to 300 persons. Its partial fulfilment had already started earlier. However, from April 1942 to its repeal in 1944, about 4,000,000 European Jews, half-Jews, Gypsies and Karaites became its victims. It must be added that alongside the Jews another "inferior" race – the Slavs – was also exterminated. The Poles and prisoners from Soviet Russia were subject to mass extermination. Their numbers exceeded the number of Jewish victims.

Asked during the Nuremberg Trials about the possibility of the occurrence of such a massacre of humans, General Erich von Bach-Zilewski replied: "I think that if for years and decades a science is solemnly proclaimed, which says that the Slavs are an inferior race and the Jews are not even human, such consequences are inevitable."

The extermination of Lithuanian Jews in German documents

Shortly before the beginning of the invasion of Poland, Reinhard Heydrich, the SD chief, and August Mueller, the Gestapo leader, organised special units which followed closely behind the Wehrmacht and exterminated all the enemies of the Reich. Later, these units were named Einsatzgruppen. They consisted of four battalions, the size of which ranged between 500 and 900 men. They were often supplemented with people from other sources – auxiliary police from the occupied areas and volunteers.

Each action group included special (*Sonderkommandos*) and specific (*Einsatzkommandos*) detachments. The units were divided into platoon-sized companies and special squads.

How were the killings carried out? A local execution team would issue orders to register all Jews, half-Jews, Gypsies and Karaites in any one district. Registration was conducted by representatives of these groups. Then, all those registered were taken to places where temporary and permanent ghettos had been set up. When the time arrived, they would be moved from there to an execution site. Executions made use of specially dug ditches, often dug by those to be exterminated, previously made anti-tank trenches, or natural depressions in the land, if such were found.

Executions were carried out by special shooting groups in a military manner. Members of these groups would take a three-week course on shooting humans. Those to be killed were taken to the place of execution in trucks in small groups, of such a size that it was possible to kill them all at once (Q. Reynolds, *Minister of Death*, pp. 113, 116). The unit commander had the task of checking whether anyone was left alive. Such people were finished off with a revolver. The victims had to take off their outer wear. They would either stand or kneel. It was only from the spring of 1942 that Himmler issued orders to murder women and children with poisonous gas (*Minister of Death*, p. 117).

After the invasion of the Soviet Union, Einsatzgruppe A entered Lithuania behind the Wehrmacht. Its chief was Franz Walter Stahlecker, an SS brigadier general and a high-ranking Gestapo officer. His area covered the Baltic states and Leningrad. His work was swift and brutal; in his reports he wrote that over the first four months he murdered 135,567 people; while over the next six months the number increased to 221,000. The figures for the neighbouring Einsatzgruppen were more modest. There was no need for Stahlecker to build special killing centres, as was done in other areas, since he carried out the extermination with automatic rifles and machine-guns. He received a just reward: he was killed by partisans (*Minister of Death*, p. 114).

A report by Einsatzgruppe A on its operations from June 1941 to 15 October has been found in the archives, which describes in detail the extermination of Jews in Lithuania:

A force consisting of the 16th and the 18th armies and the fourth armoured vehicle group, began its march on 22 June 1941. The goal of Einsatzgruppe A, which set out a day later, was the fastest possible establishment of personal contacts with the army chiefs and the rear army commander. This cooperation with the armed forces was satisfactory from the outset, and even sincere, with Lieutenant General Hoeppner, commander of the fourth armoured vehicle group. Some misunderstandings that had occurred over the first days of the campaign were resolved through personal discussion. The beginning of the campaign revealed that special Security Police tasks would have to be carried out not only in the rear, as previously agreed with the top army command, but also at the front.

Right from the start, local anti-Semitic elements were found and encouraged to organise pogroms against the Jews immediately after the army had passed through. However, the task turned out to be difficult to carry out. The Security Police were determined to solve the Jewish question by all possible means and in the most thorough manner. However, it was desirable not to give any publicity to the SD, at least at the very beginning, because the measures that were being applied made even German circles anxious. Therefore, the world had to be shown that the local population, in reaction to the Bolsheviks' atrocities committed during the occupation, were the first to begin the extermination of the Jews. The Security Police from the outset made an effort to involve the local population in the struggle against social parasites – Jews and communists – and to engage more reliable elements as auxiliary police. The different situation of each area had to be taken into account. In Lithuania, activists and nationalists organised partisan units for the struggle against the Bolsheviks and bolshevism right from the beginning of the invasion. According to their statements, about 4,000 of their own people had been killed.

After the Wehrmacht had occupied the Baltic states, the prisons there were found either empty or full of Jews and communists who had been arrested by local defence units. In areas where gaols were overcrowded, temporary concentration camps were set up.

As the populations of the Baltic states had suffered greatly from the occupying regime of the Bolsheviks and the Jews, one would only expect them, after they had liberated themselves, to render harmless all enemies who had not withdrawn with the Red Army. Therefore, the German SD tried to instigate mopping-up movements and to direct their activities.

Looking into the future, it was no less important to devise indisputable facts about the liberated inhabitants themselves resorting to the most cruel measures in their revenge against the Bolsheviks and the Jews. To our surprise, it was very difficult to provoke pogroms against the Jews on a large scale. The commander of one partisan unit gave in to our encouragement and, following the advice of an SD group that had arrived in Kaunas, conducted a pogrom with success. It was done so quickly that the incitement by the Germans was hardly noticeable.

Such actions were carried out quite regularly, as the army command, notified of them by the SD beforehand, looked on actions of this kind favourably. It was clear right from the start that it would be possible to organise pogroms only during the first days of the occupation. A little later, the partisans were disarmed, and the mopping-up operations came to an end.

It soon became apparent that it would not be possible to solve the Jewish question by means of pogroms. Its orders obliged the SD to seek the total extermination of the Jews. Therefore, special Security Police units, which included select groups – partisan companies in Lithuania and auxiliary police units in Latvia – carried out large-scale massacres in towns and villages. The work of the execution units was regular and efficient. The Lithuanians and Latvians who were appointed to special execution groups were usually those who had suffered directly under the Bolsheviks. Most of their relatives had been murdered or deported by them. Particularly cruel measures had been taken in Lithuania. In some places, for example in Kaunas, armed Jews had shot at Lithuanians in ambushes and set houses on fire. In addition to actions of this kind, Lithuanian Jews had collaborated readily with the occupying Soviet authorities.

"After the main killings of Jews in Lithuania and Latvia had been carried out," writes Stahlecker, "it became obvious that the extermination of all Jews without trace was not possible, at least for the moment. Many of the trades in Latvia and Lithuania were in the hands of the Jews, and some of them (glaziers, plumbers, stove-makers and shoemakers) were exclusively Jewish. Without these craftsmen, it was impossible to repair buildings or to do essential things for the army. Attempts to replace Jewish craftsmen with Lithuanians and Latvians, at least in the larger towns, were not successful. Nevertheless, all Jews who became unfit for work were arrested and exterminated in small groups." Stahlecker complained that some civil administration offices strictly opposed any larger killings of Jews.

During the first days of the occupation, the organisation of ghettos in the larger towns started. The matter was particularly relevant in Kaunas, with its population of 152,000, of whom 30,000 were Jews. Following the first pogrom, the Jewish Committee was called and informed that the German administration would not interfere in disputes between Lithuanians and Jews. Setting up a ghetto was the only way to create normal living conditions. The response to the Jews' protests was to say that there was no other way of preventing future pogroms. Then the Jews suddenly declared that they would try to concentrate their people in Vilijampolė, where a Jewish ghetto was to be established, as soon as possible. That part of the city lay beyond the Nemunas and the Vilija.* There was only one bridge connecting it with the city; therefore, it was easy to cut off the area. Marking the Jews with a yellow star, which they had to wear on their front and back, was carried out in accordance with a temporary order of the Security Police, which was later approved by the rear commander and afterwards by the civil administration.

The report of SS Brigadier General Stahlecker is published in the book *The Case Against Adolf Eichmann*, pages 64 to 67, by Henry A. Zeiger, published by The New American Library in 1960. It shows clearly that the Einsatzgruppen received the order to exterminate Jews, half-Jews, Karaites, Gypsies and other enemies of the Reich prior to the outbreak of the war. The report describes the attempts by the SD to involve Lithuanians in the annihilation, and their resistance to the criminal scheme. The document, on several occasions, stresses the determination of the SD to blame the extermination of the Jews on the Lithuanians.

---

* Today usually called the Neris.

The documents below relate the same tragic fate of the Jewish people.

The statement of Leib Kibart, Document D-969 from the Nuremberg Trials:

I, Leib Kibart, hereby state the following:

1. I am a Jew, and during the time of the German occupation I lived in Šiauliai, which is approximately 130 kilometres from Riga. I am a tanner by trade.

2. I was arrested in the street and forced to make women's handbags for three years. I lived in a ghetto. Every day the SA would take me from the ghetto and march me to a workshop in the yard of the office of the Šiauliai district commissar, where I and other Jews did various jobs.

6.* The Šiauliai ghetto had 4,500 Jews. It was overcrowded. In August 1941, the SA men suddenly surrounded the entire ghetto. Some of them stormed into the houses, taking women, children and the elderly, loading them into lorries and carrying them away. I saw this myself. It was done exclusively by the SA. I saw them grab the children by the hair and throw them on the trucks. I did not see what happened to them. But later one Lithuanian told me that they had been taken 20 kilometres out of Šiauliai and shot. He also said that he himself had seen the SA men strip them naked and shoot them with automatic revolvers.

7. In 1943, groups of workers would be sent from the ghetto to places of employment outside the city, and on their way back they would sometimes bring some food, like potatoes. The SA used to search them and beat up those who had food.

In June 1943, a baker called Mazaveckis (Mazaketzki) was caught with four or five cigarettes and a piece of sausage. He was beaten fiercely and brought to the district commissar's office. I and other Jews worked there. Bubas told the workers that the criminal would be hanged, because he wanted to prove that he was also capable of hanging Jews. The next Sunday Bubas hanged Mazaveckis in the presence of Jews brought together for the purpose.

8. The district commissar, in the yard of whose office I worked, was Gewecke. I saw him every day. He was an SA man.

9. The SS took over from the SA in September 1943. The ghetto became a labour unit.

I hereby state that the above is true.

Leib Kibart

10 August 1946

---

* Sections 3–5 are missing in the article.

I knew Leib Kibart. He was a short and humble individual who was inconspicuous in a crowd. He had a quiet temperament. Those qualities, perhaps, can be seen in his testimony. I also knew the district commissar, Gewecke. I will talk about him later. I was also familiar with Bubas, who was the commissar's chief of staff. Bubas distinguished himself by his perfidy and extreme cruelty. I believe Bubas was responsible for the arrest of Jonas Noreika, a great patriot and member of the resistance, in the Šiauliai district, in March 1943, and his deportation to Stutthof.

The statement of Szloma Gol, Document D-964 from the Nuremberg Trials:

1. I am a Jew, and I used to live in Vilnius, Lithuania. During the German occupation I was in the Vilnius ghetto.

2. The Vilnius ghetto was administered by the SA. The Vilnius city commissar was an SA officer called Wolff. The adviser for Jewish affairs was an SA officer called Murer.

3. In December 1943, 80 ghetto Jews, including four women, myself and my friend Josifas Belicas, by the order of an SA lieutenant whose name I forget, were allocated a spacious pit as a residence. The pit had been dug earlier and was equipped with an underground kerosene tank. The pit was 60 metres in diameter, and four metres deep. Part of it was already covered with boards. It had rooms with wooden walls, a kitchen and a latrine. We lived there for six months before the deportation. It was guarded by SA men, about whom I will speak later.

4. One morning the lieutenant, near whom were 14 or 15 SA men, standing at the edge of the pit, said to us: "Your brothers, sisters and friends are quite near. Behave yourselves in a proper manner with them, and if you fulfil your duties we will send you to Germany where you will be able to work in your profession." We did not get the meaning of his speech.

5. After that the SA threw some chains into the pit. The lieutenant ordered our foreman (we were a labour unit) to put them on us. Our waists and ankles were chained. The chains weighed about two kilograms. They allowed us to walk only with small steps. We wore them for six months on end. The SA said that anyone who took the chains off would be hanged. The four women who worked in our shop were not chained.

6. After that we had to work. We stayed in chains for five or six months.

7. We were instructed to dig up the mass graves, pile the corpses on to a fire, and burn them. My task was to dig out the corpses. My friend Belicas chopped logs and made a fire with them.

8. We dug out 68,000 corpses in total. I know this because two of our people had to count the corpses, on the Germans' order. That was their only job. The mass graves were a mixture of dead bodies: Jews, Polish priests and Russian prisoners of war. I found my brother's corpse among them, with his identity documents on it. He had been dead for two years when I dug him up, I knew that he had been in the Vilnius ghetto group of 10,000 Jews put to death by shooting in September 1941.

9. The procedure for the incineration of the corpses was wholly methodical. Parallel seven-metre-long pits would be dug. A cover of thick boards would be placed over them. Then a layer of corpses would be put on the top and poured over with kerosene. Then followed a layer of branches and firewood. Each fire contained 14 layers of corpses, soaked in kerosene. A finished fire would look like a pyramid, with a wooden funnel erected on the top. Kerosene and other flammable liquids would be poured down the funnel. Incendiary bombs would be placed around the foundations of a fire. All the above jobs were done by Jews. When that was done, the lieutenant, or his deputy called Legel (who was also from the SA), would personally set fire to one edge of a pile.

10. The guards (in particular the SA men) would beat and poke us. I have scars on my legs and neck up to this day. Once I lost consciousness from a powerful blow, fell down on a pile of corpses, and was unable to get up. My friends pulled me away from the fire. I fell ill after that. We were allowed to be off sick for only two days. Those who did not recover by the third would be taken to "hospital", to be shot.

12.* Of the 76 labourers, 11 were shot during the work. Forty-three of us dug an underground tunnel leading out of the pit with our bare hands, cut off our chains and escaped into the forest. We were warned by one Czech SS man. He told us that we would all soon be shot and placed on a pile of corpses. "Run if you can, but only when I am not on guard."

I hereby state that the above is true.

Szloma Gol

9 August 1946

---

* Section 11 is missing in the article.

Szloma Gol is probably describing the activities of commando unit 1005. After the dramatic failure at the front in the winter of 1941–1942, it became clear that victory in the war was not at all certain. Himmler was concerned about the traces of crimes left by the execution groups. Hundreds of mass graves had been poorly covered with loose soil that was washed away by showers in autumn and spring. Therefore, he decided to destroy the remnants of corpses that were already decomposing. He charged Colonel Paul Blobel with this horrible task. The latter found some chemists who succeeded in producing a special fuel which destroyed corpses at a much higher rate than gasoline. Those 1005 commandos were under Eichmann, and operated from midsummer in 1942 to the autumn of 1944. He did most of the work in Soviet Russia, Poland and the Baltic states.

Šiauliai inhabitants rescue Jews

I will now try to recall what I remember about the Jewish question in Lithuania and the rescue of Jews in Šiauliai.

The outbreak of the Second World War found me in Moscow. Guided by an unusual determination and using various legal and illegal measures, I left Moscow on the last train to Riga, which I reached on 24 June 1941. There was already no connection to Lithuania, so I continued on foot. Having reached Lithuania, I headed for Šiauliai, but I stayed for a few days on a farm in the country. The army of the Reich rolled into our area on 27 June 1941, and on 29 June 1941 I found myself in Joniškis, hoping that one way or another I would reach Šiauliai, or at least convey a message to my family that I was alive, in good health, and not far away.

On arriving in Joniškis, I went to see Fr Korzonas, a good friend of mine. The church and the presbytery had remained almost intact, but other buildings in the parish had suffered considerable damage. A lot of uprooted or damaged trees were lying around. These were the consequences of a recent bombardment. Fr Korzonas himself had also been wounded. A piece of shrapnel had gone straight through his right shoulder. The arm was bandaged and out of action. We were overjoyed at seeing each other and at having luckily avoided the problems of the first days of the war and occupation.

Our conversation was interrupted by an officer who got out of a German military car that suddenly drew up.

"Who's the priest here?" he asked in German.

"Me," replied Korzonas slowly.

"It's good that I have found you, because I have some important business. In about half an hour a general will come and will want to have a short rest. I'm giving you a small bag of coffee beans, and you will take care of the rest," said the officer, and departed.

This was my first encounter with the German army. I had the opportunity to exchange opinions with officers, and find out their thoughts on various questions, among which the Jewish question was also touched on. In reply to the German general's question "What do you think of the Jews and their future in Lithuania?" I described the actual situation that existed at that time. I stressed that they were equal citizens, who had their own schools, press and freedom of worship. That freedom was guaranteed by the constitution. Relations between the Lithuanians and the Jews had been peaceful ever since the arrival of the latter in Lithuania. Pogroms were unknown.

Having heard me out, the general patted me on the shoulder in sympathy and said: "Herr Doktor, Sie sind zu jung,* ... to understand the gist of the problem. I'm telling you that the Jews practically don't exist. The Führer has taken a different decision. The Jewish problem must be solved immediately."

The general did not make clear what he meant by "...die Juden praktisch existieren nicht". I understood from his voice and the expression on his face that the phrase was fraught with great danger for the Jews, but it did not even occur to me that he had their biological extermination in mind.

Two days after that conversation, another man from Šiauliai and I, unable to get to the city, bought a clapped-out horse and cart (a better one would have been confiscated by the brownshirts) and proceeded towards our destination at a slow trot. Troops were moving on the main road, so we took back roads and paths. In a few places we saw Jews individually, and in small groups, who, suspecting nothing, were returning to their homes, which they had abandoned.

---

* "Dear Doctor, you're too young."

Watching them, I heard the menacing echo of the words: "The Jews practically don't exist ..."

I had my next conversation with the occupying forces after my return to Šiauliai. An influential Šiauliai resident called a meeting in the first half of July that was attended by some Germans and a few Lithuanian social figures. I was among the latter.

After dinner, conversations began. I was sitting next to Colonel Loeffler, a member (there were three of them) of the Šiauliai *Militaerregierung*.* He told me that he had been an officer in the First World War. After the war he became a pastor. When Hitler assumed power, however, he became fascinated by the leader's teachings, gave up preaching and joined the army again. A long time before that he had become interested in theories of race. He used to travel to Scandinavia and Palestine to study these questions. Therefore, he was extremely curious about what we, the Lithuanians, thought of the Jewish question, and what ways we envisaged for its solution.

I repeated the thoughts I had expressed to the general in Joniškis. In reply to the question about how we, the Lithuanians, would win back the positions taken by the Jews in the economy and trade, I said that this could be done with the help of various cooperatives. That is why Pienocentras, Maistas, Linas and hundreds of other small local cooperatives and banks had been created. Finally, I added that the facts showed that we had chosen the right course, that in five to ten years these questions would be settled, and that there was no need to resort to other measures.

The colonel was not satisfied with my conjectures. Maybe wishing to instruct me, he claimed that the Jewish question had been researched scientifically. To this end, the Institut fuer Rassenkunde** had been founded in Frankfurt. The institute had established that racial groups were not equal. Nordic-Scandinavian blood was rated the highest, Germanic blood was in second place, and the Lithuanian-Latvian tribes came next. The Jews were a foreign element among the German people and on the European continent. They had to be eliminated in the shortest possible time and by all possible means.

----

* Military authorities.

** Institute for Race Research.

World Jewry represented a powerful obstacle to universal peace. In Western Europe and the USA the Jews were powerful in terms of capital; while in Central Europe, especially in Lithuania and Galicia, they were strong from the point of view of biological capital, which showed in the form of a great population rise. If European and American Jewry were not supplemented with continuous immigration they would soon, over 50 years, die out, as their natural increment was insufficient to cover their death rate. Therefore, the Führer had issued orders to destroy the Jews' hatching places ("Judische Bruttstaette ausrotten") in this country and elsewhere.

The Führer had started a fateful struggle. No changes or compromises would be accepted in solving the Jewish question. All those who actively opposed the execution of the Führer's plan would be exterminated along with the Jews. My plans for solving the problem were naive and romantic. They had been tested in Germany and other countries, but the results had been insignificant.

Such were Hitler's general principles for solving the Jewish question. Listening to this lecture, I stated timidly that the Lithuanian people did not feel any mass hatred towards the Jews, and that it was difficult to imagine the Lithuanian community approving of these plans.

Later, our talk digressed. The whole conversation was interesting. A great amount of humanity shone through. I could not understand how such opposing ideas could fit in one person: flashes of nobility, and unbridled brutality, verging on bestiality. The implementation of everything that Colonel Loeffler had said soon began.

The commencement of the Jews' extermination in the city and district of Šiauliai made the Lithuanian community very nervous. The mood was probably noticed by the Nazi security forces. During these days, I met an SD chief, Lieutenant Bucalski, on Vilniaus gatvė. He stopped and asked me reproachfully:

"So, the Lithuanians are unhappy?"

It was clear to me that he was referring to the extermination of the Jews. At the time the entire Šiauliai district was in panic after the shooting of 2,000 Jews in Žagarė that had been carried out in a particularly cruel way.

"Mr Bucalski, I think you too would agree that one cannot be happy when one knows what is happening in Žagarė and other places."

My acquaintance with Lieutenant Bucalski was formal and official. But he was usually favourably disposed towards me. However, this time he cut me off and retorted angrily:

"Doctor, if you talk like that you will undoubtedly fall into the same pit. And no one will save you. The Jews doomed themselves by saying: 'May his blood be on us and on our children'. The Führer is fulfilling their own curse on themselves."

Talking to someone who had such perverse views was both meaningless and dangerous. Wishing to end the conversation in an inoffensive manner, I said:

"Would you refuse if I asked you to save a lovely Jewish girl?"

Calming down, Bucalski said:

"I understand you, we will do that."

We bade farewell to each other and parted. I did not meet him again. The Germans whom I met on business told me that he had gone to the front, where a mine had torn off both his legs.

It is important to recall one more conversation that happened at the beginning of the German occupation. In the period of independence I had been chairman of the Lithuanian Red Cross Šiauliai section. The Bolsheviks did not have enough time to destroy the Red Cross organisation. With the outbreak of the war, it was able to restore its activities immediately, to care for those who were suffering in the war and gather information about arrested and deported persons.

One day, I got a summons to go to the SD office. I was received without delay. The conversation was short.

"I am Gotschalk, Gestapo chief in the Šiauliai district. You probably know what the Gestapo is. I just want to stress that our institution operates absolutely independently, and reports only to the Führer. A dispute is going on now. It is affecting not only the soldier at the front but also the destiny of people in the rear. I want to tell you that from time to time you, as chairman of the Red Cross, will receive messages with either my signature or that of my deputy, which will indicate that somebody has gone away for a long time, an indefinite period, and that his family needs relief or care. Your office will do that."

I stated that the Red Cross provided relief to all those who find themselves in trouble. "The families listed in your messages will also be taken care of to the best of our ability." Gotschalk was satisfied with my answer. He thanked me and I left.

All the above shows that the anti-Jewish attitude was one of the most important principles of National Socialism and that it was imparted to the masses through propaganda and turned into an imperative commitment for the SD, the SA, the Gestapo and all the members of the Nazi Party. The principles for the solution to the Jewish question were formulated before the Second World War. Therefore, the main responsibility for the crimes committed falls on Hitler and his government. At the outset of the occupation, separate Lithuanians – some taking revenge for the participation of many Jews in the deportations of Lithuanians, others wishing to avoid punishment for their own collaboration with the Bolsheviks, and others who were mentally disturbed – were deceived by the SD into perpetrating these crimes. However, Lithuanian society as a whole and the Church hierarchy remained faithful to humanity and loyal to the Jewish people. The isolated instances of submission to the criminal influence of the SD were extremely short-lived. Their numbers decreased rapidly, and later they petered out altogether with the restoration of organisations that became the driving force of Lithuanian society and which paralysed SD activities with their dignity and moral authority. The Lithuanians soon not only totally freed themselves of the Nazis' corrupt influence, which had all the marks of psychosis, but also undertook separately and together measures which improved conditions for the Jews, who were subject to persecution and destruction, and saved large numbers of them from death. However, they were not able to take charge of the fate of all Lithuanian Jews.

Postwar research carried out in various countries that were occupied by Hitler shows that no one could save the Jews where Hitler's SD reached them directly. Not even the larger nations such as France and Italy could manage this. The final statistics reveal that, in terms of percentages, the Jewish survivors in Lithuania were more numerous than in some other states.*

---

* The author was writing in 1962. It is possible that the facts about the true extent of the Holocaust in Lithuania had not by then come to light.

The Nazis began implementing their plan for the solution of the Jewish question in the very first days of the occupation. The Šiauliai Jews, who before the Second World War had numbered about 6,000, were driven into a ghetto. This was set up, according to orders from the commandant, between Frenkel's factories and the station, on the so-called "Caucasian Slope", by the Prūdelis district. The Lithuanians were moved out of it to other parts of the town. The ghetto was surrounded by a high barbed-wire fence. It had to have only one entrance and exit. It was strictly forbidden for anyone to come near the fence, talk or sell anything. For a short time at the beginning, the ghetto was guarded by mixed units, German SA and Lithuanian police; while in later years it was guarded by Ukrainian partisans under SA supervision. Internally, the ghetto was administered by a Council of Elders, elected by the Jews themselves but approved by the Germans. The ghetto had its own police. The city government appointed a commissioner for Jewish affairs to deal with their concerns and liquidate assets not taken into the ghetto.

The Jews from the surrounding district were placed in a ghetto in Žagarė.

The German military authorities made their base in the building of the Hospital Fund; while the civilian authorities (the district commissar and his units) took over the large District House; and the SD and the Gestapo established themselves in Dr Luncas' hospital (Aušros alėja).

Šiauliai was taken without a major battle; therefore, the number of casualties was extremely low. However, the relief felt by the population was brief, as the first half of July saw the beginning of mass executions of both Lithuanians and Jews.

The hard labour camp in Šiauliai was overcrowded. It was crammed with communists, their close associates and also probably many innocent citizens denounced by malicious people. It was managed by the SD, who started carrying out nightly executions of the arrested. It was not possible to find out who provided the lists of victims, but all the signs pointed to the Gestapo. It became clear that the shootings were conducted without a court judgement. There was talk that the number of victims had reached 600. On behalf of the Šiauliai community, Fr Justinas Lapis, Feliksas Bugailiškis and Domas Jasaitis went to District Commissar Gewecke and asked him to stop these shootings and administer punishments only with a court judgement. He refused to halt the executions, but promised that in future they would be carried out only after a decision by a court. The commissar failed to keep his promise. The shootings went on as before, according to decisions made by the SD, the Gestapo and the commissar himself; however, they were not so numerous.

A much crueller fate befell the Jews. In mid-July the SD began their mass murders. The first victims were the elderly, the sick, the disabled and orphans. They were brutally herded into lorries, taken out of town and killed in the woods between Kuršėnai and Gruzdžiai (see the testimony of Leib Kibart). At that time a rumour went round that they numbered about 1,500. The killings caused widespread panic in Šiauliai.

The first appeal by the representatives (Fr Lapis, Orlauskas* and Jasaitis) of the Šiauliai population to Schropfer, chief of staff of the Šiauliai district commissar, requesting an end to the extermination of the Jews was unsuccessful. He cut short the conversation and warned them not to interfere in the affair, as it was for the exclusive knowledge and within the jurisdiction of the Germans. However, the killings of Jews, although less frequent, still continued. The Jewish Council of Elders continued to call for assistance. Therefore, the same people appealed to District Commissar Gewecke several days later, and asked him to stop the executions of innocent Jews. He gave them his word, which he kept.

By the end of the occupation there were no more large-scale massacres, with the exception of the execution of children in 1943.

In the majority of towns in the Šiauliai district the Jews experienced the worst suffering in the first days of the occupation. Many fell victim to squads commanded by Petras Požėla-Kolokša. Under instructions from the SD, the survivors were all taken to the ghetto in Žagarė. Their fate is described above.

Petras Požėla not only carried out the extermination of the Jews planned by the SS but was also an NKVD agent during the Bolshevik occupation (1940–1941). This fact was discovered in the spring of 1943. The Gestapo had him shot.

---

* Sic.

The Jews' life in the ghetto was hard. The place was overcrowded, and the sanitary conditions were dire. The "Caucasian Slope" had neither a sewerage nor a water supply system. Food rations were very small and were not distributed regularly. Most Jews were put to forced labour in factories, workshops or specially established enterprises. If they did not die from hunger and did not fall ill from malnutrition it was only because Lithuanians willingly supported them. All had one or two acquaintances among the Lithuanians. On their way back to the ghetto from work they would manage to meet and get food. Quite often the Lithuanians would give them food for nothing. Moreover, the Lithuanians helped them organise smuggling into the ghetto of food in larger quantities. This was an illegal trade involving great danger. Many Jews and Lithuanians who were caught suffered for it (see the testimony of Leib Kibart).

Jewish females were forbidden to bear children. Every pregnancy had to be terminated. Pregnant mothers risked death. This recalled the terrifying times of the Pharaohs.

The Jews were ordered to give all their gold, money and valuables to SD officers, but they gave up only a fraction of it. They entrusted most of these assets to their Lithuanian friends. It was all returned to them later.

I had close contacts with the Jewish representatives. They did not express a single complaint about the Lithuanians abusing their trust or misappropriating the treasures entrusted to them. The Lithuanians' loyalty to their Jewish neighbours is shown by the fact that Šiauliai did not witness a single instance of a Lithuanian reporting another who supported or maintained contacts with Jews.

The solidarity of the two peoples became especially strong in the spring of 1943, in late February or early March, with the Final Solution of the Jewish question under way, when a large task force suddenly rounded up the entire ghetto. Several dozen SD men came and demanded that the Jews give up their children. The official explanation was that the living conditions in the ghetto were too difficult for babies and children, and damaging to their health, and that therefore they were all going to be taken by train to Switzerland where they would be put under the care of the International Red Cross and various international Jewish organisations. The mothers had already suffered too many German atrocities and injustices to believe these words. Not a single mother agreed to give up her child. The SD then grabbed the children and threw them on to lorries. The victims numbered several hundred. However, some mothers still managed to hide their children in cellars, in pits dug in advance, in attics, in latrines, behind stoves or in other hiding-places.

Panic and screaming rose in the whole ghetto. The call for help spread to all corners. Struggles broke out between the unhappy mothers and the SD. The men were not in the ghetto, as they had been taken out to work. Maybe the struggles prevented the Germans from conducting a more thorough search of the ghetto, and made them content with several lorries loaded with terrified and screaming infants. The ghetto elder, Kartūnas, protested against the action and expressed his doubts about the official explanation for the deportation. The unit commander then suggested that he accompany the children, to see their new living conditions and tell the mothers of them, and comfort the women on his return. Faithful to his people, the dutiful and noble Kartūnas went on a doomed journey ... from which he never returned.

Several days later, the news came from reliable Lithuanian railway workers that the entire group of children had been sent to the extermination camp in Oswiencim.* There was no return from there. From there one would escape to freedom only in smoke.

After the news of the kidnapping of the Jewish children had spread round the city, the Lithuanians became involved in a mass rescue action. Over the next few nights nearly all the children (about 100) hidden by the mothers were taken out of the ghetto in sacks with the rubbish or with other loads, or in carts designed to transport horses, or were thrown at night over the barbed-wire fence, beyond which they ran into the hands of waiting Lithuanians.

There were a lot of problems with the rescue. Since a great number of Jewish families spoke Russian or Yiddish at home, their children did not know Lithuanian. Some showed the physical features of their race extremely clearly, therefore people would recognise them immediately, and it would be impossible to hide them. It was especially difficult to save boys. It sometimes happened that mothers

---

* Auschwitz.

who had given away their children in panic would ask some time later that they be returned. Also, some grown-up Jews who had already been freed and hidden would give in, break down psychologically, and return to the ghetto themselves.

Unlike the ghettos in Kaunas or Vilnius, the Šiauliai ghetto was not destroyed. It survived until 1944, with small fluctuations in the number of inmates. That spring large numbers of able-bodied Jews (which was all there were in the ghetto) were sent to work in the Rėkyva peat bog near Šiauliai, the sugar refinery and the Daugėliai brickyard near Kuršėnai. Smaller numbers were sent to various other sites. On the second occupation of Lithuania by the Red Army, they were taken to Germany. Since in October 1944, Himmler issued orders to cease the extermination, the Jews from the Šiauliai ghetto, finding themselves in the Reich, had a good chance of remaining alive. Information that came to light after the surrender of the Reich confirmed this assumption.

It is appropriate also to mention other kinds of aid provided to the Jews. Šiauliai had about 40 Jewish doctors. According to an order from Heinrich Lohse, Reichskommissar fuer Ostland,* they were forbidden to provide treatment to the Aryans. I, as head of the Health Department, presented a letter to the district commissar in which I explained that the removal of 50 per cent of doctors from their work was impossible even under normal conditions and dangerous during wartime when the threat of various epidemics was hanging in the air. Gewecke agreed, and allowed all Jewish doctors to work as laboratory assistants. It was a great victory for health care and for the doctors. If I am not mistaken, it was the only city in Lithuania which managed to achieve such conditions for its Jewish doctors.

However, there were people who reported me to the Chief Health Administration for it, but a short explanation was enough to make everything clear and have it approved. And when in November an epidemic of typhus broke out in Šiauliai, the district commissar was happy about his farsighted policy.

The Jewish doctors retained their position until the disbanding of the ghetto. Of those in the city, only Dr Gecas was killed. That

---

* Reich Commissar for the Eastern Territories.

happened long before the establishment of the ghetto. One night several armed men invaded his flat and took him away. The next day he was found outside the town shot dead. Attempts to find the perpetrators were unsuccessful. In 1943, Dr Kamberis perished under circumstances unknown to me.

Later another important issue arose, the supply of medication to the ghetto. The Germans were not interested in the health of their slaves (especially as a secret understanding allowed the extermination of those more seriously ill); therefore, they did not provide the inmates with medicines. I think the ghetto had several sources of drugs. I was one of them. Kartūnas, the neighbour mentioned above and a friend, maintained contact with me.

The ghetto needed mostly sedatives and painkillers, cardiac preparations, sulphanilamide substances, serums and vitamins. The anti-diphtheria serum was especially valuable. It was not easy to provide, because there was a general shortage of medicines. As head of the Health Department, I used to get permission from the district commissar to go to Karaliaučius* to purchase drugs for the city and district of Šiauliai. In addition to his permission, I would also procure recommendations from him. Moreover, I used to take some good flitch and ham with me. Sometimes I would give them some essential medicines from the chemist's shop in Šiauliai City Hospital, or I would buy them from the German War Hospital. I am pleased even today to recall the happy expression on Kartūnas' face when he used to get a large quantity of valuable drugs. It is important to stress that, despite the appalling living conditions, there seemed to be no epidemics in the ghetto. It is even more amazing that the typhus epidemic, which raged in the city in January and February 1942, did not spread to the ghetto either. The Jews were silent about it. Nor did the Germans know anything about the fact.

It must be stressed, in conclusion, that the Lithuanians' loyalty to the Jews lasted through the entire period of the occupation. It increased with the growth of Nazi atrocities against the Jews, and was universal. It came as a great pleasure for the people of Šiauliai to get the news from Kaunas that the Church hierarchy had condemned

---

* Koenigsberg, now Kaliningrad.

the extermination of the Jews. The same impact was produced by the memorandum presented by Aleksa, Grinius and Krupavičius to Lithuania's regional commander, von Renteln.

The opposition among Šiauliai inhabitants to the issue of the execution of the Jews was expressed by the Šiauliai and District Resistance Council underground newspaper *Lietuva*, which carried an article condemning the killings of the Jews and pointing out that all accomplices to such deeds would, after the war, be tried for the murders committed or complicity in them.

In this atmosphere all that was necessary was determination, goodwill, bravery and, probably most importantly, an absence of fear of reprisals by the SD. The formation of any committees or organisations at the time was forbidden. Therefore, assistance could only be provided by individuals. The Lithuanians rendered such assistance whenever the occasion arose. Quite a large number of inhabitants of Šiauliai provided it regularly on a small scale. Only this could ensure its success, as the SD and the Gestapo would not find out about it. It was known only to those who provided it and those towards whom the assistance was directed. Secrecy is a major requirement to any successful underground activity, but it is the enemy of history in that it does not usually leave any documented information.

I know that long-term and far-reaching assistance to the Jews was conducted by Sofija Lukauskaitė-Jasaitienė. The house that she lived in had two entrances from Vilniaus gatvė. It was good for a secret operation, as it had the offices of a doctor and a dentist, which were visited every day by several dozen people. Beyond them was a large garden full of trees and bushes from which one could get to Aušros alėja.

Not a single day passed without several Jews coming to the house to get some food, leave possessions for safekeeping, request mediation or some other assistance, or leave a message for another Jew. The mothers of the children rescued from the ghetto and hidden would also come for news. Sometimes the house would serve as a meeting place for Jews who lived in different areas and who did not have any other chance to meet each other. Sofija Lukauskaitė-Jasaitienė would provide temporary shelter in her home to a Jew who had been saved from the ghetto or who would come to her of his own accord. These people would be taken out of town by various means as quickly as possible. In special cases a hospital ambulance was used. They would be taken to points from which they could be picked up by further helpers.

It must be emphasised that farmers were less afraid of the risk and the punishment for sheltering Jews. Those who were rescued first had to be provided with passports or ID cards proving that they were Lithuanians and Catholic, and the children had to get birth certificates. About 150 personal identification cards, with the required signatures and seals, were obtained from the local government with much trouble and a lot of luck. Nearly all of them were used to rescue Jews. Only a few of these documents were issued to Lithuanians who were forced to hide from the SD or the Gestapo.

Identity documents were distributed to well-known and reliable people, and most Jewish doctors received them. Those with these documents would flee from the ghetto, or from their places of employment, which were guarded less strictly. Help in procuring birth certificates for children came from parish priests. The first and last names, and the date and place of birth of dead children would be taken from parish records. When issuing birth certificates to rescue Jewish children, the year indicated on a document and the age of a child receiving the document had to be taken into account.

The trouble would not end with a rescued child's removal from town and his or her settlement in a safe place. Sometimes it happened that those sheltering them or the Jews themselves would be overcome with a well-grounded or only imagined fear that the SD would discover what they were doing, and would demand that the Jew they were hiding be returned as soon as possible. In such cases, any changes were extremely difficult and dangerous. Sofija Lukauskaitė-Jasaitienė's intermediaries and messengers were often her son and daughter, and her sister's two sons.

I have already mentioned that large numbers of Lithuanians rendered assistance. I know that Fr Lapis, Fr Byla, Fr Dzegoraitis, D. Venclauskaitė and her mother, Deputy Mayor V.P., Dr Prialgauskas, H. Kildišius, Dr J. Luinienė, who was head of the Children's Unit at the City Hospital, and others were very active in this.

From 1929, Šiauliai had a convent of the Order of the Sacred Heart of Jesus, with about 20 nuns working at a primary school run by them. After the Bolsheviks invaded, the convent was destroyed, the school was shut down and the nuns were driven out. Luckily, they were taken on at the City Hospital as nurses, cooks and matrons. Having several of them in her unit and making good use of their devotion and help, Dr J. Luinienė managed to save over 30 Jewish babies and children. These children would find themselves in hospital as foundlings left at the hospital door or as would-be patients, where they received protection and treatment. Within a week or two guardians for them would be found, or they would be placed in the orphanages at either Vaiguva or Kuršėnai.

A great deal of assistance came from Fr Kleiba, the priest at Kužiai, who at critical moments would always find a way out. Kleiba was an ordinary and modest person who had an absolutely kind and noble heart full of Christian humanity. I beg the forgiveness of those people who contributed to the struggle but whose names I have not mentioned here due to forgetfulness or ignorance.

The rescue of Jews and their support created highly dangerous situations and required special efforts. However, Providence blessed those efforts: many dangers did not destroy them but passed them by.

The Lithuanian people had just regained their own freedom after a long enslavement. They not only enjoyed that freedom for 20 years but also shared it with all the other people living on Lithuanian soil.

In 1940, Lithuania was overrun by the Red terror; and in 1941 it was overcome by a brown plague. Over that period, when the Jewish nation found itself in mortal danger, the Lithuanians rescued Jews to the best of their abilities.

An important task rests on the shoulders of all those who rescued Jews, which is to record objectively their memories of those times and their actions. A huge job is awaiting our historians, to gather documents, take down the statements of witnesses, and portray in historically correct terms a picture of the terrible tragedy that befell our country. Although much delayed, it is not yet too late …

Draugas (Chicago): 25 September 1962

2. Series of articles "Lithuanians
in the Struggle for the Freedom of the Jews"
by Juozas Šalna (Liudvikas Šmulkštys*)

Chicago, USA: 1948–1949

Lithuanians in the struggle
for the freedom of the Jews

On 22 June 1941 the German army, after occupying Lithuania, immediately embarked on the massacre of all Lithuanian Jews. No distinction was made between young or old, intellectual or blue-collar, or laity and clergy; in a word, the Germans used the most atrocious means to shoot all Jews without distinction. The survivors were those whom the Nazis were simply physically unable to destroy in one fell swoop, and those who had enough time to hide somewhere at the beginning.

Quite a large number of Jews had been involved in the first Bolshevik Russian occupation of 1940–1941. They were also quite active in the Communist Party, the NKVD and the MOPR, and in government institutions and agencies, as well as in all areas of public life. Even former millionaires had pretended to be active supporters of Lithuania's cruel occupation and advocates of the new order. The Russian newcomers often relied on local Jews, and expressed their confidence in them. Quite a few Lithuanians noticed this identification of the majority of Jews with the Bolshevik government, to say nothing of the general discontent with the fact that in Lithuania the Jews were becoming more numerous than the Lithuanians themselves. True, in Bolshevik times Jews were also thrown into prison, and on 14 June 1941 some were deported in cattle waggons to Siberia along with

---

* LIUDVIKAS ŠMULKŠTYS (1902–1989) was born in Bardauskai, near Vilkaviškis. He studied at the Law Faculty of the Lithuanian University, and between 1928 and 1944 worked as a lawyer in Kaunas. In 1944 he fled to Europe, and in 1949 emigrated to the USA. He was one of the founder members of the Society for Acquaintance with the Culture of the Nations of the USSR. In 1943 he became a member of the VLIK's Rights Commission. He contributed to the press under several different names.

Liudvikas Šmulkštys (Chicago, 1966)

tens of thousands of Lithuanians. However, more level-headed Jews, and especially their rabbis, had warned during the Bolshevik period that their people's overly great involvement in the Bolshevik system might cost them a great deal in the future.

Thus, by the time the Nazis arrived in Lithuania, and with the beginning of the persecution of the Jews, the Lithuanian community was no longer favourably disposed towards them. The general opinion was against them, especially since hardly a week earlier, on 14 June 1941, mass deportations of the Lithuanians had been carried out, and some Jews had participated in this terrible undertaking, as NKVD officers or as Communist Party members. I have touched upon general opinion, as in the uprising of 23 June 1941 against the Bolsheviks, the masses – workers, civil servants and ordinary citizens – were the most active participants. It is these people who would prove more active in the difficult times to come. Intellectuals were always more reserved.

Despite this situation, many Lithuanians from various social groups immediately became involved in the rescue of Jews, saving them from death, and hiding and standing up for them wherever possible. This kind of assistance was provided regardless of the threat of imprisonment or execution. Only a tiny group, made up of the dregs of society, acted unfavourably towards Jews who had found themselves in trouble. However, there were also some heroic events, when a Lithuanian, pressed by the Nazis to kill Jews, would resist or even commit suicide ... All these facts will be recorded in detail, verified and described by unbiased historians in the future. I will describe a few separate incidents concerning the Lithuanians' struggle for the freedom of Lithuanian Jewry, and of the Lithuanians' assistance to the Jews in their tragedy, which are familiar to me. I know very well that my modest pen will hardly be able to describe the entire period with accuracy, but there are many Lithuanians and Jews living who will be able, of their own free will, to confirm, correct and supplement my statements, and in this way present an accurate picture of the aforementioned historical events. I believe deeply that the editorial office of *Naujienos* will not refuse space in its pages to this painful subject. I must also note that the effects of the Second World War are not yet over, and that it is thus necessary to take into account present conditions and to constantly be careful that in speaking of the misfortunes of the Lithuanian nation we do not cause suffering to another significant group of fellow countrymen.

General attempts to rescue Jews

With the outbreak of the war, some Jews made their way east. They moved slowly in the direction of Russia on foot or by any other way possible. The first ones to arrive at the border with the Soviet Union were stopped and forbidden to go further into Russia. Some tried to get in by some ruse, while the majority lost heart, surrendered to fate, and returned to their previous places of residence. This was especially common among those who had travelled a short distance from their homes. Those who had not made any attempt to escape, hid wherever possible, and tried to avoid being seen in public in the early days. The Nazis caught them, took them out of town, and shot them. This was common in the larger towns in particular. The Lithuanians began rescuing Jews. Prominent social figures and the clergy appealed to German military institutions, demanding an end to the extermination of the Jews. This way Z.T., who had just got out of a Bolshevik prison, saved a number of Jewish lawyers from death in the Seventh Fort in Kaunas. Rescues were also carried out in other towns and cities. Lithuanians hid especially large numbers of Jews from the first German strikes. They supplied Jews with food, clothes and money, and issued them with documents. The Germans immediately noticed these actions and, following the orders of their commanders, announced restrictions on the movement and lives of Jews, deprived the Lithuanians of all jurisdiction over them, and applied harsh punishments not only to anyone who aided them but also to anyone who held conversations or had any contact with them. In short, they themselves began to manage all Jewish affairs and removed them from the competence of Lithuanian officials. Shortly afterwards, they even set up their own special German institutions for the extermination of the Jews and the plunder of their assets. The heads of these institutions were sadists who could not live without shedding blood. Kaunas had an SA officer, Jordanus, who was well known for his savagery. The city commissar, Brigadier General Crammer, was not far behind.

Some Lithuanian officials made attempts to mitigate the Jews' fate by applying limited restrictions to them. The draft rules were shown to Simanas Bieliackinas, a well-known figure in the Jewish community and a professor of civil law. When he said "If such rules were to be the end of all the persecution of the Jews, we would be able to thank God," attempts were made to reach an agreement with the German military commandant. At the beginning, the German officer approved the rules; but several days later he stated: "New officials for Jewish affairs have arrived, and neither you nor I, Gentlemen, can do anything about it ..." Unprecedented killings and torturing of the Jews, and looting of their assets – gold, silver and jewellery – and their deportation to Germany began.

Then the Lithuanians made a verbal protest to the Germans about the persecution of the Jews, and the underground press, especially *Nepriklausoma Lietuva*, began to attack the Germans for the extermination of Lithuanian Jewry. In addition, they issued a strict warning to all Lithuanians not to contribute to this terrible undertaking, and to use all possible means to rescue the unfortunate Jews. A mass action of assistance to them ensued.

Shortly afterwards, a former president, Dr Kazys Grinius, Fr Mykolas Krupavičius and Professor Jonas Aleksa presented a memorandum to the German regional commander, Dr von Renteln, in which they also touched upon the horrible persecution of Lithuanian Jews. It was mostly for this that the three were arrested and interrogated brutally. Due to his age, Grinius was exiled for the whole period of the war to a village near Marijampolė; while Krupavičius and Aleksa were deported to Germany. All three were strictly prohibited from any public activity, and were kept under close observation by the Gestapo. The persecution of other Lithuanian intellectuals also began.

Secret Lithuanian anti-Nazi resistance organisations assumed responsibility for Jewish affairs and developed a rescue plan. Repeated measures were taken by Catholic leaders to use monasteries to hide Jews. As a result of this, more than one Jew was saved from a terrible death. Public opinion was also favourable to the Jews. Lithuanians forgot the negative words uttered to their Jewish neighbours, and expressed their deep sympathy for them everywhere. Hiding Jews in the country was common, due to which a number of farmers found themselves in prison or in concentration camps in Germany. In a village called Virbaliūnai, near Kaunas, two families of farmers were arrested and taken to an unknown destination by the Gestapo; several farmers were arrested and exiled from a village called Būdežeriai, near Vilkaviškis; similar things happened near Marijampolė. Farmers also lost their farms, which were turned over to the Germans.

To step up the actions in support of the Jews, a meeting was organised between Professor Mykolas Biržiška and the lawyer Levas Garfunkelis, a responsible figure in the Jewish community. The meeting took place in private in the office of a Kaunas lawyer, B. Many issues were discussed in detail, but the outcome of the meeting is not known to the author of these lines, only that attempts were made to promote support for the Jews.

Furthermore, foreign countries were warned about the extermination of Lithuanian Jews. Secret messages were sent to Berlin and Stockholm, and from there to the rest of the world. After this, the lawyer Rapolas Skipitis established contact with foreign countries and developed a project to send about 20 prominent figures from the Lithuanian Jewish community out of Germany. The suggestion was immediately conveyed to Garfunkelis in the Kaunas Jewish ghetto through the lawyer Aronas Makovskis. Some time later, the following reply was received from Garfunkelis: "These Jewish men will be the last to leave the ghetto". The motivation for this reply was that the Germans, if they found the list of the 20 Jews, would immediately put them all to death, and also that the 20 Jewish activists could by no means leave several thousand members of the Jewish community in the ghetto; they had to be the last to leave.

Action to rescue Jewish children also developed on a large scale after the news that the SS was getting ready for the horrible deed had spread. It yielded some positive results.

Details of support for Lithuanian Jews

At the beginning, the situation with clothes and food in the Jewish ghettos was very difficult. Donations were collected and distributed. Later, the food situation improved slightly. Most Jews did not complain about food shortages.

Kaunas lawyers frequently raised money to support their counterparts in the ghetto. I know well that such assistance was provided to Professor Simanas Bieliackinas, the district prosecutor Lurje, and the lawyers Viktoras Cimkauskas and Aronas Makovskis. Viktoras Cimkauskas was in a particularly difficult situation and received continuous support. Permanent contacts were maintained with Aronas Makovskis. His daughter was aided and hidden by a Kaunas tradesman, J.K. She was rescued, although both her parents perished. The lawyer Šmuklerytė was regularly hidden and supported by private individuals. A friend of hers, a former secretary of another lawyer, was also granted similar assistance. The tradesman J.K. took care of and supported the dentist O.G. on a permanent basis. Dr Kazys Grinius also for a long time hid and supported one of his Jewish acquaintances. Throughout the occupation, the late Dr J. Krikščiūnas hid in his own family a Jewish girl who is alive and well today. Especially great support for the Jews came from the bank employee and engineer Š., currently residing in America. The economist J.A. even risked his life when saving two Jewish children. Hunted himself by the Gestapo as an activist in the political resistance, he went into hiding and sheltered Jewish children. He sacrificed himself willingly in order to save others. He carried out honourable humane work.

The late Dr Ladas Natkevičius maintained constant relations with responsible persons in the Jewish ghetto, provided support to them, and notified them of impending dangers, as he had reliable sources of information among quite senior German officers.

Two lawyers from Kaunas spent several months in the Pravieniškės concentration camp, and lost their belongings simply for entertaining some Jewish girls. It was only due to the efforts of their relatives that they managed to avoid a crueller fate.

During the rescue of Jewish children, about 50, mostly orphans, were sheltered in the Kaunas Children's Home. All of them were saved.

I know that the following children were rescued through the efforts of Lithuanians:* a girl called Gar, both of whose parents survived and now live in Palestine; Ariva Tkač, whose parents are alive and living in Munich; Bracha Atlas, whose parents are living in Munich; Liuba Zilberg, whose parents were killed and is now being raised by a relative, called Zilberg, in Landsberg; Pupa Lifšic, whose mother died and whose father lives in Munich; Rūta Karnowski, both parents are alive, the mother living in Palestine and the father in Munich; a girl called Mincer, whose father died in 1945, and whose mother is still alive; Asra Ludwinowski, whose mother is alive and whose father is dead; Debora Kalvariski, whose father was killed and whose mother resides in the USA; Sara Weiss, whose father is alive, the fate of her mother is unknown; Eta Levin, both of whose parents are alive in Munich; Rita Gaison, whose father is dead and whose mother is living in Munich; Fira and Boris Nementschik, their parents are alive in St Ottilien; Ilona Ludwinowska, whose parents died; Miki Bukanc, whose father is alive and lives in St Ottilien, and whose

---

* Spellings are given as in the original.

mother was killed; a boy called Gringauz, whose father, a lawyer, lives in the USA, and whose mother perished; Dalia Vilenčuk, whose parents are alive and live in Oslo, Norway; Daniel Gold, whose father lives in St Ottilien and whose mother is dead; a boy called Lurje and his brother, whose parents live in St Ottilien; Sulamit Lewi, whose father died long ago, and whose mother resides in St Ottilien; and Imanuel Grinberg, whose parents are living in Palestine.

This list is far from complete. Through the greatest personal risk and continuous effort taken by the Lithuanians, another large number of Jews got back the greatest treasure of their lives – their own children. The Lithuanians who took this risk for the sake of humanity, and the Jews who are grateful to them, will certainly be able to add to this list.

Much support for the Jews came from Catholic priests, who issued them with birth certificates. The parish priest of the Kaunas Carmelite church was sentenced to three years of hard labour by the *Sondergericht*[*] for christening a Jewish girl. Jews were hidden in presbyteries, and priests also organised shelter for them with farmers. Their attitude towards saving Jews led other believers to get involved in it as well.

More detailed accounts of support for the Jews

I will give a few examples which show clearly how Lithuanians rescued Jews in their difficult situation. The following are the words of someone who organised rescue actions himself:

> During the German occupation I worked for the Textile Trust[**] in the capacity of factory director.
>
> This was a small factory set up in Bolshevik times, which at the beginning of the war had only ten workers and three clerks. There were plans to close it due to the shortage of raw materials, but the

---

[*] Special Court.
[**] In Kaunas.

cold winter of 1941–1942 made the Germans change their mind. In early 1942 large orders were placed, and by instruction from the top, the factory was granted priority immediately after the arms industry. The *Arbeitsamt*,* procurement offices and other institutions received an instruction to give priority to the factory. After the question of labour had arisen, 40 Russian prisoners were sent to the factory in the spring of 1942. They arrived in a deplorable condition. Most could hardly stand, and they immediately ate all the grass from the yard, and although only a few of them were able to work, they were kept at the factory out of sheer compassion. After a little encouragement of the workers, I collected some food and we began to make lunch for them every day. Over a short time, they all recovered and became an exemplary labour force. However, due to a typhus epidemic in the winter of 1942–1943, the prisoners of war were not allowed to work. But under pressure from the top, more and more production was demanded ...

The Lithuanian workers, whose number had by now reached 40, and myself, did not want to support the Germans at all. Therefore, work progressed very slowly, the products would come out extremely badly, and so on. To justify this to management, I would always point to the shortage of skilled labour, the poor raw materials, and the like. Then an inspector from Germany, Georg Dimmel, was sent, who, after a short while, reorganised the labour, but arrived at the same conclusion that I had. Unable to get Russian prisoners of war again, Dimmel asked about Jews. The Arbeitsamt gave its prompt approval, and Dr R., a representative of the ghetto Arbeitsamt, whom I had known for a little while before, arrived at the factory. The work conditions were rather harsh, but I promised to help the Jews as much as I could. Several days later, a group of 20 women arrived. It was headed by Dr Zalmanas Grinbergas, a 30-year-old born in Šiauliai. He had studied medicine and done his thesis at Zurich University. I had not met him before. Not knowing with whom I was dealing, at the beginning I was slightly reserved, but that lasted for a short time, the more so that Dimmel was a man of reasonable views who did not cause trouble or create any obstacles. After Dimmel's departure for Germany a couple of weeks later, we were left completely without restrictions. A black market was organised at our factory immediately, which was the only way of buying food for the Jews. Officially, it was all strictly prohibited, and I, as the person responsible, had instructions not to let Jews work

---

* Employment Office.

with others in the same room, to talk together, and so on. However, after certain measures had been put in place so that we would not be taken unawares, I allowed free trade under controlled conditions. Another very important issue was meetings between Jews and the local population. Most had left their savings and valuable possessions in the town long before being driven into the ghetto. They would maintain contact with the Lithuanians who kept their belongings.

I always used to have the best and most accurate information about life in the ghetto. The Jews would hide nothing from me. For about half a year, life in the ghetto was normal, if such a life can be described as normal at all. However, towards the autumn, things began to turn. One day the ghetto was converted into a concentration camp. At the beginning it was just a change of name, but soon the true nature of a concentration camp became apparent. The appointment of a new commandant, SS Lieutenant Colonel Goecke, did not promise anything good, as among Jews he was known as a liquidator of ghettos. He immediately undertook various kinds of reform, but I will not speak about that, leaving it to the Jews themselves. I will only mention the issues which had a direct impact on the Jews who worked at the factory under my management.

One day I received an official letter saying that within a few days the Jewish group would be recalled. At that time all Jewish labour units employed outside the ghetto were being recalled. I applied to the top. However, no one helped me to rescue the Jews and to create humane work and living conditions for them, as everybody was afraid of having anything to do with the SD and the SS, upon whose orders the Jews were being withdrawn.

The withdrawal was a big blow to the Jews, because they would be isolated from the town, which would mean their slow starving to death. After a few meetings with Dr Grinbergas, I called on the ghetto Arbeitsamt and happened to find Goecke there. Through the same Dr R. as an interpreter, I demanded a reply to the question whether the Jews would really be taken away, as I had to know, due to the orders from the army and so on. Thinking it over for a while, Goecke answered that in a couple of days he would himself come to the factory to familiarise himself with the work and the place. That was already a major victory, as the very question of recalling the Jews from the factory had become debatable.

On the date set, I sent the Lithuanian workers home early, telling them to tidy up their work areas accordingly, to change things slightly, and so on, in a word, to get ready to welcome the guest. At the agreed time, a car drove into the factory yard, from which Goecke and his adjutant got out. After spending a good hour on the site and familiarising himself with the work quite thoroughly, Goecke must have gained a good impression of our "village Potemkin", as we later called it, and put to me a totally unexpected question on leaving: "How many labourers do you need now?" Grasping the point, I replied: "I need about 100 people for a full team." I had not expected it at all, and began to modify the answer by saying that the total labour capacity could not be fully utilised at the beginning, that I could develop labour only gradually, and so on. Then he changed his decision in my favour, so that I had the right to get up to 100 people on terms and conditions set by me. That exceeded all my expectations. The victory was complete. In fact, the Jews were only recalled elsewhere, with the exception of a few places, probably a total of about ten in the whole city, instead of the previous couple of hundred.

In October 1943, I believe, the ghetto received the news that in Šiauliai the so-called "children's action" had been conducted: the Jewish children had been brutally rounded up and taken away into the unknown, to Auschwitz as it turned out later. Panic broke out in the ghetto, and everybody began to look for ways of hiding their children in safe places. The factory became a centre for meetings: not only would people meet there the Lithuanians they knew, but also complete strangers used to come who wanted to meet free citizens of the town. This way a good number of children were rescued.

I myself, after asking the advice of my family, on a dark November evening went to the barbed-wire fence of the ghetto to fetch the two-and-a-half-year-old son of Dr Grinbergas. Moreover, I personally helped a number of people to establish contact. I would make phone calls, go there in person, search through my own reliable acquaintances, and by other ways look for people who could help the Jews. My office, not to mention other more secluded places in the factory, was accessible to anyone who wanted to talk freely.

At Christmas in 1943 some prisoners from the Ninth Fort who had to dig up and burn the corpses of the Jews killed there in 1941, escaped. One of the escapees hid in the factory the whole day. Only Dr Grinbergas knew about him, and warned me that if by chance the Gestapo tracked him down, I should know what to do. According to him, in the evening the man left for Moscow. I have not heard about him since.

In early 1944, Ernst Hofmann was suddenly appointed to the factory as a technical manager. Special precautions had to be taken again, as he said from the very first day that he hated Jews. It was very difficult for me, because I managed to identify at the factory a few people who had been recruited by the Gestapo. Hofmann was a really awful person. I found out that he had been a private in the SA, and probably later joined the SS only to get rich. He dreamed constantly of victory, of how he would then reorganise the factory, how much he would be able to earn, and so on. He sometimes talked about it as a fait accompli. We used to laugh about it a lot in private. He knew that the only way of becoming wealthy was through the greatest possible exploitation of the Jews. He immediately set about abusing Jews for his own benefit: he would order them to give him food daily, which cost no less than 100 RM per day, to sort out his private quarters, deliver curtains, pictures, and so on. In his turn, Hofmann made no concessions towards the Jews, but would pressure them relentlessly, introducing larger and larger labour quotas.

March 1944 ended with the "action" of the ghetto children. As the factory was near the ghetto, we could see and hear well what was happening. Our German turned up at the factory. Pulling out his pistol, he ran throughout the factory, making the people work twice as hard, threatening to shoot them on the spot, and otherwise terrorised the crying mothers and fathers.

Not all children fell into the hands of the brownshirts. Some succeeded in hiding. Again, searches began of places where it might be possible to hide children for a long period. This time, it was even worse because every move was scrutinised and people were terror-stricken by the searching eye of the Germans. However, a number of Jewish children were rescued. Again there was a lot of telephoning and running about. The Jews themselves could already see that the end of the war was approaching, so many made a special effort to hide. A number succeeded in leaving, with the help of my factory. I personally assisted several people. With the beginning of the Allied landings in France, I would go home every day to listen to the radio in secret and, writing down the news, I would bring it to the ghetto.

I tried to do all this secretly, usually by myself, so that if I was caught I would not cause any trouble to others. Therefore, I often did not even know who I was talking to. For example, I would make a phone call to the German General Commissariat itself, and convey the regards of a Zosé to a Petras, and would say a couple of totally innocuous sentences, which, of course, were a secret code. Usually I would not even know who the people were and what the sentences meant, nor would I try to find out. I must note that the Jews were very good conspirators.

I was known among the Jews as an absolutely reliable person. Here are a few examples.

As I was standing one day in the factory yard, the guard let a young man in and pointed to me. The man approached me and asked, "Are you Director X?" and handed me a letter, only after I replied "Yes", and said, "The priest is sending you a personal letter." I must confess that I did not know any priest in the city, but the letter had my full name and exact address. Without opening it, I gave it to Dr Grinbergas. As far as I remember, this was very important news from a Jew who was in hiding, if I am not mistaken, with the Jesuits. The letter was addressed to the Council of Elders in the ghetto.

One day the Jews received quite a lot of meat at the factory. This came to Hofmann's notice, who said he would go to the ghetto to find out about the conditions. After his departure, half an hour later, the telephone rang and someone asked for me. A female voice said that when returning the Jews would be searched, because someone had reported them. It turned out that the caller was a ghetto employee, and the informer was Hofmann himself.

When going to Germany, I took Dr Grinbergas' son with me, and, finding the father there by chance, returned the child to him.

As I provided assistance without any material interest, now when meeting those survivors whom I managed to help, I feel a great moral satisfaction.

In conclusion, I would like to note that I have intentionally mentioned only Dr Grinbergas throughout this story; I have disguised the other names that I remember, Jewish and Lithuanian, on purpose, in order to prevent them from falling into the wrong hands. Dr Grinbergas is currently in Palestine, and he has promised to write his memoirs of the ghetto, in which a significant place will be devoted to the small factory under my management. Some of the other Jewish survivors are in Palestine, some are in North America, and quite a lot are also in Bavaria. They could also say much about my factory, which was well known to them ...

***

The fate of another Jewish family:

Chijena Šereševskienė came to my factory as an ordinary worker, a member of the Jewish labour group. She was a doctor of humanities from Jena University, and the owner of a knitwear factory called Beja. Her husband had gone to England just before the war and had got stranded there, while she was managing the plant and raising her two sons on her own. In the Bolshevik period of 1940–1941 she was put in prison as a former factory owner, and was only freed thanks to her good connections shortly before the famous deportations to Siberia of 13–17 June 1941. Warned by her friends, and wishing to avoid deportation, she hid in a remote place in eastern Lithuania. When the war broke out she found herself in Byelorussia, from where she later returned with various adventures to recount to the children she had left.

In the autumn of 1943, after the "children's action" in Šiauliai, Šereševskienė decided to hide, to go to a *malina*,* to use the ghetto slang. At that time she worked as a typist at my factory, which was officially forbidden by the Germans, as the Jews were supposed to do only hard physical labour. She began to ask for assistance for her children. I advised her to make contact with one of my old acquaintances. After a long deliberation, we chose Professor Jonas Šimkus, may his memory live long. He was ill then, and had been in bed for a long time, but he sent a relative, an engineer called S., who met Šereševskienė several times in my office and discussed the whole issue thoroughly. S., with the assistance of his brother, a priest (I think a Jesuit), provided her with a malina in the Rumšiškės district. She was to live there with forged documents. I knew the whole plan well, as I had discussed it with her many times and would give her moral support, advice and whatever else was necessary. All contacts were maintained through me, or else I would send a reliable person "on personal business". Before her departure, Šereševskienė left some of her more valuable possessions with my guards. She stayed in the malina with her children for three or four months. One day I heard that the Gestapo had found and arrested her and the children. I was greatly upset, because I knew that the Gestapo shot, without hesitation, all Jews arrested hiding with Lithuanian families; while the latter were arrested and sent to concentration camps in Germany, all their property confiscated and transferred to the ownership of the Germans. However, a few days later, Šereševskienė was released and returned to the ghetto, it seems for 5,000 RM. Such a low sum aroused my suspicions, especially since her two children had also been freed.

Several days later, Šereševskienė visited me with the Jewish ghetto labour force. The story of her arrest and of that of her children, which she told me, and the story told by others, tallied. Those people could

---

* A hiding place.

not have suspected that I had contributed to hiding her. Therefore, the entire story of the arrest was totally believable to me. The story itself goes like this.

One evening the house where Šereševskienė and her children were in hiding was visited by an SS patrol looking for partisans who were operating quite actively in the area. They checked the documents of all the residents, did not find anything suspicious and were about to leave. However, a Ukrainian, who had been a Russian prisoner of war, and who was with the German SS police, suddenly had a suspicion that Šereševskienė was a Jewess. He went to the bed where her two sons were sleeping, inspected them thoroughly, and called the Germans over immediately. They took Šereševskienė and her children away with them, and turned them over to the Gestapo. There she succeeded in ransoming herself quite cheaply. The Lithuanian helper was also arrested by the Gestapo and kept in prison for a long time, but somehow he too managed to escape any worse misfortune. The priest who had given Šereševskienė refuge under the name of his sister-in-law went through a long and difficult period of hiding. I knew him well, because several times S. sent him to me dressed as a civilian to discuss the issue of Šereševskienė.

My suspicions about the low price for Šereševskienė's ransom soon proved to be true. In less than two weeks, the Germans again conducted a new "children's action" and took both her sons away to be killed. This terrible misfortune had a tremendous impact on the mother, and sometimes she seemed to be mentally disturbed. Unable to find peace, she considered leaving the ghetto again, but at the same time she was afraid. She began to seek my advice. We arrived at the same conclusion, that the best thing for her to do would be to leave for Germany as a labourer from the east. At that time, the Germans would take by force a lot of the *Ost-Arbeiter** to take them to armaments factories, and would find volunteers very easily. Šereševskienė spoke perfect German, and so it was not too difficult for her to be included with the Nazis' other slaves. All that was missing were Aryan (non-Jewish) identification papers. We again engaged S., the documents were obtained, and Šereševskienė left the ghetto. She spent a few nights with my family, but her permanent place of residence for a while was in Didžioji gatvė. My wife used to take her possessions and letters there.

Around May 1944, Šereševskienė mysteriously disappeared from our world.

---

* Eastern labourers.

I got a message that she had left the ghetto. I did not hear anything about her falling into the hands of the Gestapo. This meant that our plan must have succeeded. I have to note that we had an excellent grapevine in the Gestapo. Nothing disappeared into the unknown. I received detailed information that Šereševskienė was to go to Vienna. She refused to go to Saxony, because quite a lot of Lithuanian workers had already been taken there, which might not be safe for her.

With the ups and downs in the course of the war, we eventually also found ourselves in various remote corners of Austria. I would often joke to my wife that we might meet Šereševskienė somewhere. The war came to an end. I met a handful of Lithuanian Jews, but no one knew anything about her. Suddenly one day I was called to the telephone. I heard the following words: "This is Šereševskienė, calling from Landsberg ..." That was 15 kilometres away from where we lived. The surprise was indescribable. The next morning she came personally to see my family. She told us her whole story. We learned that she had reached Vienna safely, and stayed in a factory there until the Russians arrived. While working at the factory, she had been reported to the Gestapo by a Russian worker, but it seems that the Gestapo had not believed it and had only asked the factory director for his opinion. The latter had not known anything about Šereševskienė, had not suspected her of being a Jewess, and defended her vigorously. After the arrival of the Russians, she had worked as an interpreter at the commandant's headquarters. She located her husband, who had fled from England to North America during the war and lived in Worcester, Massachusetts. Later she had left Vienna for Landsberg, from where she intended to go to Nuremberg, to the trials, to ask Rosenberg where he had sent her two sons ... I tried to put her off this. Although she had survived apparently sound, she discussed the question of her children like an insane person. Shortly after that, she went to join her husband in the USA, and I have not heard about her since. I know her address though.

I must note that Dr Šereševskienė is the lawyer Levitanas' sister, Levitanaitė. Levitanas survived and now lives in Paris. She left for Vienna with the help of a Lithuanian woman. Later that woman also lived in Vienna and moved to Bavaria just before the arrival of the Russians, and currently lives somewhere near Regensburg. That woman helped Šereševskienė find her husband.

***

Ona Šimaitė

Ona Šimaitė was a very modest and attractive girl who lived in Kaunas. She enjoyed the theatre and literature, and studied at the Lithuanian University. She did not shirk her social duties either. She participated in the work of the Lithuanian Teachers' Union, and in particular supported the activities of the socialists. She professed a deep idealism, and was for a long time a convinced socialist revolutionary. The motto of her life and work was: "Rights are only won through struggle!" She adhered to this maxim from the very beginning of her adult life and implanted it in others, and seems not to have renounced it even today. Šimaitė liked young people and worked with them. The Lithuanian authorities were not too approving of her goals and her public work. It had not been easy for her to find a livelihood until, assisted by friends, she got a job at the Lithuanian University Library. There she worked devotedly arranging books, which she liked so much. Professor Vaclovas Biržiška, the founder and director of the library, and a famous bibliographer and scholar, could say a lot of positive things about Šimaitė's activities. In this context, I want to say a few words about her work in the struggle for the freedom of Lithuanian Jewry. Guided by her idealistic socialist principles, a modest Lithuanian woman, an ordinary librarian, became a true heroine when it was necessary to provide aid to Lithuanian Jews who had found themselves in great trouble. She was selfless, and risked her life to rescue her Jewish neighbours, who were being tortured and murdered in the Vilnius ghetto. Newspaper columns are not enough to describe her deeds. It would require a whole book. I believe that this will be done in due course.

[...]* the journalist Šmulevičius from Paris wrote in a New York Jewish newspaper of 7 June 1948, issue No 18, 426, the article "Heroic Lithuanian Woman Helped Jews in Vilnius Ghetto". Let us read the words of this genuine witness:

---

* Line illegible.

Many years before the war, Šimaitė had worked at the Kaunas university library. When the war broke out she was living in Vilnius, where she also worked in a library. After the Jews had been rounded up into the Vilnius ghetto, on the third day, Šimaitė arrived with Gadliauskas, the head of the library, to find out personally how they could help the victims. Here is the story of how she got into the ghetto. E. Tit (?), vice chancellor of Vilnius University, asked her to go to the ghetto and collect any valuable books for the library. The Germans issued her with a pass. The vice chancellor was a Lithuanian woman, who knew that the purpose of Šimaitė's visits was not to collect books. In the ghetto she met many old acquaintances who were socialist revolutionaries, and a group of students that had attended the library. Taking advantage of the opportunity, she would take letters out of the ghetto and bring back answers, bring news about the war, and take custody of valuable documents, manuscripts and the like, for storage. She especially helped the poet Suckeveris, whom she used to meet by the building of the YIVO* when he was leaving after work. The Gestapo sensed that this Lithuanian woman was frequenting the ghetto not only to gather books but also for other purposes, and took away her pass. The wife of Jakobas Gensas, the Vilnius ghetto leader, would also come to the university library. Gensas himself was a tragic personality. A while ago he had fought for Lithuania's independence. When the Germans marched into Vilnius, the Lithuanians wanted to save him, and appointed him chief of the ghetto police. Gensas' wife was a Lithuanian, but officially he divorced her so that his nationality would not harm her. He could have rescued himself and hidden with his Lithuanian acquaintances. However, he did not, because he thought he might be able to help the Jews. What he did, like his personality, has remained a mystery to everybody ...

Thanks to Gensas' wife, Šimaitė obtained a pass to visit the ghetto, but on 23 April 1942, Gensas came to her and warned her not to come to the ghetto again. He said that the Gestapo knew about her assistance to the Jews, and if they saw her in the ghetto, ten Jewish policemen would be shot. However, Šimaitė continued to keep in touch with Jews who used to go to work outside the ghetto. At the beginning of the liquidation of the ghetto, she started to rescue the children. This way she saved the daughter of a Kaunas Jew, Bermann, and others. The Gestapo found out and arrested her on 28 April 1944. They tortured her for a full 12 days in order to get the names and places of

---

* Institute for Jewish Research (Yidisher Visenshaftlikher Institut).

residence of the rescued children, but she kept silent, and the Gestapo sentenced her to death [underlined by the author, Juozas Šalna]. Senior officials at the Lithuanian University made every effort to have the decision reversed, which they finally achieved. However, with the next deportation of Lithuanians, Šimaitė was sent to Dachau where, luckily, there was no room for them. Therefore, they were all sent to the Lidelange camp in occupied France. She spent four months in the camp and worked at unloading carriages. On 1 September 1944 the French army liberated her.

In Vilnius, Šimaitė had stated to friends that if she survived she would write a book on the Jews' suffering in the city. Now she is working on her memoirs ...

Šimaitė currently lives and works on the rue de l'Ouest in Paris. She is preparing to go to Israel to study Yiddish and Hebrew. She likes Jewish literature, especially the writer Bialik. In Paris she reports on literary and social issues. No one questions her commitment to the persecuted Jewish people. It would be highly desirable if she could describe in more detail her struggle for the freedom of Lithuanian Jews in the Lithuanian press as well.

The felt boot factory

Last year *Naujienos* carried coverage of the deeds of the felt boot factory's director in the struggle for the freedom of Lithuanian Jews. He organised the liberation of Jews from the Kaunas ghetto and their shelter after the escape. In the slang of the Kaunas ghetto, a hiding place was called a *malina* (Russian for "a raspberry"). I will give a number of true stories.

Aronšteinas worked at the felt boot factory. He was in a malina near the Medical Faculty of Kaunas Vytautas Magnus University, on the bank of the Neris. About 20 people were hiding there, all of whom survived. Aronšteinas survived, but he was later betrayed and is now in prison. Desleris survived as well. The names of the Lithuanians who hid the 20 Jews have been forgotten.

Bela Frenkelytė, the daughter of Vulfas Frenkelis, the famous owner of the horse-drawn trams in Kaunas, was saved from the Kaunas ghetto along with her son, and hidden. Everything was organised by her former nanny, a Lithuanian. Frenkelytė and her son survived and now live in Kaunas. Vulfas Frenkelis worked at the felt boot factory, and was deported to a concentration camp in Bavaria. The dentist Baronaitė, who had an office on Savanorių prospektas, was rescued along with her mother in the summer of 1944 by the owner of the Vilrita firm, whose name, I believe, was Mickevičius, and who now lives in Augsburg. Mickevičius is a person of democratic Christian principles. The women he rescued live in Palestine. Before that, Baronaitė had already been in a malina, but she fell into the hands of the Gestapo; however, she ransomed herself and went back to the ghetto again. Her father and brother perished in the first days of the war.

Ira Subockytė, the daughter of the famous Kaunas physician Dr Subockis, whose mother had worked at the felt boot factory and was later killed in the Nazi concentration camp in Stutthof, was taken by Lithuanians from the ghetto to a malina, escaped, got to Munich and there worked at the Jewish Central Committee. She may be living in the United States now. The girl Kleinaitė, whose mother had worked at the felt boot factory and later perished at Stutthof, and whose father, the engineer Kleinas, had been killed in the first few days of the war, hid with a Lithuanian family in Kaunas, on Miško gatvė, and survived.

For four months Šimaitė hid a young female Jewish writer called Sala Wachman, whose pen name was Ktana. The money for her subsistence came from Professor Mykolas Biržiška. He used to allocate every month a certain amount of cash for the support of other Jews in the Vilnius and Kaunas ghettos. He sent the money right up to the time of the liquidation of the Vilnius ghetto. Šimaitė collected money and food from Professor Biržiška, Fr Alfonsas Lipniūnas, and a number of other Lithuanians and Poles who made contributions. She would also supply Jews with documents, and maintain contact with those hiding in the woods. Every step in helping Jews involved great risks, but she ignored them and worked with great devotion.

Apart from these people, a number of Lithuanians assisted Šimaitė in her activities. She published an article in the American newspaper *Litvisar Idiš* on the work of Catholic priests. The poet and priest Mykolas Vaitkus used to help the well-known Kaunas librarian Balošeris, and christened Baugriauskis' daughter, Baugriauskaitė, in order to save her life, rather than to convert her to Catholicism. The poet Kazys Jakubėnas cooperated actively with Fr Vaitkus. They were both poets, one held deep Christian views, while the other had socialist ideals. Both provided assistance to the Jews. A soloist from the Kaunas State Opera, Jadvyga Vencevičaitė-Kutkuvienė, also helped the Balošeris family and other Jews a lot. Professor Biržiška visited his friend, the mathematician and poet Leo Bernstein, in the Vilnius ghetto. He was also a supporter of the Jews. A Lithuanian carpenter and Professor Bieliukas each hid Professor Movšovičius for two weeks, who was later taken in by Poles.

The poet Suckeveris writes in his book *Die Vilnaer Ghetto** that the archivist, Fr Juozas Stakauskas, rescued 13 Jews. Some Jews consider Fr Stakauskas to be a Pole for some reason. In fact, he is a pure Lithuanian, from the Vilnius area, who until 1922 went to the Rygiškių Jono Gymnasium in Marijampolė, studied history at foreign universities, and has always written scholarly papers in the Lithuanian language. For some time he was also head of the State Archive at the Seventh Fort. He is a wonderful man. He is a person of great moral stature, tolerant and totally devoted to learning. It is not at all surprising that he worked hard and risked a lot to rescue Vilnius Jews. Suckeveris also writes about the feats of the Lithuanians Jankauskas and Kazlauskas in supplying the Vilnius Jews with weapons. He mentions the work of the poet Kazys Boruta and Ona Šimaitė as well.

As evidenced by Ona Šimaitė, particularly great energy, ingenuity and determination in rescuing Jews were demonstrated by the Lithuanian official Rutkauskas. He issued false papers to a great number, and saved the lives of more than 100 Jews. He used to organise sending Jews to various jobs in Germany. Those operations were extremely dangerous, but they helped to rescue Jews from death. Convincing documents and constant pretending by the Jews allowed them to avoid trouble. Rutkauskas adopted a little Jewish girl, but in order not to let her remain an orphan he went to Riga and brought her mother back secretly ... That was a daring deed and a great risk to his own life and those of his family. In the opinion of Šimaitė, this was almost the only case when an Aryan managed to get into the

---

* *The Vilnius Ghetto.*

strictly controlled Riga ghetto and get a Jewish woman out of it. Rutkauskas reunited the mother and the girl and kept them both at his house. After the liquidation of the Vilnius ghetto, there was not a single day without ten or even more Jews hiding in Rutkauskas' home, and whose affairs he looked after himself. The most interesting thing is that, using his daughter's birth certificate, he obtained a passport in the name of Margarita Rutkauskaitė for the Jewish girl Zana Rann, and found a translator's job for her in a German office in Minsk ...

Eimaitytė, who worked at Vilnius University Library, worked especially hard to obtain forged documents for Jews, with which they could leave the ghetto and hide with Lithuanian families in and around Vilnius.

The Jews had earlier shown a lot of loyalty towards Lithuania, especially in legal circles in Vilnius and Klaipėda, in diplomatic activity, and in their writings and social work. Dovydas Eichornas, Dimantanas and Kacenelbogenas who translated Lithuanian *Dainos** into Yiddish and English, deserve a mention. The Lithuanian Ona Šimaitė and all her famous co-workers rescued Jews in deep trouble, hiding them and preserving their culture.

***

A few introductory remarks

The Lithuanian Jewish Society in America has accused Lithuanians, and even the entire Lithuanian people, of participation in the massacre of the Jews. I have not heard or read anywhere about the Society revoking this terrible and unfair accusation. Nor have I heard of Jewish figures publicly condemning the outburst from the Lithuanian Jewish Society. On the contrary, this official institution of American Jews has responded to my articles in *Naujienos* about the struggle by Lithuanians for the freedom of the Jews by accusing the Lithuanians severely, and making every effort to belittle the facts about support rendered to the Jews described by me and to show them as totally

---

* Songs.

incidental and useless. They have also claimed that the little help that was given allegedly came from the Tartars or the Russians, rather than the Lithuanians.

This situation forces me to continue to write on this theme and to present to the public more facts about the struggle by Lithuanians for the freedom of the Jews. I have been assisted by Ignas Vytenis, an indefatigable worker for Lithuanian society, and an honest man, who suffered for years in the Nazi hell that Stutthof was, and who has provided a lot of new material for my articles, which I, making use of the kind offices of *Naujienos*, continue to make public. Some material was also provided by generous readers of *Naujienos* who read my articles and sent me their reminiscences and experiences. I hereby express my sincere gratitude for this support, both to Vytenis and to the kind readers of *Naujienos*.

There are some people who, after reading my articles, claimed that the issue had been raised prematurely. They said that on the one hand it could cause unnecessary conflicts with the Jewish community, and on the other the people mentioned in my accounts who felt unsafe might suffer. I have an explanation for this as well. When the Jews are accusing the Lithuanians so terribly, writing in newspapers and even in books about the crimes of Lithuanians against them, how can we not write about the heroic help from the Lithuanians for the Jews in the truly horrible misfortune that befell them? Can't those who are unfairly attacked and accused not defend themselves? Of course they can! We have to explain to the public how things really were, and what the role of the Lithuanians was. Certainly, there was a small group of criminal and Bolshevik elements who collaborated with the German killers; but are all Lithuanians to be blamed for that, even the entire nation? There were some people among the Jews themselves who mercilessly persecuted their own Jewish brethren, so can we accuse all Jews of murder? My articles are not only timely but maybe even a little late, because the defamation of the Lithuanians by the Jews has become widespread and has harmed them in the pursuit of their own goals. Furthermore, the Lithuanians mentioned in my articles can by no means be in danger, for they, risking their own lives, property and status, and that of their families, did much good to their close neighbours, the Jews, and no one can be accused, persecuted or harmed for making such a sacrifice. On the contrary, all these people must be properly recognised and honoured. We must not remain silent about them. We must record their names and make them known, so that they are not forgotten and so that they remain a virtuous example to future generations. Certainly, my modest pen cannot record them all. This is not one man's work. In fact, recording and disclosing the names of the Jews' rescuers will probably never be done. Therefore, the statement from *Dirva* that Juozas Šalna has named all the rescuers of the Jews is incorrect and misleading. There are thousands of them, and I have mentioned only hundreds, and not in proportion to what they did for the Jews, but only those about whom I have received information.

I would like to take the chance to request that honourable Lithuanians and Jews either correct or fill in mistakes or details in my articles, and in this way explain the true facts about assistance from the Lithuanians to the Jews. I appreciate this co-operation in advance.

More about Ona Šimaitė

I have already written in *Naujienos* about the great acts of Ona Šimaitė in relieving the Jews' problems and misfortune, and on her death sentence and its commutation to imprisonment in a German concentration camp. Now I would like to give a more detailed account of the heroic deeds of this dedicated woman.

All the time, Šimaitė lived and worked in Lithuania's historic capital, Vilnius. She is currently in Paris and is getting ready to leave for Israel.

With Šimaitė involving a number of people in the action of rescuing Jews in Vilnius, and with much support coming from the writer Kazys Boruta, they succeeded in getting out of the Institute for Jewish Research and hiding all the letters of the Jewish writer Perecas, several rare incunabula, and some photographs and manuscripts. In addition, Šimaitė managed to save the Vilnius ghetto chronicle compiled by G. Šuras, written in great secrecy, which depicts the development of events in the ghetto. Songs from the ghetto written by the poet Suckeveris, and about 30 songs by unknown authors, were also saved. These songs used to be sung in the ghetto. They also hid 200 letters written by Jews in hiding during the war, and another 30 composed after the ghetto's liquidation. The 16-page article "The Old and the New Ghetto" by the Jewish historian Heller was also saved. The article contains statistics about how many Jews were killed by the Nazis, and when.

At the time of Šimaitė's arrest, the Gestapo discovered the archives of the well-known Jewish director N. Eljaševas and the manuscripts of Movšovičius, a professor of botany and an authority on Lithuania's flora. Movšovičius had earned his doctorate for his thesis "The Flora of Paneriai", in which he described in a scientific manner the flora around Paneriai, which became the site of mass graves for the Jews. There is a certain irony in that.

Šimaitė also saved the memoirs of Sala Wachsmanaitė about the Germans' arrival in Warsaw, and her mystical drama about the Vilnius ghetto.

From 14 September 1941 to 26 April 1943, Šimaitė visited the Vilnius ghetto both legally and illegally. Later, she used to meet with Jews only outside the ghetto. She would travel on important business to Kaunas and Riga, and meet with imprisoned Jews. For several days she sheltered in her apartment the Polish Jewess and nurse K. Zaborowska, a teacher of English called Taper and her 13-year-old daughter, Ana Abramovičienė, the wife of H. Abramovičius the director of the Vilnius Jewish Crafts School and a writer, and others. She obtained documents for Alė Bermanaitė which recorded her as her relative under the name of Aldona Daujotaitė, and placed her in the Antakalnis orphanage in Vilnius. This ten-year-old girl spoke excellent Lithuanian because her parents thought that living in Lithuania they had to know the language well. Šimaitė was arrested by the Germans along with this girl.

***

The work of Bronius Gotautas

In Petrašiūnai, a suburb of Kaunas, there lived a simple craftsman called Bronius Gotautas. As a matter of fact, he was a man with a very kind nature. His goal every day was to help other people as much as possible. He was a deeply religious and just man, and kept in close touch with the Capuchin friars. Terrible days befell his brothers, the Jews. The monks helped to hide and rescue Jews, and their most active helper was Gotautas. He would take on the most dangerous and difficult jobs. He used to run errands and transport people. A number of Lithuanian Jews found refuge in the friary. Many were saved from death. A significant number of Jewish children found compassion through the efforts of these good people. Lithuanian residents in the area were also eager to join in the rescue of the Jews. The friars and Gotautas had quite a strong influence on them and involved them in rescuing Jews. The friars themselves were encouraged in this by their charitable goals and by their spiritual leaders, the bishops. Moreover, the Gestapo, with all its gangs of spies, did not interfere so much in the activities of the friars either. The Germans still respected the Catholic clergy, and therefore it was a little safer for them to rescue persecuted Jews. The activities of Gotautas deserve a fuller description.

With the invasion of the Bolsheviks, Gotautas has found himself in exile. A number of Jews rescued by him also escaped. Their gratitude was boundless. The Jews who he had hidden and saved from starving to death made every effort to reward their benefactor. They sent letters of gratitude, clothes and food to him from various countries. Gotautas has recently received a parcel from South Africa. He has also received news from Palestine from people he rescued. A sick man himself, he is in a German hospital now. He is suffering from epilepsy and serious kidney disease. Material assistance from the Jews to their benefactor is now particularly important. They also ought to describe more thoroughly the deeds done by Bronius Gotautas and the Capuchin friars of Petrašiūnai in aiding and hiding Jews. This would provide quite a lot of important historical facts about Lithuanian-Jewish relations and give a more detailed view of the role of Lithuanians at the time of the persecution of their Jewish neighbours. Maybe then the irresponsible accusations and attacks on each will become fewer. The surviving Petrašiūnai and Pažaislis monks should also take up their pens and describe their deeds.

The helpers of Bronius Gotautas

Gotautas' chief aide was Sofija Binkienė, the wife of Lithuania's best-known poet, Kazys Binkis. Her flat in the Žaliakalnis district of Kaunas became an office for Jewish affairs. It was frequented by Jews who were in hiding and Lithuanians who provided assistance to them. Gotautas was a regular visitor too. He would find Jews who needed assistance and provide them with documents and hiding places. Binkienė received a particularly large number of internal passports and other types of papers, as well as extracts from registers of births and marriages. Such documents might give the name Jonas Petraitis instead of Mordchelis Šeinas, Lithuanian rather than Jewish nationality, Roman Catholic instead of Jewish, a birthplace in a village like Žagariškės instead of the city of Kaunas, and so on. With these documents, Lithuanian Jews found it much easier to hide, and they caused less danger to the Lithuanians who harboured them. Gotautas used to get these documents in the towns of Vilkaviškis, Marijampolė and Tauragė and from various parishes. Birth and health certificates were readily issued by the director and a doctor at the Kaunas Red Cross Hospital Women's Clinic whose name I do not remember. He sheltered and gave jobs in his hospital to four Jewish girls. One of them worked as a nurse. With the assistance of this courageous hospital director, false documents were provided to five Jewesses who were sent to factories in Austria along with deported Lithuanian girls. They survived, while in the Kaunas ghetto they would have been sent to their deaths.

Binkienė used to give the documents to persecuted Jews. She received much support from her children in this humane work. The Jews themselves could say a lot about the dedication of Binkienė, because everybody knew her well. Often Jews would get the documents of deceased Lithuanians, in which only the pictures would be replaced.

Jews were much aided by the Capuchin, Salesian and Franciscan communities. Fr Paukštys was especially prominent in these undertakings. According to the rules, Jews were not allowed to come into the monasteries and could only visit the guest rooms, but otherwise they helped Jews a great deal.

The student Juozas Gražys was a close associate of Gotautas in giving assistance to the Jews. He rescued many Jewish children in particular. Along with Gotautas he was also involved in the circulation of anti-Nazi publications. Once a Gestapo officer caught them by surprise in a room and was about to arrest them. Two thousand copies of a small newspaper *[Laisvę* were also hidden there. Either not wishing to conduct a search alone or being afraid of the two men, the Gestapo officer reached for the phone to call his headquarters and ask for help. The student kicked the man in the groin, grabbed the package with the banned literature, and dashed through the door. Gotautas did not hang around either. By the time the Gestapo man came to his senses, the two brave men had vanished ... They both continued their secret work in assisting the Jews and circulating illegal publications.

Dr Steponavičienė also helped the Jews a lot, together with her maid. They both rescued Dr Mendelovičius from Kretinga. They helped other Jews and supported Bronius Gotautas.

Vincė Jonuškaitė-Zaunienė, a soloist at the State Opera, also sheltered Jews in her family. She hid a chemist from Kaunas, called Vaksas, and his wife. Vaksienė was a maid. Vaksas was later arrested, and his fate is unknown.

At the rehabilitation centre for consumptives in Aukštoji Panemunė, a Jewish girl was disguised as a nurse, and a Jewish boy worked as a stoker. That required several people's assistance and involved great risk.

The engineer Antanas Šapalas was the most active helper of Gotautas. He rescued a great number of Jews. He fell out of favour with the Gestapo, was arrested and died in the terrible concentration camp at Stutthof.

I have mentioned here only a few examples. The helpers of Gotautas were hundreds of ordinary Lithuanians whose good deeds and dedication were not valued properly and which were not recorded in time. Their names are known to just a few people, and will soon disappear.

Letters from Jews to Bronius Gotautas

Appreciation of the actions of Bronius Gotautas can be seen in letters from Jews. These letters are quite typical, and I want to quote from some here. Two were received from Lithuania, and one even came from South Africa. Let the Jews speak for themselves:

Vilnius
8.8.1948

My Dear Brother, Companion and Benefactor,

My name is Bronė Kukytė [the name has been changed, for obvious reasons – J.Š.] and I am writing to you from Panemunė. I have learned about you from the pharmacist. I am so glad that you are alive, and I hope that we will meet again. You must be having a hard time in a foreign country, far from your homeland. I have written about you to Lithuanian Jews in Africa. There is a committee of Jews from Raseiniai, the chairman or secretary of which is our acquaintance, B. Fridmanas. He has also written to you and asked you to give him your correct address, so that the committee can help you. Please do not feel shy, and reply to them immediately. They write that it is a real joy and a great honour for them to help such a humane benefactor as you.

I live now in Vilnius and teach at the university. Benutis goes to school, and Jadzė manages the house. Our life is quite good, and I often remember you with gratitude and love. Take care and please write a few words about yourself to me.

Formerly Bronė Kukytė.

The letter also contains a postscript:

You can write to Fridmanas about yourself. He has also written to you.

Moreover, my honourable brother, I have just received a letter which says that another committee, that of the Triškiai Jews, has already sent two parcels to you: one with clothes and the other with food. They all write that it is a great pleasure for them to help you, and they will send more if only they know that those parcels [...]* the following contents:

---

* Line illegible.

Another letter goes:

Vilnius
15.9.1948

Dear Brother, Bronius Gotautas,

Not getting a reply to my first letter, I am writing once again and hope that this time, even if this letter does not reach you, it will reach some of your friends who will be kind enough to tell me where you are now and how you are. There are very many people wishing to help you, but they refrain from doing so only because they do not get answers to their letters. The pharmacist has visited me, and all our talk, of course, was about you. I hope at least you can take a short rest after the hardship experienced and be able again to support and help the poor, as you have always been accustomed to doing.

Goodbye, dear brother, I wish you all the best.

Formerly Broné Kukyté.

This is what the letter in Yiddish from South Africa says:

Dear Friend, Bronius Gotautas,

I have heard about the good things that you did for many Jews in Kaunas. And I am writing and asking you: what do we have to do in order to help you? Mr Benjaminas Fridmanas has recently sent you a parcel with food. Please reply to him after you get that food parcel. Tell him what he has to send you in the future: food parcels or something else, maybe money directly? So, please write to me as well. Would you like to come to Africa, to Johannesburg? If so, we will tell your friends here. I am writing to you in Yiddish because I do not know Lithuanian. A Jew must read the letter to you and write the answer. We want the Catholic Church to look after you, and if you want you will be able to come to Johannesburg. What do you think of that?

Mrs Kagintan from Viekšniai has told me that she has received a letter from you. Write to me about your friends and people whom I know from Lithuania. I want to find and help them. If you write to me please also write to Doctor If. I will find him and give him the letter, or you can write directly to him. Describe your condition in detail. How are you doing? How is your health? Do you have enough to eat? Do you need clothes? Please reply by air mail. I hope you keep healthy.

I am thinking about you.

Joseph Schain.

Give me the names of your Jewish friends whom I know in Johannesburg. And if you have their addresses then give them to me. I know Dr If. here from Vienna. Does he also know you?

Bronius Gotautas received two parcels with food from his Jewish friends: one from Mrs E.K. and the other from Mrs Kaganton* .

Gotautas received more letters, and it is impossible to mention them all here. The Jews looked for him very actively, but he sent only a few replies to their letters, for various important reasons. So far, the Jews' assistance to Gotautas has been quite modest.

The eventual fate of Bronius Gotautas

By taking constant risks and rescuing Jews, Gotautas did not escape a cruel fate either. The Germans hunted for him relentlessly. They put up large sums of money for this. However, they failed to catch him. Only with the Bolsheviks approaching Kaunas, did the German police seize Gotautas on 22 July 1944 by sheer chance in Aukštoji Panemunė on his way back from the Pakuonis district. The Russians entered Kaunas on 30 July 1944. Before this, everything was evacuated to Germany. They took Gotautas too. At the beginning he was ordered to dig trenches, and was later confined in the horrific concentration camp at Stutthof. He suffered terribly there. He is not a very healthy person, so all the insults, torture and persecution by the SS were hardly bearable to him. Several months later, the Russian army approached, and the Germans evacuated the concentration camp too. Gotautas was taken to Baden Baden. There he was also made to do hard labour. Finally, in April 1945, the French army freed him. This way, this prominent figure found himself in exile. He had Certificate No 5,000 issued by the Lithuanian Anti-Nazi Resistance Political Prisoners' Society. He was granted Displaced Person's rights and received maintenance from the United Nations Relief and Rehabilitation Administration; now he receives aid from the International Refugee Organization (IRO). His health has been damaged by so much suffering. He has a chronic intestinal ulcer and also suffers from epilepsy. He did not remain idle, but worked as much as he could for the Chief Administration of the Lithuanian Red Cross. He was known for his decency, and especially for his fairness. Certainly, he is not fit to emigrate, as he is unable to do hard physical labour any longer. All

---

* *Sic.*

his life he has distributed mostly religious books, and made his living that way. Now the IRO office has resolved to place him in a camp for non-emigrating and ailing deportees in Bad Jardan or Biberach.

Bronius Gotautas' important anti-Nazi deeds and humane rescues of Jews will not be forgotten soon by the self-respecting Lithuanian community. However, Bronius Gotautas was not the only decent activist in Lithuania during the German occupation. There were hundreds, and maybe thousands, of them. One needs only to find and honour them and record their heroic deeds. Then Lithuanian Jews, who have suffered a lot, will also cease making accusations against the Lithuanian people for the persecution of their Jewish neighbours who were in great trouble. Maybe they will then come to their senses, will start supporting their benefactors more, and understand the Lithuanians' national and political goals. Instead of sabotaging them, the Jews will support their efforts, as most of them did in 1918–1922 when creating the independent Republic of Lithuania.

Naujienos (Chicago): 21–27 April 1948, 30 March 1949, and 13 June 1949

3. Report of 15 May 1946 by Sofija Lukauskaitė-Jasaitienė* to the VLIK on the rescue of Jews

Tubingen, Germany: 15 May 1946

The report of Sofija Lukauskaitė-Jasaitienė

Everyone had known for a long time about the aggressive anti-Semitism of the Nazis, but we saw it in its most terrible form only after their occupation of our country. The extermination of the Jews started in Lithuania immediately after the arrival of the SS and SD

---

* SOFIJA LUKAUSKAITĖ-JASAITIENĖ (1901–1981) was born in Šiauliai. She studied to be an agronomist at the Berlin Higher Agricultural School, and also in Denmark. From 1926 to 1940 she was chairman and a member of the central board of the Šiauliai section of the Lithuanian Children's Society. In 1950 she emigrated to the USA.

Sofija and Domas Jasaitis

troops. All those not brutalised could not witness the massacre of innocent people without being horrified. With the beginning of the extermination their rescue also started.

Why was it so difficult to save Jewish children?

1. Jewish children generally did not know other languages: they spoke only Yiddish, and those who had known some Lithuanian before forgot it completely in the ghetto. Even if they knew a foreign language (Russian or German), listening exclusively to slang over those three years, they would speak it with such an accent that one could recognise them from afar. Thus the absence of a knowledge of the Lithuanian language was the main obstacle to the rescue of Jewish children.

2. Jewish children were often spoilt, had difficulty in adjusting to a strange environment, would not take a single step without their mothers, and would keep repeating the word "ghetto" in their conversations.

To be fair, we must stress that Jewish children had a strong instinct for self-preservation and a certain slyness, which often saved them from death.

Why was it so difficult to save a Jew?

1. The Jews were very irresolute: if an escape involved risk, they would back out. They would leave the ghetto only if everything had been organised well in advance. More than one Jewess told me openly about that trait.

2. If after an escape Jews were arrested and interrogated by the Gestapo, they would give away all the details about their rescuers, including the names, which posed a great threat.

Rescuing a Jew was always full of danger to the person and his or her relatives. Meanwhile, the circumstances of a rescue were so difficult and complicated that at least five people had to be involved. Entire families were put in danger for one rescued Jew. However, there were quite a lot of Lithuanians who did rescue them.

How would an escape be organised?

1. A birth certificate for a child or identity documents for an adult would be obtained.

2. A safe place for residence and determined people who would agree to accept a citizen deprived of rights would be found.

People would rarely rescue for material reward; usually they did it out of religious principles or for humanitarian reasons.

Birth certificates were prepared as follows: blank forms already with a seal would come from parish priests. They only had to be filled in appropriately and signed with the name of a priest who was not in Lithuania or who was even deceased.

In most cases, the steps were as follows: the name of a dead child whose age approximately matched that of a Jewish child to be rescued would be found in parish records, and, after learning the name, surname and date of birth of the selected child, an application would be made to a registry office, which (not suspecting anything) would issue a real birth certificate. The issue of a birth certificate alone required at least three people ready to break the law: a trustworthy person who would apply to the priest; the priest himself; and an inconspicuous person who would not be questioned at the registry office.

An adult's identification papers required the following:

A blank passport form with a seal would be stolen from a local government, or a person in the local government found who would have the courage to put a seal on the appropriate form with a picture. Creating the text of the document was not so difficult!

This work also could not be done by one person.

Various old passports of dead people and others were also sometimes used for the purpose.

These and similar methods rescued the following people:

1. Jerusalimskienė, the wife of a gymnasium teacher, with two boys six to eight years old, was taken 60 kilometres from Šiauliai to the farm of Jaloveckis, and was later transferred to several places near Kužiai.

2. Kamberienė, the wife of Dr A. Kamberis, and her five-year-old son, was taken by horse 75 kilometres to the home of the Zubovas family, a farm called Judreliai, near Akmenė, where she lived until the Germans retreated.

3. Chanė, Janė according to the new birth certificate, the eight-year-old daughter of an electrical engineer, at the beginning stayed with Ona, a laundress; but she twice had to change her place of residence and was later taken to a farmer in the Padubysis district, to be looked after by E. Liutikienė; there she had to change twice again, and was finally moved to the Mažeikiai district, to the farm of a certain Bugonis (the sister of Č. Liutikas), where she lived until the German retreat.

4. A female worker from Frenkel's tannery, whose name I do not remember, brought two children to my house and fainted. On coming round again, she said: "If you do not save my children, I will go directly to the SD, because I do not have any strength left." Such a move would have meant death, so I decided to rescue them. The rescue of the older one (Jonukas) required changing guardians four times. Finally, he found refuge in a village near Vaiguva, in the Šiauliai area. The younger one (Petriukas) was first placed in the Šiauliai city hospital. It was noticed that the staff had begun to talk about his background: so he was taken away immediately and placed in the care of a woman, after much pleading. Still later, with another Jonukas, the son of a foreman at Frenkel's tannery, who had also been sent to the children's hospital earlier to be rescued, they were taken by horse to the Vaiguva orphanage (60 kilometres outside Šiauliai).

Documents certifying them as orphans had to be organised for them in various ways.

5. Volodia Petrov was a boy of 12. His father, a Russian émigré from Paris, was dead; while his mother, a Jewess called Gurvičaitė and the daughter of a chemist from Šiauliai, was in the ghetto with her son. Her other child had already been taken to Auschwitz. He had to get documents saying he was an Orthodox believer. To do this two trips were made to Kėdainiai, in order to see an Orthodox priest. Finally a blank form with a seal was obtained, which I myself completed at home. A little later, I managed to find his uncle, his father's brother, in Daugavpils. I invited him to come, and gave the child over to him. For some time the threat loomed that the child would be returned to me, so documents had to be prepared in Kaunas quickly, to state that the father had been living there that year. The document was sent by post and disappeared, so a new one had to be furnished. Eventually the matter seemed to have been settled after the provision of the document, because I did not get any more threats that the child would be sent back. (When he left the ghetto, I placed him in the Lietuvos vaikas kindergarten, which he attended daily.)

6. Rudmikaitė, the daughter of the director of the Šiauliai Jewish Gymnasium, who was 16, was taken in at my request by the family of the forester Dauginis. Unfortunately, she was returned to the Šiauliai ghetto a week later because she missed her own family too much. The escape, which was organised with care and dedication, and fraught with danger, came to nothing.

7. Šifmanaitė, this was her mother's maiden name, who was an engineer's daughter, found refuge in the family of a teacher near Kužiai, in the Šiauliai district. Her escape was organised in the following manner: she was brought to our house by her mother; and from there she was taken to her new guardians by a hired coachman. Of course she had also been supplied with identification papers. All this happened during the daytime.

8. The five-year-old son of a Kaunas tradesman was brought from Kaunas by train by his former nanny and lived at my house for some time, but later he was placed in the care of the agronomist Mikolaitis in the countryside. We rescued this child thinking him to be the son of our colleague, the agronomist Girševičius, though it turned out later that the child was only his relative. A person came from Kaunas twice

with a pleading note from our colleague. After everything had been arranged, as agreed, the child was thrown over the wall from the Kaunas ghetto in a potato sack and found himself in Šiauliai.

9. The wife of an engineer and architect who had studied in Paris, and their six-year-old son, were saved from the Kaunas ghetto by Binkienė. She came to Šiauliai, where the Jesuits were to take care of her. She had a letter of recommendation from Bishop Brizgys, but they could not provide a permanent refuge for her immediately, so Fr Borevičius sent her to me. The woman was desperate and close to suicide: "When I was in the ghetto I had no idea that life at large was so complicated and that to save oneself was so difficult. If it had not been for the child, I would be dead long ago." After several long and complicated attempts, she became a housekeeper on the farm of P. Taišerskis (she spoke fluent Lithuanian and had an Aryan appearance).

10. The nine-year-old son of the owner of the Star paint factory in Šiauliai, whose father was a philanthropist and a very popular figure in the ghetto, was furnished with documents and, through D. Venclauskaitė, was sent to guardians in a village in the Vaiguva district.

Here I would like to note that his brother, a disabled child, was taken by the SS during the "children's action", which took place on 5 November 1943,* when about 800 Jewish children and handicapped people were most brutally torn from their mothers and taken from the Šiauliai ghetto. The consignment documents of the train that were noticed at the railway station gave Auschwitz as the destination. Overcome with terror, the Jewish mothers hid about 200 of their children in various hiding places in the ghetto. Most were eventually rescued by Lithuanians.

11. Dr Pikas' son got the documents of a student, a Lithuanian secondary-school boy. The school-leaver decided to organise his escape himself at the last minute.

12. Zinaida Blimentalienė, a well-known photographer in Kaunas, obtained identity documents there and was taken to my farm (Lopetiškiai, in the Padubysis district). She stayed there till the end of the war.

13. Another two unknown women were saved. One beautiful morning early in May 1944 the bell rang at 200 Vilniaus gatvė in

---

* Other sources indicate that it took place in the spring of 1943.

Šiauliai (where I lived). I went to open the door. I had hardly opened it when two women, who were clearly Jewish, flew in. "Are you Jasaitienė?" "That's correct," I said. They both dropped to their knees and tried to kiss my feet and hands ... I shied away. "Please save us, help us, we have only three minutes. An armed guard is standing right there behind the door who promised to let us escape if we give him 1,000 marks. Hurry up! Hurry up! Our lives are in danger."

They were strangers, unknown women, their speech so unclear that it could hardly be understood ... My first thought was that it was a trick. I ran into the next room to ask my husband what we should do (Dr V. Sruogienė, who had arrived from Vilnius, was also there). We suggested that the women be let out through the other door into the backyard, through the garden and into another street from where they could easily get out to the fields. They refused: "We cannot do that, as the others in our column will suffer because of us. Please rescue us, otherwise we will perish; the only way and chance to be saved is now, quickly, we beg of you!" There was no time for thinking ... and we took the risk. I gave 1,000 marks to the guard, and they rushed back into the street like mad ... An hour or so of tense waiting passed ... The SD? ... The SS? ... An arrest?

Everything went well this time again ...

These facts about rescued Jews have stuck in my memory. In all this rescue work I was faithfully assisted by my husband, Dr D. Jasaitis. Various jobs, such as that of scout and others, which were often responsible and fraught with danger, were also done, with the help of the children of my sister, Ona Lukauskaitė-Poškienė.*

14. At least 15 people, mostly men, were furnished with identity papers.

These documents made it easier for them to escape the ghetto at the right moment, and this way to save themselves.

Farmers were less afraid of sheltering people with proper documents.

15. For three years whole families were systematically supplied with food from our family supplies. Deliveries to workshops in the city where Jews worked also involved great danger.

---

* The words "of my sister, Ona Lukauskaitė-Poškienė" are written by hand.

The most dangerous things were the Jews' visits on some pretext, often even with armed guards, who had to be bribed with a cigarette, an apple or something.

We also took care of jewellery and other possessions of the Jews, which they entrusted to me for protection when sensing they would be sent to the ghetto. Later, they would find ways to leave the ghetto, sell some of these things, and use the money to buy the food that they needed so much. Many Lithuanian families who could not contribute directly to rescuing the Jews helped them in other ways, to avoid starving at least.

16. The following example shows how sometimes entire groups of people were involved in the rescue work. The lawyer Gecas and his family were in the Šiauliai ghetto. He was a person of great moral stature and very cultivated, a member of the Rotary Club, and a man respected by Lithuanian lawyers. There was a plan to rescue him from the ghetto. He refused, because he had debts: he could not leave until he had paid them. The same day a collection was organised, and within a couple of hours it had raised 1,200 marks (he still demurred, unwilling to be separated from the rest and, I think, he died with his family).

17. At the very beginning of the German occupation, three representatives of the Šiauliai community – the lawyer F. Bugailiškis, Dr D. Jasaitis and Fr Lapis – went to Schropfer, the commissar for the Šiauliai district and chief of staff, and with various arguments tried to intercede for the Jews, and expressed their indignation at the brutal killings. The chief of staff rejected the intervention indignantly, broke off the conversation, and threatened that anyone interfering in the matter would meet the same fate as the Jews, while the SD chief, Bozalskis, in another conversation on the same issue, told Jasaitis the following: "If you interfere in this matter you will fall into the same pit as the Jews".

I would like to note, in conclusion, that we rescued not only acquaintances but also total strangers; therefore, a lot of the events and circumstances of the rescues have been forgotten. I am also convinced that in Šiauliai, Jews were rescued by and received general support from hundreds, and maybe thousands, of Lithuanians.

Of the people I knew in Šiauliai, similar rescue work was carried out by the family of the late lawyer K. Venclauskas, Dr Luinienė,

Fr Lapis, Fr Byla, Fr P. Dzegoraitis, the Jesuits, Dr Prialgauskas, the parish priest at Kužiai Fr Kleiba, the deputy mayor Pauža, H. Kildišius, the agronomist Ibianskis, and J. Sondeckis.

As the undertaking risked the penalty of death and had to be done with great care and in complete secrecy, the list given above is far from complete.

As far as I know, a lot was also done by a woman in Kaunas called Binkienė. In Vilnius, V. Sruogienė was active in issuing passports.

Tubingen   S. Lukauskaitė-Jasaitienė [unsigned]
15 May 1946

From GRRCL archives: copy, typewritten

4. Letter from Bishop Vincentas Brizgys* to Domas Jasaitis about the conduct of priests during the Nazi occupation

Chicago, USA. 25 November 1976

Chicago, Ill.
25 November 1976

My Esteemed and Kind Doctor,
I have not had the time to write to you for a few days. My days are still quite full. I regret that I am not sending you the things you want.

---

* BISHOP VINCENTAS BRIZGYS (1903–1992) was born in Plyniai, near Marijampolė. In 1930–1935 he studied at the Gregorian University in Rome. Between 1936 and 1940 he taught at the Vilkaviškis Seminary. He was ordained a bishop in 1940. In 1940–1941 he was rector of the Kaunas Seminary, and in 1941–1944 dean of the Theological Faculty of Vytautas Magnus University. In 1944 he left for Germany, and from 1951 lived in Chicago. In 1960–1968 he was chaplain to the Lithuanian community in exile. In 1965, Pope Paul VI awarded him the title of Episcopal Assistant to the Pontifical Throne. He published many articles in Catholic periodicals.

I subscribe to *Baltic Studies*, but I do not keep the copies and give them to the bookshop of Maria H.S. I believe it has *Darbininkas*, and the Franciscans get this publication.

I do not have the *Philosophical Library* and do not know where I might find it. I think that the best thing is to apply to T. Jackevičius at Fordham University. You would certainly find it there.

Neither the bishop of Kaunas nor the bishop of Vilnius made any decrees on Jewish affairs. It is true that measures were taken by the government, and that people were encouraged and even organised to rescue Jews. You will find more information about this in my paper, which is now being typeset in Lithuanian at *Draugas*. Its English translation is under way, and it has been agreed that it will be completed before Easter. I hope that by the summer, both editions – Lithuanian and English – will be out. In addition to the actions carried out for Jewish affairs mentioned in the form of a chronicle, at the end there is a separate article describing the general mood and situation, and reacting to the accusations made against the Lithuanians. That is all.

I wish you and your wife good health and the peace of God.

With sincere respect,   V. Brizgys [unsigned]

From GRRCL archives: original, typewritten

5. Letter from Vanda Sruogienė* to Fr Juozas Prunskis** about the rescue of Jews in Vilnius

Chicago, USA: 16 January 1977

Highly Esteemed Father,

In reply to your request to provide information through the press about Lithuanians who rescued Jews during Nazi times, I am sending you something that concerns me and my husband.

---

* VANDA DAUGIRDAITĖ-SRUOGIENĖ (1899–1997), a historian, was born in Pyatigorsk in the Caucasus. In 1916–1918 she studied at the Moscow Trade Institute. From 1921 to 1923 she was a student at the Philosophy Faculty of

On 7 September 1972, I received a letter from Israel in which the wife of Algirdas, the son of the writer Jurgis Savickis, wrote to tell me that my husband, Balys Sruoga, had saved her and her daughter from death in the Stutthof concentration camp.

My husband helped Jews a lot at the time of their persecution by the Nazis, both those he knew and some he did not know. However, I would not now be able to say accurately whom he rescued, or how in such turbulent times we would often keep our underground work secret from each other, as we were both liable to be arrested (he as a famous person in Lithuania, and me as a director of a gymnasium).

I myself tried to rescue the wife of Colonel Štencelis. While she was hiding in Vilnius, in an attic in the Old Town, late in the evening, in darkness and evading the watchmen, I would climb the old stairs and bring her money, food and clothes (provided by Marija Nemeikšaitė), which Siegfried Stoessinger, a German officer and adjutant to Commandant Justus (yes!), had delivered from Kaunas. Unfortunately, one day in winter the woman could not bear it any longer, left her hiding place and went to Mass at the Cathedral. There she was seen by some evil people, who reported her to the Gestapo, and she perished.

I took care of Professor Horst Engert's wife, a Jewess from Kavarskas. She used to spend the night at our home, and my husband and I tried to talk her into going to a safer place in the country, but she kept putting it off, until finally, when on her way to her own flat, she was arrested and taken to the Vilnius ghetto. Through our efforts,

---

Berlin University; she also graduated from the Faculty of Humanities at the Lithuanian University. In 1939–1944 she was director of Gymnasium IV and Duchess Birutė Gymnasium in Vilnius. From 1944 she studied at Bonn University, and later in Chicago. She was a regular contributor to the press, and published monographs on Lithuanian history.

** FR JUOZAS PRUNSKIS, a priest and editor, was born in 1907 in Žvilbučiai, near Utena. In 1932 he graduated from the Theology and Philosophy Faculty of Vytautas Magnus University; in 1932 he was ordained a priest. Before the war he worked in education and publishing. In 1940 he left Lithuania and, after arriving in the USA, worked at St George's Church in Chicago. From 1948 he was the editor of *Draugas* and from 1953 of the journalism section of the *Lietuvių enciklopedija*. He was also a sponsor of various prizes.

Jonas Bertašius gave her a job at Lietūkis and tried to help her escape, but she was killed, as a result of carelessness.

I helped to rescue the daughter of a Jewish lawyer from Alytus, a gymnasium student, who had fled the ghetto and was seeking help from Kazys Janavičius. I gave her a gymnasium certificate and took care of her for a couple of weeks while she lived at the place of a Lithuanian (K. Barauskas, a former son-in-law of the Biržiška family), and together with Janavičius sent her to his mother in Alytus. There she stayed with a farmer and survived the war. I do not remember her last name, but Kazys Janavičius will.

The mother of the aforementioned engineer is already dead, but she rescued Dora Petrovienė and more Jews in a truly heroic manner.

As the director of a girls' gymnasium in Vilnius, I would take groups of unfortunate women from the ghetto, supposedly for work, but in fact to feed and help them.

I helped a number of people who were in hiding, but I do not remember their names.

I know for certain that Sofija Čiurlionienė* worked with a priest, and by issuing birth certificates saved quite a few people. She sheltered in her house, hid and fed a professor from Vytautas Magnus University, but unfortunately I do not remember his name. Her daughter, Danutė Zubovienė, could give a more detailed account of it.

Regrettably, the matter has been delayed. Information should have been gathered immediately on arrival in the USA and published long ago. Now, sadly, we are on the defensive.

Here are a few more words about the "review" of Vt.Vt. (Vaitiekūnas, alias Katilius) in the magazine *Į Laisvę*.

Some people are really angry! After looking at the accusations, I found that only three out of 50 of them had any foundation. The

---

* SOFIJA KYMANTAITĖ-ČIURLIONIENĖ (1886–1958), a writer, was born in Joniškis, near Šiauliai. In 1904–1907 she studied at Cracow University. She taught the Lithuanian language at various schools. From 1930 she participated in the Lithuanian delegation to the League of Nations and was a member of the Social Affairs Commission. She was a regular contributor to newspapers and magazines, wrote dramas and translated Molière and Homer.

reply will come in *Séja*. J. Puzinas recommends not worrying, but this criticism will harm the circulation of the VLIK's book, even though the aforementioned magazine does not have a wide readership.

Please accept my best wishes.

Respectfully, [Signed:] V. Sruogienė

PS. If necessary, I can send you the letter from J. Savickienė from Israel.

[Attachment to the letter:]

This is an extract from M...aitienė's* letter from Lithuania:

"... I happened to study for several years at the Kaunas School of Art with Algirdas Savickis, under the painter Vienožinskis.

"In 1938, Algirdas married a Jewish girl, Julija, and on 20 November 1943 the brutal Germans killed him: they shot him in the spine, which left him paralysed, and a few days later he died (the shooting was carried out in the ghetto on the bank of the Neris in Vilijampolė, on the other side of the cemetery) ... Julija and her little daughter Regina were taken to the Forest of the Gods.** There only starvation and a crematorium seemed to await them. She is grateful to your husband Balys Sruoga for rescuing her daughter. He shared his last morsel of food with her. After returning to Lithuania, Regina grew up to be a beautiful young lady, and studied medicine. In her fourth year she contracted cancer and died."

The story here refers to the writer Jurgis Savickis' son and his family.

[Signed:] Vanda Sruogienė

From GRRCL archives: original, typewritten; postscript written by hand

---

* Part of the letter is torn off, and the name is illegible.

** A reference to Balys Sruoga's novel *Forest of the Gods* describing the Stutthof concentration camp.

6. Account by Vanda Sruogienė of the hiding of
Jews in Alytus and Vilnius during the war

Chicago, USA: 15 February 1971

How Vanda Janavičienė
saved Dora Petrovienė

Dora, the wife of Dr Petrovas, was a Jewess. She was a friend of the
Janavičius family in Alytus. When the Germans came they made a
list of all the Jews in Alytus. Janavičienė learned from a young man
whom she knew and who served in the Gestapo that they also had
a file for Petrovienė among the other records in the Gestapo office.
One night she and that young man went there and stole Petrovienė's
file. They hid the woman herself with her faithful maid. Dr Simas
Janavičius had already been arrested and deported by the Russians.
Vanda was turned out of her house, and the Petrovas clinic was
nationalised and taken over by the Germans. Both sons of the
Janavičius family were somewhere else, Stasys stayed in Vilnius.
The Germans allowed Janavičienė to return home, but they
themselves occupied most of her house. Despite that, Petrovienė
hid there. Once she and Janavičienė came to us in Vilnius, but it
was not safe, because we had a female yard-keeper who had served
in Polish security, and later spied for our security service, the
Bolsheviks and the Germans. Petrovienė saved herself; when the
Russians returned, she lived modestly somewhere. On finding
herself with her sons in the USA, Janavičienė kept sending parcels
and medication to her friend, but some ten years ago Petrovienė
died of cancer in Lithuania.

Janavičienė never told her sons about the risk she had gone to
to save her friend. She told me, and sometimes I also helped her a
little, but I do not remember the details.

The fate of Professor Horst Engert's* wife

Horst Engert, a professor of German literature at the Lithuanian University, after divorcing his German national socialist wife, married a student of his in Lithuania, a Jewish girl from Kavarskas. They got on very well, and often came to see us in Kaunas, and later in Vilnius. She knew Lithuanian well and helped the professor to improve his language skills.

As soon as the Germans occupied Lithuania, Engert's daughter arrived and was appointed to a senior position in the Nazi office in Kaunas. In her own name and on behalf of her sister and mother, she demanded that the professor divorce his second wife. She threatened to report the wife to the Gestapo. Both my husband and I urged the professor to send his wife without delay out to several places in the country we had proposed to him, but he could not bring himself to part with her and did not believe that his daughter would denounce him. Several times we persuaded the professor, almost by force, to leave her at our house for the night. Neither of them were careful, and one night Engertienė was arrested by the Gestapo. For a while she worked at Lietūkis in Vilnius, and the professor visited her, bringing food and clothes. But finally she disappeared. The professor was distraught, he went everywhere looking for her, hoping she was still alive. It became clear that the daughter had hastened her end.

As director of the Duchess Birutė Gymnasium in Vilnius, I tried to do everything I could to protect my Jewish students, but we did not have many, and I forget their names now. I used to visit the Vilnius ghetto, taking food and other things. I was once a witness to how Maurer, an adjutant to Vilnius City Commissar Hingst, on coming to the ghetto, beat brutally unfortunate ones who were then probably sent to their death by firing squad. The scenes were horrible ...

---

* PROFESSOR HORST ENGERT (1888–1949) was a linguist specialising in Germanic languages. In 1927 he was invited to the Lithuanian University, where he taught Germanic languages and literature.

I once succeeded in getting a group of women out of the ghetto, on the pretext of cleaning the premises of the gymnasium. We fed them and gave some the chance to escape on their way back to the ghetto after work, but I do not know their names: I do not remember to whom I gave money, or how much.

***

While living in Bonn, Germany, in 1947 or 1948, I received a letter from Australia with a picture enclosed. I recognised my former student Šiukšteliškis from Kaunas Gymnasium III (it seems that his father was a lawyer). The letter was signed by a different name, with the explanation that he now had another name, for obvious reasons. He asked for a certificate showing that he had really been to Kaunas Gymnasium III, but asked to have his new name put on it. Remembering this student well, and the good marks he had earned, I complied with his request. Some time later I received a letter with an acknowledgement and a photograph of him and his fiancée. I have not heard from him since.

Štencelienė

Colonel Brunonas Štencelis* , born on 27 May 1892 in Gudžiūnai, near Kėdainiai, returned to Lithuania from Russia after the First World War and joined the Lithuanian army as a volunteer. He was the local military commander for Kaunas and Raseiniai, and later headed the Senior Officers' Course. In 1929 he held a senior position in the Ministry of the Interior and at some trading and industrial companies. He was well known in Lithuania, prosperous, had a small mansion

---

* COLONEL BRUNONAS ŠTENCELIS (1892–1943) was born in Gudžiūnai, near Kėdainiai. In 1914–1918 he served in the Russian army. On his return, in 1919 he joined the Lithuanian army as a volunteer in Kaunas. He took part in battles at Suvalkai and Trakai. In 1929 he left the army and became general secretary of the Ministry of the Interior. He was awarded the Vytis Cross Grade II third degree.

near Kuršėnai, and was married to a Jewess, a daughter of the Šiauliai lawyer Cimkauskas. In 1941 he was arrested and deported to Vorkuta by the Bolsheviks. With the arrival of the Germans, his wife and daughter stayed in Kaunas. When the persecution of the Jews began, they hid in the homes of acquaintances, and finally, probably in the winter of 1944, they found themselves in Vilnius. They were taken under the care of a German officer, an adjutant to Commandant Justus, Siegfried Stoessinger, whose wife was the sister of Brunonas Štencelis. I had known him since 1918. He arranged a small room for Štencelienė in the attic of a large old house in Vilnius, and maintained contact with her through Marija Nemeikšaitė and me: Nemeikšaitė would bring to Vilnius money, food and other things provided by him, and I would climb the dark wooden steps up to the attic in the evenings, reach Štencelienė's hide-out among the piles of old pieces of furniture, and, on saying the agreed password, would hand over the things to her and stay with her for a while. We would talk, and I would try to reassure her as much as I could. But she, spending all day and night alone and in permanent fear, was very nervous and agitated. One day, when visiting her, I met her daughter Irena who was hiding somewhere else.

One cold winter evening I came to see her, and she told me: "The sun was shining so beautifully on Sunday that I could not help going outside and visiting the Cathedral during Mass."

Concerned about her carelessness, I told her that she had taken a great risk and asked if anyone she knew had seen her. She replied that she had met the lawyer Nargelavičius and his wife. They had invited her to their home, where she had spent the night.

I asked and pleaded with her not to leave her hiding place again until Stoessinger and I could find another shelter for her. However, Nargelavičius already knew her hiding place.

Soon, maybe a couple of days later, I met Nargelavičius at Krėvė's place, with whom I had lived in the same house, at 21 Tauro gatvė. There I heard Nargelavičius tell them about the meeting with Štencelienė. Feverishly, he repeated that both his wife and he had insistently asked her: " 'Gde vashy dengi, gde vashe zoloto?'* But she would not let on! This is how she repaid us for our favour, for the

---

* Russian for "Where is your money, where is your gold?"

risk of putting her up for the night! Can you imagine, when I escorted her to her attic she gave me a small bottle of Benedictine! That's all!" I will never forget those words …

I did not tell anyone that I was seeing Štenceliené. But shortly afterwards, when he came to Vilnius, Stoessinger told me agitatedly that the Germans had found Štenceliené and taken her away with them. None of her acquaintances ever saw her again. There is no doubt that she was betrayed by Nargelavičius.

However, Stoessinger saved Štencelytė:* he found her a job in Rosenberg's office in Riga; from there the girl managed to leave for Switzerland, where the money of the Štencelis family had been deposited in a bank. Later she reached Canada, married there and now lives in Montreal. She seems to be keeping her origins secret, therefore I would prefer not to reveal the name of her husband.

Chicago   [Signed:] Vanda Sruogiené
15 February 1971

From GRRCL archives: original, typewritten

7. Letter from Viktoras Perminas to Fr Juozas Prunskis about the rescue of Jews in Vilnius

Detroit, USA: 30 December 1976

Detroit
30 December 1976

Dear Father Prunskis,

In response to the December 30 issue of *Dirva* concerning the gathering of information about the fate of Lithuanian Jews, I can provide here some facts:

1. In 1941, Paulina Papečkiené, her brother Alfonsas Mickevičius and myself lived in apartment No 2 at 4 Kudirkos gatvé in Vilnius. Papečkiené is now called Yelich. Mickevičius, an employee of the

---

* Štenceliené's daughter.

Vilnius Criminal Police, was deported to Siberia on the second occupation of Lithuania by the Russians and died there.

Papečkienė, the owner of the apartment, and I were witness to how a young Jew, an employee of the Lithuanian police, used to come to Mickevičius and hide at his place. The hostess would feed him and put a piece of food in his pocket on his way out. It should be remembered that at that time the situation with food in Vilnius was very difficult; therefore, I think that the Mickevičius family used to share their last piece of bread with the young Jew ...

Regrettably, I do not remember either his surname or first name, as so many years have passed and they have escaped my memory ... I also do not know his subsequent fate. Mickevičius was transferred to Mažeikiai, while I was mobilised for labour service into a construction battalion. The owner of the apartment may have more information; if it is very important, ask her. If he is alive he will also know about more people who helped.

2. The Jews themselves have published the names and photographs of some of their Lithuanian benefactors in Volume 2 of *Lietuvos Jeruzalė*. This material will be very useful to you, therefore I am sending a review of it. The material comprises three books, in English, Hebrew and Russian. If the book covered all of Lithuania, part of the work would be done, but regrettably it mostly applies to Vilnius.*

3. In any case, I would also like to express my opinion as to why such a large number of Jews suffered in Lithuania. In other countries, according to the article by Dovas Levinas in *Tėviškės Žiburiai* No 28, the death toll was much lower.

Let us consider why. I think the main thing was that Lithuanian Jews led a life of their own, were isolated from society and differed totally from the Lithuanians and ethnic minorities in Lithuania. In addition to their religion, they differed in their language, customs, appearance and even the pronunciation of the letter "r", which came out as a gurgle; if you had doubts about what a person was, you just had to wait for him or her to talk, and you would know immediately ... For that reason it was very difficult for them to hide and pretend to

---

* The book mentions a total of 12 people.

be Lithuanians or anything else. They kept themselves apart, and showed little interest in the life of independent Lithuania; and therefore, they never knew the language very well. They had their own synagogues, schools, banks, hospitals, organisations, sports clubs, and so on. I never heard of one family speaking the Lithuanian language at home. They avoided Lithuanian organisations, friendships with Lithuanians, and intermarriages, and preferred to speak Russian at home. There was a tendency in Lithuania to give Lithuanian forms to surnames that were either not Lithuanian or not obviously Lithuanian: I did not hear of a single Jewish family doing that ... In other countries they became so integrated with the local population that it was very difficult or nearly impossible to identify them: take the USA, for example. Therefore, in other European states it was difficult to distinguish them from the local people.

Had the Jews mixed more with the Lithuanian people, more of them would have survived: their fate would have been closer to that of the Lithuanian people ... The accusations against the Lithuanian people are unfounded. The Lithuanians have shown their goodness throughout history. A very clear example of this is the sharing of bread with interned Polish refugees and soldiers during the Second World War. At a time of trouble, the Lithuanians forgot that the Poles had occupied our capital, Vilnius, and came to us for bread ...

Also, the Lithuanians brought food to hungry Russian prisoners, exposing themselves to danger; and there was much sharing of the last piece of bread with the famished German prisoners on their way back home! Those who returned to West Germany remember the Lithuanians' kindness with tears in their eyes ...

[Note:] Wishing you success in your work. Respectfully,

[Signed:] V. Perminas

From GRRCL archives: original, typewritten; note written by hand

8. Reminiscences of Bronius V. Galinis*

Norwell, USA: 31 May 1971

Vilnius under the Nazis

It is not only interesting, it is important to write reminiscences of this period, even if they relate to the experience of a single person only, for by putting together writings by various people, the image becomes clearer. Here I shall try to share my reminiscences and experience of Vilnius during the Nazi occupation, and particularly in respect of my relationship with Vilnius Jews and the terrible tragedy that befell them.

Unfortunately, it is impossible to write about the period in great detail, as much time has passed since then. Another important thing is that, living in a distant foreign country, it is especially difficult to gather together all the necessary documents and records, which, with the passing of time, become vague or sometimes even get lost altogether.

Bronius V. Galinis

* BRONIUS GALINIS was born in 1911 in Vilnius. He studied at the construction faculty of Kaunas Vytautas Magnus University, and was a member of the Riflemen's Union, the Union for the Liberation of Vilnius and the Lithuanian Society of Technologists. After emigrating to the USA, he participated in several Lithuanian and American organisations.

Jews in Vilnius and Lithuania

Historical documents show that Jews were living in Vilnius as far back as 1320*. We can assume that a few Jews had come to Vilnius even before that time. Speaking about the legal situation of the Jews in Lithuania, it should be mentioned that in a document of 24 June 1388, Vytautas the Great granted the first privileges to the Jews of Trakai.** Later, the Jews in Brasta and Gardinas*** were granted similar privileges, which shows that the number of Jews in Lithuania had grown and their rights had to be protected. In 1514 the Jews were granted new privileges by King Žygimantas the Old. In 1529 these privileges were recorded in the Statute of Lithuania.

From the 17th century the Jews had tried to settle in separate blocks in towns in Lithuania called ghettos. The ghettos were not completely closed, and came into being not because the government made the Jews settle in such a manner. It was the choice of the Jewish communities (*kahals*) themselves. They formed a close-knit community, seeking to preserve their Jewish customs, religion and language.

Over time, the size of the Jewish population of Vilnius, the capital of Lithuania, was as follows:

1550 – 3,000; 1600 – 7,000; 1650 – 12,000; 1700 – 13,000****; 1750 – 11,000; 1800 – 10,700; 1850 – 23,091*****; 1900 – 63,250; 1914 – 73,420; 1916 – 61,265; 1941 – 70,000

The contribution made by Vilnius Jews to Jewish culture is so large and so exceptional that for centuries the Jews have called

---

* The writer is mixing dates. The first mention of Vilnius in documents was in 1323, when Grand Duke Gediminas wrote to several cities in Germany inviting merchants and craftsmen, including Jews, to come and live in Vilnius, and promising them religious freedom.

** A reference to the Karaites, a Turkic tribe from the Lower Volga that converted to a branch of reformed Judaism, whom Vytautas the Great brought back from his 1398 military campaign to the Black Sea.

*** Brest and Grodno, in present-day Belarus.

**** 3,800 Jews died in the plague in 1710; therefore, their numbers were reduced significantly [author's note].

***** This accounted for 41.4% of the population of the city of Vilnius [author's note].

Vilnius the "Jerusalem of Lithuania". This name dates from 1650, when the Jewish population in Vilnius amounted to about 12,000; however, it already had a Jewish institute for religious teaching, with 40 rabbi scholars who were famous in the Jewish world for their explanations of the Talmud and other scriptures. All this gave Vilnius its character as the "Jerusalem of Lithuania", which has persisted up to the present day.

In 1938, according to statistics, 168,000 Jews lived in independent Lithuania. The following year, after Vilnius and the surrounding region were returned to the Republic of Lithuania, another 82,000 Jews were added to that figure, including 20,000 Jews who were refugees from Poland. These had fled after the remaining Polish territory had been occupied and divided between Germany and Soviet Russia.

By the summer of 1941, after the Germans had occupied Lithuania, the total number of Jews amounted to 250,000. Only small groups managed to escape to Russia, they were mostly Soviet officials and party functionaries. Both Polish and Lithuanian Jews came under the attention of the Gestapo. The extermination of the Jews gained pace, and methods became crueller every year. Due to the genocide nightmare, the number of Jews in Lithuania totalled only 25,000, only ten per cent of its former figure, after the war. This figure is given in 1959 statistics. However, it is not clear what percentage of that the old Jewish inhabitants of Lithuania constituted, and how many Jews were new arrivals from Russia and other Soviet republics.

The last decade has shown that the Jewish population has not increased in number. Despite a natural increase in population, the number of Jews in Lithuania even dropped to 24,000 (according to the 1970 census).

The Lithuanians under the Nazis

When the war broke out between Germany and Russia, the sudden uprising by the Lithuanians against the Russians that erupted in June 1941 made it easier for the German army not only to advance through Lithuania but also to work its way deeper into Russian lands. Wherever the inhabitants could not or did not try to organise uprisings, the German advance was delayed, and the army could only march forward at a much slower pace, suffering greater losses.

The Provisional Government of Lithuania proclaimed by the insurgents took measures without delay to declare Lithuania's sovereignty, establish law and order, and manage the economy, which was in a state of absolute chaos. It was clear from the very beginning that Lithuania's aspirations for independence and statehood were at odds with the objectives of the Third Reich. The Provisional Government could not do its work, as the brownshirts and the Gestapo interfered in all its actions. It soon had to step down, and its place was taken by a Nazi government installed by Berlin, called the *Ziwilverwaltung*, headed by an official of the Nazi Party, a Russian German, Adrian von Renteln, as the Generalcommissar for the Lithuanian "region". Lithuania, together with Latvia, Estonia and Belarus (Gudija), constituted the large colony formed by the Nazis in the east called Ostland. A senior official of the Nazi administration of northern Germany bearing the title of Reich Consul, Heinrich Lohse, who was little known to the Lithuanians before, was appointed its "viceroy".

The fate of the Baltic nations, their everyday life and existence, depended on the actions of these "overmen". The fact that the territories were to be turned into lands of the great Nazi empire and inhabited by Germans, who expected to win the war, was no secret. Perhaps some of the local population would remain if the people were loyal to Germany and agreed to be germanised in the immediate future; however, others would be moved further east. The Jews would have to be exterminated.

The plan began, and was carried out without delay. Estates, large farms, and farms belonging to people who were missing or had been deported to Siberia, were taken over and put under the direct control of the German army. All economic enterprises, major branches of trade and industry, were put under the command and supervision of the Germans. With this in view, secret agents within companies, called *Treuhändern*, were appointed.

Large companies such as Pienocentras, Lietūkis, Linas and Maistas were the first to receive secret agents. Construction companies and their activities, which I can talk about, were regarded as less important (because they did not store goods in warehouses, and they could not be plundered); however, they were needed for construction work related to the war and everyday life. So they were also put under the control of the occupying Nazi authorities.

At the beginning of the occupation, a German called Ratner was appointed secret agent for the Construction Company; but later, in the autumn of 1943, he was sent to the Ukrainian front. Fortunately, our company seemed to be forgotten, and was left without a German boss. However, a number of German institutions would not leave us alone, and often demanded, even gave orders, that the company carry out construction work of some kind for them.

The headquarters of the Construction Company was in Kaunas, and it had divisions in Kaunas, Vilnius, Šiauliai and Panevėžys. One of the German military institutions in Vilnius which meddled in the work of the company and demanded various services was called *Ruestungskommando* ("the armament team"). Its head in Vilnius was a Captain Klueppel, who was trained in the Fifth Infantry Regiment on an exchange scheme before the Second World War when he was still a lieutenant. He had learned to speak Lithuanian quite well; however, now, under the occupation, he concealed his knowledge. However, at one reception, after drinking too much and forgetting himself, he suddenly started to speak Lithuanian. Earlier people had thought that the German official could understand only German, even though after saying something indiscreet or against the occupying forces in Lithuania they always used to be punished or fall out of favour.

Another German institution that would not leave us alone was the Ministry of Culture from Berlin. One of its many tasks was to increase the number of cinemas, to build more of them, so that conditions for showing more German films and newsreels could be created. In this way, the Germans sought to spread Nazi propaganda in the occupied countries, circulate the idea of the "New Europe" and instil the philosophy of the Third Reich in the subjugated nations.

A third German military institution which became especially active when the fighting approached the Baltic states, was called Organization Todt. Its governing body was granted special rights to allocate construction material, thus it could control our activities directly and take decisions on any work undertaken by the

Construction Company. For example, our company wanted to obtain a permit to cut timber for the roof of one of the buildings of a joiner's shop. A permit was issued for the material; however, with a very unfavourable condition – to use only round logs, that is, without making use of the services of a sawmill.

It is known that Germany, before declaring war against Soviet Russia, had to recruit large armies; and that it was incapable of equipping and supplying the armies itself. Therefore, having occupied Lithuania and other countries, the Germans started to demand that these should provide labour. The Germans took workers to the Reich for labour (usually to work in the more dangerous places, which were subject to bombardment, or to do the hardest and heaviest work for the lowest pay).

None of our people wanted to go to Germany. A legal way of avoiding it was to obtain *Unabkoemmlichkeitsbescheinigung* (UK) certificates, which provided exemption. These certificates were issued only to enterprises which were seen as important in providing military services in Lithuania. Workers from construction companies were entitled to UK certificates. Hence we were not short of labour, there were more people offering their services to us than we could ever employ. Many people tried not to come under the Arbeitsamt (the German institution managing workers' affairs) because it immediately deported workers who had no UK certificates to Germany for hard labour.

A total of 680 employees working for the Vilnius division of the Construction Company had UK certificates, and their number increased so rapidly that at the beginning of 1944 the number of those who had obtained UK certificates to avoid being deported to Germany amounted to 1,025. This increase could be accounted for by the ever-growing number of people working in the forests. They prepared the material for construction work that was in progress and work that was planned. Earlier, raw material had been supplied by specialised wood processing enterprises. Now we had to do it ourselves. Also, there was a lack of skilled workers to carry out basic construction work.

The Jews and the Gestapo

The Nazis had a special political agenda: to exterminate the Jews. Therefore, in every occupied country, the Jews were placed under the control of the Gestapo. Two months after the beginning of the war, two ghettos were established in Vilnius, and 50,000 Jews were herded into them.

The first, which started in Arklių gatvė, ran along Karmelitų, Rūdninkų, Ligoninės and Pylimo. Mikalojaus and Ašmenos went through the houses across the block as far as Arklių; the front houses along Vokiečių were excluded. The entrance was on Rūdninkų. About 30,000 Jews were herded into that ghetto.

The other one started in Vokiečių gatvė, ran along Didžioji as far as Švarco, then along Gaono and Dominikonų and turned back in the direction of Vokiečių. The front houses along Didžioji, Dominikonų and Vokiečių were excluded. The entrance was on Gaono. Some 20,000 Jews were herded into this ghetto.

Vilnius Ghetto No. 2

In addition, two camps housed several thousand Jews. One was the camp near the fur factory in Vivulskio gatvė (in Soviet times the factory was given the name Vito). The other camp was in Subačiaus gatvė, and there the Jews who were capable of working worked at the H.P.K. (Army Vehicle Park).

The Jews who were taken straight to Lukiškių gaol were liquidated immediately in the Paneriai extermination site, about seven miles from the centre of the city. The Construction Company had been building underground petrol tanks in Paneriai, and many ditches had been dug to install these tanks in. The place was taken over by the Germans and put under the supervision of the Gestapo. About 80,000 people were killed there by the Gestapo during the occupation. Lithuanian, Polish and Russian prisoners of war, and Jews, who are supposed to account for about 55 per cent of the total number of individuals killed, were annihilated there.

Agreement with the Judenrat

In the spring of 1943 I was informed that representatives of the *Judenrat* of the Vilnius ghetto (the Jewish Council formed with the permission of the Gestapo to maintain order inside the ghetto) wanted to meet me. I was told that the meeting should be as secret as possible, and that it should not draw the attention of people who were or could be negatively disposed towards the Jews. Although the Jews had notified the Gestapo of the meeting, their desire for discretion was understandable and right.

The headquarters of our company were on Vilniaus gatvė, which ran into Vokiečių, where it bordered on the ghetto. It took only a few minutes to get there on foot.

It was not too convenient to receive a delegation of the Judenrat at my work, because they would have to go through the office, where a number of employees worked and where there were always a lot of customers and other people. We also had to avoid the telephones in the office. Moreover, it was not clear how many people would be in the delegation. To avoid all these inconveniences, I chose a place in the accounts department, which had a separate entrance.

We agreed to start the meeting at 4 pm when the working day was drawing to a close. Tvirbutienė, who worked as an interpreter in our office and was in charge of telephone calls to German institutions, arranged all these small matters. She was a serious and reliable woman, she lived in Vilnius on her own, and her knowledge of languages was especially useful to the company in a place like Vilnius, which at that time was like an international city.

At last it came to the agreed hour. The Judenrat delegation consisted of only two people – the lawyers Buršteinas and Rabinovičius. A young Gestapo escort accompanied them. He sat down on the bench by the door and seemed to be absolutely uninterested in our conversation: he probably did not understand Lithuanian.

I asked the ghetto representatives to come to the table, and shook hands with each of them, as was common in Lithuania. Buršteinas said right away that he had been transferred from the Kaunas to the Vilnius ghetto, and Rabinovičius explained that he had been born and had grown up in Vilnius. Both of them confirmed that they had been authorised to talk to me about Jewish matters and the Vilnius ghetto.

I asked them to sit down. I was impressed by the respect of the Judenrat from their very first words: both delegates spoke perfect Lithuanian, thus showing respect for the Lithuanian administration in Vilnius, which teemed with a mixture of languages and cultures, a city which at the time was occupied by the Germans, had been seized by the Soviets some years before, and had been run by the Poles who had tried to make it Polish before that. Between those periods, the government of independent Lithuania had governed Vilnius for no more than half a year.

Both lawyers were of medium height, about 45 and 50 years old, neatly dressed, and it was only the Star of David on the lapels of their suits that showed their bitter fate as Jews. I asked them to tell me the reason for their visit. Both started to speak at almost the same time, interrupting each other:

"We ask you to save us from death. We Jews are starving in the ghetto ... We cannot wait any longer ..."

After the first few emotional sentences, Buršteinas continued in a quieter and calmer way. As far as I remember, his words went like this:

"When the Germans issued the order on 6 September 1941 to drive us into the ghetto, we were given only fifteen minutes to get ready and take what was necessary. We were allowed to take as much as we could carry. In panic, we grabbed what was to hand, without thinking what was more important. It was a hot day. Sweating, tired and nervous, the weaker Jews were unable to carry their bundles. They had to leave them on the way, and it was mostly heavier bundles containing food that were left behind. Therefore, the inmates of the ghetto had no supplies of food from the very first days. Some people had taken clothes or valuable things with them, and these could not replace food. We survived last year because many of us worked outside the ghetto and in this way helped those who stayed inside. However, this year the situation is catastrophic. We cannot procure more food, what is given to us at the ghetto has been reduced, and is hardly enough to keep us alive, so the weaker people are dying of hunger. We cannot find work. Since UK certificates were introduced, most large enterprises have had no need for Jewish labour. There are enough other workers. Therefore, we have now been abandoned to our fate, and are dying without food. We have come here, on behalf of the whole ghetto, to ask you, Lithuanians, for help. And of course we address you personally ..."

The matter was clear, and I believed it all. However, I had to ask them to elaborate:

"How, in your opinion, can I help you in this untold misery?"

Then the delegates started explaining the possibilities.

"Your company is building an extension to the fur workshop on Vivulskio gatvė, and it is also rebuilding part of the workshop which was burnt down. Your people work there and you alone have the right and power to ask to hire Jewish workers. This would create the possibility for people working on the construction site to obtain food and take it to the starving people in the ghetto ..."

"At present about a thousand Jews already work in the fur workshop. They could help the starving with food," I interrupted, knowing that many skilled workers worked there. The delegates explained to me immediately what I did not know:

"The Jews and their families who work at the fur workshop for military purposes are accommodated in a special camp. Those who work with fur are strictly separated from those who work in construction. Only if we can join in the construction work will we be able to establish contact with the public."

"Let us say," I said, "that I ask, and permission is given to you to work on our construction site. Are you sure that people will be so altruistic as to bring food for you free of charge? There is already a lack of food in Vilnius, there is no surplus."

"Director, we are realists. Despite the difficulties, we will arrange payment. We will pay black market prices for what we receive. We understand that it can't be done any other way. We won't bore you with the difficulties that might arise later. The most important thing is to get your consent in principle to get permission from the Gestapo for us to work. In this way, we will be able to help our people."

In order to make some time to think it over, I asked another question:

"The Construction Company needs various skilled workers, carpenters, bricklayers, electricians and plasterers, for example. How many people who are able to do this kind of work do you have?"

By asking such questions I was only trying to make time; however, I was on tenterhooks. What could I do, and what answer should I give them right then? For reasons of personal security, nobody wanted to have anything to do with either the Gestapo or the Jews, who were under the special supervision of the Nazis and the Gestapo. Interference in Jewish affairs or attempts by Lithuanians to hide or help them were strictly forbidden. Those who broke the ban were punished severely.

At that moment I saw the engineer Vytautas A. Daniūnas in my mind's eye. The director of the Vilnius Construction Company, my predecessor, was arrested by the Gestapo on 23 April 1943 and deported to Germany to the concentration camp in Stutthof. Tortured and exhausted, he died in Ragainė prison. Daniūnas was killed by the Nazis for his underground activities in Lithuania. I had also participated in underground activity, running the risk of being caught. And now, all of a sudden, I was faced with the Jews' problems, with a request to help them. This meant new risks and new dangers.

It was extremely difficult to decide in such a short time. Today, so many years later, everything seems different. Now it looks crystal clear, there was no need to think at all. However, then, in wartime, in the bleak atmosphere of Vilnius, with the Gestapo rampant, and with the nervousness of the Nazis increasing due to their failures at the front, it was not so simple to pretend to be brave and to subject oneself to new risks.

Being more or less a normal citizen of independent Lithuania, belonging to the younger generation, having been brought up in a family with strong moral and humanistic principles, not recognising any foreign occupation, and being horrified by all the atrocious and pointless acts of terror committed by both Red and brown invaders, I did not hesitate for long to make the decision to help the Jews, former and perhaps future citizens of Lithuania, who were doomed to death and with whom the Lithuanian nation had got on better than our larger neighbours did.

At that moment I remembered my years spent at school, where there always used to be Jewish children. Later, at technical college, I had made friends with Abraomas Šusteris, who was born in Auštadvaris, near Trakai. I last saw him marching across Aleksotas Bridge in Kaunas with other Jews, humiliated and abused. Our eyes met, and when he gave me a smile I felt a pang of guilt at remembering how we had been friends and seeing how I could not help him then. His column, guarded by the Gestapo, was marching back from hard labour to Vilijampolė, where there was a ghetto. By that time, Šusteris was already married, had a son, and before going into the ghetto had lived in Kaunas, on Italijos gatvė. I was supervising the construction of a building on that street then, so we quite often used to meet and have a chat.

After the work was completed, I moved to Vilnius and got a job with the Construction Company. At first I worked as an engineer, and later became director. The position gave me a certain prestige; however, at the same time it obliged me to carry out a lot of responsible tasks related to problems in the war years. If there was proved to be any negligence, the consequences would have been disastrous. Therefore, trying to find to correct and careful words, I hesitated between fear and courage, between selfishness and moral responsibility, between hatred of the deeds of the invaders and dreams about Lithuania's freedom: in short, between acceptance of the genocide and my duty to humanity.

I received the following explanation to my last question:

"We speak with trust and openness. We want as many ghetto Jews as possible to take part in construction work. We have found out that it would be possible if our people could be appointed to do labouring jobs. For example, to carry materials, clean out work places, dig pits, and the like. We can provide several hundred people for that kind of work at once."

Everything was clear, without a need for further explanation. The work itself was not the most important thing for them. They wanted to save as many people as possible. The decision had to be taken, and the answer given, right away.

I concluded the meeting saying that I would try to find work for the ghetto Jews not only at the fur workshop but also on other construction sites. The German military and civil administration often demanded that the company I headed perform various kinds of work, and set short deadlines. Since I could not be too sure about the confidentiality of our conversation, as I did not know what the delegates would report to the Gestapo about our meeting if they were asked, I tried to give the impression that I was interested first of all in my own company, and that the fur workshop was another matter.

The experiment worked out

A four-storey building for making Velfa electronic equipment was one of our larger jobs at that time. The engineer Kęstutis J. Jesaitis ran the factory and was its director. Our company was doing the construction work. The factory was important for the country's economy.

I had recently appointed Jonas Oleinikovas as work superintendent. He was a man of about 50, of medium height, broad-shouldered, balding, with a round face and regular features. He had a lot of experience in organising construction work, but the main feature of his character was his ability to communicate with people. Besides, he had worked in Vilnius for a long time, and his circle of acquaintances in the field was very wide. He had never had any disagreements or disputes with his workers, which is usually difficult to achieve.

I asked Oleinikovas to come and talk, and explained to him the situation at the fur workshop, as it was from there that he had moved to Velfa. He was not surprised when I told him about the need to look into the possibility of employing Jewish workers and to organise a supply of food. He gave me a brilliant idea. It turned out that before he had moved to Vilnius, he had had Jews among his workers. At that time, according to the rules issued by the German administration (Circular No. 1, signed on 15 October 1941 by a certain Ross) employers were obliged to provide hot soup for Jewish workers for lunch. That order had not been revoked, or else it was forgotten about, and we could make use of it. The order would make it possible to bring food to the workplace, or, to be more exact, it would help disguise the operation and its real nature. The only thing that was to be done was to get permission for the ghetto Jews to work.

I began to draft a letter to the Gestapo asking for permission to hire 180 workers from the ghetto to work at the fur workshop, and 30 workers on the construction of the Helios cinema being built on Gedimino prospektas, claiming that these buildings had to be completed as soon as possible. They were important for military purposes on the Eastern Front ... I also specified that our company was doing construction work on 17 different sites, and that we needed labour. The company employed over 1,000 workers, and 200 of those were in joinery and machinery shops; however, this number, excluding office staff, was distributed around 17 places, and was not enough to complete the work on time and to prepare the buildings for use. Therefore, it was necessary to increase the labour force sent to work on these construction sites, which, according to the order of the Reich, had priority over other construction work.

From an official point of view, it seemed that the contents of the letter were absolutely convincing and aimed at contributing to the war effort. But its essence and purpose were quite different. It involved danger and risk, if somebody in the Gestapo saw "where the shoe pinched", according to the Lithuanian saying, or if somebody denounced us.

I gave the letter to be translated into German to Nikodemas Antanavičius, who was responsible for the affairs of the company.

He was a young and educated man, with experience in journalism, and he carried out all tasks irreproachably. I signed the letter, so different from all other letters, as it dealt with miserable, suffering people rather than building issues.

An answer came back in no time, and, to our great satisfaction, it was positive. The request made by the ghetto Jews to help them had been heard. Jonas Oleinikovas was immediately sent back to the fur workshop. I appointed Beresnevičius, a Lithuanian from Lyda, to take his place at Velfa. He was also a good superintendent, and the construction of the Velfa factory was completed in April 1944.

Oleinikovas, a person of great ability, organised the construction work at the fur workshop and managed the new workers so well that soon food started flowing into the ghetto. This lasted till 16 September 1943. That day about 2,000 Jews from the Vilnius ghetto were moved to the fur workshop site. Conditions were better there and they had more freedom. Most people in the camp were Jews working for our company and their families, and people who knew how to work with fur and their families.

Some of the buildings were completed in spring, and work on other objects was continued and finally completed in June 1944, as the Soviet army was approaching Vilnius. On 30 June I went on a business trip to Kaunas; however, I never went back. I embarked on a journey to the West, and several years later finished it in Boston, USA.

The attitude of the Jews

More than a quarter of a century has passed since those events. We sometimes come across views, impressions and reminiscences about those days in the writings of Lithuanians, both émigrés and those who remained in Lithuania. However, the Jews themselves, survivors of the Vilnius ghetto or witnesses, have written about those tragic events the most. This is quite understandable, since it is they who were affected most, tragically and painfully.

I want to mention in passing only one work out of many, which deals with the fate of the Jews of the Vilnius ghetto and the attempts to rescue them.

It is a big book, illustrated with photographs and documents, running to more than 400 pages, published by New York Central Guide Publishers in 1969. Its author, Isaac Kowalski, a Jew born and brought up in Vilnius, was still a young boy during the occupation. He was the son of a Jewish printer and himself skilled at printing, who had been in the Vilnius ghetto, a witness to all the tragedies, until his escape to Rūdninkai Forest to become a partisan. He belonged to a partisan division led by the well-known Genrikas Zimanas, and published and edited newspapers for the division in Polish and Lithuanian.

The title of the book is *A Secret Press in Nazi Europe – The Story of a Jewish United Partisan Organization*. On the whole, the book is interesting and worth knowing about.

There is no hatred of Lithuanians in Kowalski's book. He records everything that he experienced, and describes the Lithuanians' friendliness and the help they provided to ghetto Jews.

Kowalski mentions the Jews who worked in the fur workshop, writes about their problems and their attempts to free themselves, and discusses the attitude and help of the Lithuanians. The author relates what happened to Jews in the ghetto and the workshop when they organised a secret press and formed a military organisation. The Jews ran to the forests to join the partisans not only from ghetto No. 1, but also later managed to escape from the fur workshop camp as well.

In writing my reminiscences I have disclosed another side of these events. From my own experience, I can say that companies and enterprises at that time, headed by Lithuanians who put their lives at risk, contributed greatly to helping the Jews, and helped many of them to survive.

31 May 1971   [Signed:] Bronius V. Galinis

From GRRCL archives: original, typed

9. Account by Ava Saudargienė of rescues of Jews in Kaunas

Sidney, Australia: 20 February 1977

The German occupation and the Vitman girl

One morning my sister, Marytė Bieliukienė, phoned and asked me to come over immediately. My sister lived in Žaliakalnis, and I lived in Karmelitai. When I went there I found my mother and sister in a panic. A nine-year-old Jewish girl, the daughter of Vitman, the bookkeeper at the Drobė factory, with whom my sister worked (she was a cashier) and had lived in the same house next to the factory for some time, was with them.

When the Vitmans had asked her to hide their daughter, my sister brought her home. The following morning the Vitmans and their two-year-old son were taken to the ghetto, where they later died.

What could we do? We couldn't hide the girl. It was too dangerous. I decided to go to the chaplain of the school where I worked.

The following morning, full of fear, I talked to the chaplain. He agreed to help. However, we had to hide the girl until he could prepare a birth certificate and find a place for her.

In the evening I brought her to my place, and in the morning I took her to my sister's again, knowing that it was not only I, but also my mother, sister and our husbands who were threatened with imprisonment and even execution.

Some days later the chaplain brought a birth certificate for Danutė Vitkauskaitė, nine years old, and told me to take "Danutė" to the orphanage run by nuns in the Old Town.

I ran to Žaliakalnis, to get the Jewish girl. I knocked on the door of the convent in the agreed manner. A nun let us in. After a brief conversation, I left Danutė with the nuns.

Some days later I visited the convent again. Danutė looked quite well. When she saw me she threw her arms around me, sobbing bitterly. The nun on duty and I could not help crying too.

With the front line approaching, the nuns moved the children from the orphanage to Pažaislis. After the war I learned that the Vitman girl, Danutė Vitkauskaitė, was alive and living in Kaunas.

Adina Frumkinaité-Segel

During those turbulent times I met a young Jewish girl called Adina Frumkinaité in the street, with whom I had studied at university. She looked ill, unkempt, and had a yellow star on her back. After going to work she did not go back with the others, but spent the night in the park. Her mother, the doctor Frumkinienė, and Adina's young husband, Segelis, were in the ghetto.

From that day on Adina used to come to us to spend the night. My husband and I looked for a way to help her.

My husband procured a passport for Adina, as a maid, under another name. Adina went to a provincial town to another friend from her university days, but returned without receiving any help. She spent the nights with us again, and sometimes went to the ghetto to stay with her mother and husband.

In June we got ready to go to the country, to my husband's village. We gave Adina the keys to our flat. On the day we left, Adina, her mother and her husband came to live in our flat, where they stayed until the second Russian occupation, after which they emigrated to Israel. As far as I know, they now live in Ramat Gan, Israel.

Sydney   Ava Saudargienė [unsigned]
20 February 1977

From GRRCL archives: original, typed

10. Letter from an unidentified person to Domas Jasaitis about saving Jews who escaped from the Kaunas ghetto

New York, USA: 20 April 1971

New York
20 April 1971

Dear Doctor,

There you are, many a time I have told myself to hold my tongue because nothing good ever comes of it, and now, here you are, asking me to write about saving Jews. What can I write? I do not even know their first names. I know that they were two brothers, Solskis by name, and had a farm in Drebulinė (near the road, five kilometres from Garliava, in the direction of Prienai). They were not only farmers but also businessmen: farmers from the neighbouring villages used to buy fertilisers from them, and they used to sell whatever they had a surplus of on their farm: birds, animals, corn. Nobody ever complained that Apčikas (the father's name was Abelis, so the neighbours called the whole family "apčiks", I don't know why they didn't call the family Abeliai. Perhaps the name was too difficult for them to pronounce) charged too much for the fertilisers, or paid too little for farm produce. On the contrary, people spoke only well about him.

My late father told me the following. Long, long ago, in the times of serfdom, the grandfather of these two brothers gave an order to birch a labourer who had not raised his cap to a passing priest. Old Apčik himself took up the rod, and between each blow he said: "Apčikas is the master. Obey him. Joselis is a supervisor. Obey him. And the priest is the superior of all of us. We all have to obey him."

Coming back to those two boys, many Jews from the ghetto in Vilijampolė had escaped and hidden in the villages and forests. Perhaps they had sensed trouble. The two Solskis brothers took refuge at my brother's place. My brother was called Juozas. Since it was too dangerous to keep them on the farm, Juozas made a dugout for them in the forest. And so, from the summer of 1942, both of them lived undisturbed in the dugout. However, towards autumn they used to come to the farm more and more often, to dry their clothes or to get something warm to eat.

In the autumn of 1942 the Germans noticed that numbers in the ghetto were low, and organised a hunt for people in the Pajiesiai villages and forests. Both Solskis brothers were shot and wounded in the forest, but they managed to evade the Germans. The wounds were serious: one of them was shot in the shoulder, the other in the hip. They had nowhere to go to wash or dress their wounds. A few days later, after the hunt was over, Juozas, taking some supplies of food, went to see them one night. He found them hungry, wet and trembling with fever ... On learning that they had both been wounded, he returned home without delay, harnessed a horse, and brought them home. They were too weak to walk. While dressing their wounds, Juozas saw they would die without a doctor's help. Therefore, he went to fetch a doctor the following day. He told the doctor that his wife had suddenly been taken ill and felt very bad. He only told the doctor the truth as they were approaching his house. The doctor understood the situation. He provided the necessary help, and agreed to come and see the patients again because their condition was very serious.

It was extremely dangerous to keep the patients at home, but to take them back to the dugout would be the same as killing them. Juozas sided with danger. He made a hideout for them in hay in the barn, and concealed the entrance so well that it would be impossible to find it if you didn't know where it was. The two brothers would spend the whole day in the hay, where they were warm and dry, and at night Juozas would bring them into his house, dress their wounds, feed them, and let them rest comfortably.

That is more or less the whole story. The doctor was brought three times. I do not know what happened to them eventually. The only thing I know for sure is that the Germans did not catch them.

The Shneideras family

I not sure about the first name; however, he was a wealthy goldsmith on Vilniaus gatvė in Kaunas. Young parents. They were sent to the ghetto with their newborn son. When they sensed danger they tried to rescue at least the son.

My sister Ona was married to Ignotas Žegunis. They lived in the village of Degimai, near Šilavotas Wood. They had no children. Ignotas' sister was married and lived on Jonavos gatvė in Kaunas, not far from Vilijampolė Bridge. The Shneideras planned to save their son with her help. She told her husband Ignotas about it, and he agreed to take the risk. In 1942, just before Christmas, the boy was taken out of the ghetto in a suitcase and anaesthetised at Ignotas' sister's place. At night Ignotas threw the suitcase on to a sledge and took it home. The boy was about two years old. It did not take long for the child to get used to the new place; however, he spoke with a clear Jewish accent. The neighbours started saying that Žegunis had taken in a

Jewish child. Although he tried to deny it, saying that the child had come from the orphanage, it was difficult to convince them. In the summer of 1943 the Žegunis took in the Dvareckis girl. They thought the boy would learn Lithuanian better by playing with her.

Ignas Žegunis was killed by a former landless peasant of his, a communist, in 1945. His widow Ona lives at our brother's now, in Utena. I do not know the boy's fate. I only know that the Germans did not kill him.

If the original names of those children of Israel are needed, I could try to ask my brother or sister if they could provide them.

My best regards to you and your wife.

[Signature indecipherable]

From GRRCL archives: original, typed

11. Letter from Marija Žymantienė to Domas Jasaitis about saving a Jewish girl

Los Angeles, USA: 7 February 1977

Los Angeles
7 February 1977

Dear Doctor,

I am sending back the letters that you wrote to my husband Stasys Žymantas.* The first letters from deportation are warm, sincere and very nice. Soon it will be four years since Stasys passed away, and I have nobody to save these letters for. You might need them to recall some events or dates.

I feel a deep gratitude to your family for taking care of me at the Red Cross in Tübingen during those years that were so difficult for me. Give my best regards to Sofija. I hope you are both in good health.

---

* STASYS ŽYMANTAS (1908–1973) was dean of the Department of Law at Vilnius University from 1941 to 1944. He was one of the organisers of the 1941 uprising, and after the war took an active part in the struggle for freedom.

I have read in the newspapers that you are collecting material about Jews that the Lithuanians saved. I do not know whether Stasys wrote to you about a young Jewish girl whom his mother* smuggled out of the Kaunas ghetto and brought up with her own daughter in Kaunas until 1946. Doctor Zacharinas had asked her to take the girl in. He handed the anaesthetised girl to her over the ghetto wall. She was the daughter of a Kaunas tailor, Dovydas Vilenčukas.** She was given a birth certificate in the name of Dalia Petrauskaitė, which was later changed to Dalia Jablonskytė (after the name of Stasys' sister, Jadzė Jablonskienė). She was two years old, and at first she spoke only Yiddish, but Jadzė taught her Lithuanian. My Stasys loved the girl to distraction, and she called him Uncle Stasys. By a miracle both the parents of the girl survived, her father was in Dachau and her mother in Stutthoff. Her mother was put on a boat and taken away from Stutthoff. She recounted terrible things about weak people being thrown overboard. Dr Zacharinas' wife was among them. On their return they found us in Wuerzburg at once and looked for the girl. When they heard that Stasys' mother and sister had stayed in Lithuania, the girl's mother went to Lithuania immediately and took her to Germany. She would have taken Stasys' mother as well but Jadzė had already been imprisoned (she died in prison on 22 December 1948). Actually, she had stayed in Lithuania because of the girl, hoping that the parents would survive the Kaunas ghetto. She did not know that they had been taken to Germany. They lived in the Jewish camp of St Ottilien in Germany, near Munich, where I visited them.

The girl was seven years old and spoke about her *motulė* ("granny", Stasys' mother). She spoke only Lithuanian, so they did not emigrate to Israel but went to live in Norway where they still live, in Oslo. The girl is still called Dalia, and remembers only one Lithuanian word, "motulė".

We still correspond with the Vilenčukas now and then. Dalia is married to a Norwegian with fair hair and blue eyes. Her name is Dalia Wilentschuk-Jackbo. The whole Vilenčukas family survived.

---

* Marija Žakevičienė.

** Or Vilenčuk (p. 77). See also p. 33.

Some of them stayed in Lithuania and took care of Stasys' mother right up to her death. They wanted to buy the tombstone for her grave.

They were all worried about the fate of their relatives who had stayed in Lithuania, and I should ask them if they have anything against their names being mentioned.

I know neither the first name nor the surname of the Jewish student who stayed in our flat in Vilnius. He left for Warsaw to be with his mother; however, you know about the events that took place in Warsaw ... I know nothing about him.

These memories keep coming back to me now.

This is all for the time being.

[Signed:] Marija Žymantas

From GRRCL archives: original, typed

12. Letter from Matas Janušauskas to Domas Jasaitis about problems between the Jews and Lithuanians

O'Halloran Hill, Australia: 11 March 1977

O'Halloran Hill,
South Australia
11 March 77

Dear Compatriot,

Excuse my delayed answer, due to unavoidable circumstances.

Your letter has reopened old wounds and made me think over those tragic days again. Your letter reads: "It is very painful that the Jews, who the Lithuanians rescued by putting their lives at risk, now angrily accuse all Lithuanians of collaborating with the people who shot Jews." However, is it not also very painful that the Lithuanians who contributed lack the moral conviction to openly admit their deeds, and thus take responsibility and shame away from the names of the honest Lithuanians?* At least the fanatical Nazis and fascists do.

---

* Underlined, here and further, by the author.

I do not know you and I do not know if we have any acquaintances in common (J. Vilčinskas never mentioned your name to me), so I do not know how much you know about the genocide of the Lithuanian Jews. It would not be boasting to say that I am probably one of the best informed, because after the end of the war I found myself at the very heart of the Lithuanian Jews who had survived (in Germany), where I was able to learn more. I will not conceal the fact that while still in Lithuania I was convinced that the country would be "free of the Jewish yoke for years and years" (the words of one of the councillors) and I started collecting facts about the systematic extermination of the Jews. This was a secret, and not a single soul knew about it; however, having found out that a Jew was being hidden in the Jesuit house in Kaunas, whose aim was the same, I destroyed the material.

I am not sending you the information you asked for, because first I want to know more about your future book. Will it be: A) just a collection of facts about the rescued Jews (a very small number); B) a desire to justify the tarnished name of the Lithuanians by claiming, for example, that the Jews were (all?) guilty of killing and persecuting Lithuanians under the Bolsheviks, a fact that is still emphasised by many people; C) an attempt to place all the blame on the Germans, as if "we knew nothing, we were forced, etc"; D) a serious academic work, with an introduction which considers historical facts illustrated from the point of view of "good" and "bad"? Take, for example, Dr Kaganskis (whom I knew personally) from Virbalis, standing in a lieutenant's uniform by a ditch and giving the order: "Lithuanian soldiers, shoot the Lithuanian officer" and was shot dead, together with other Virbalis Jews, by Lithuanians in uniform. Or, in 1949, in the transit camp at Bonegilla (Victoria, in Australia) a young Jew came up to a group of Lithuanians and said: "Good afternoon, Captain Šimkus, do you remember the time when you supervised the shooting of Jews? I managed to run away from the very edge of the ditch. I remember you very well." I have to add that according to the narrator, Captain Šimkus "evaporated" from the camp the very same day.

I saved a Jewish boy; however, it was only part of the struggle against violence and injustice.

In Germany I was encouraged by acquaintances to provide similar material, which was published in the Lithuanian press in the

USA. I later understood that it was done for the purpose of improving the prestige of a certain political group, but I have never been a member of any political party.

To conclude my letter, I declare that I will agree to provide any relevant information (see D) if it is going to be a serious academic work, rather than a "political football"* or similar nonsense for publication. Such publications are sometimes distributed in the USA in the name of the Lithuanians (at whose expense?) and they fall into my hands.

I want to say that I personally do not want and do not seek any honour.

Looking forward to your reply.

With best regards,   [Signed:] M. Janušauskas

From GRRCL archives: original, handwritten

13. Letter from Matas Janušauskas to Domas Jasaitis about problems between Jews and Lithuanians

[...] 4 April 1977

4 April 77

Dear Compatriot,

Since I do not know what you know about me, I shall provide some information. From 1932 to 1936 I took a course in political economics at Vytautas Magnus University in Kaunas. In 1936 and 1937 I worked at the Bank of Lithuania in Kybartai, and later in Kaunas. As I have always been anti-fascist, under the Soviets I was appointed, against my will, to senior positions (if necessary I could give more interesting facts about those circumstances), which gave me the chance to get a profound insight into Lithuanian-Jewish relations. Though I did no harm to anybody during the Bolshevik period, when the Germans came a certain element started to persecute

---

* Quoted in English.

Imanuelis Grinbergas
was rescued by Matas
Janušauskas (1945)

me. After losing my job, I worked as chief accountant for one of the nationalised factories. Later, after the Germans took over the factory, I was appointed director; however, my persecution went on, and thanks to good friends and with the German authorities interceding for me, I managed to avoid anything worse, though I was surrounded by spies at the factory.

I tried to remain impartial in Lithuanian-Jewish relations, and I viewed the historical, social, political, religious and other circumstances from an academic point of view. Perhaps this is why I keep apart from Lithuanians. Now, as in the past, I have good reason to avoid people I do not know or cannot trust. However, this is a subject for another time; now, I am coming back to the subject in question.

I am enclosing information about a child saved by my family. I mentioned in my first letter that I had already written about my activities in […],* which was published as a part of the article "Lithuanians in the Struggle for the Freedom of the Jews" (*Naujienos*, 21–27 April 1948). I have to add that I was not sent the article – I learned about it accidentally through a third person. Also, an article was published in the St Louis *Star-Times* (December 1944–1945, page 35, and 17 December 1945, page 15). The information in it was provided by Dr Grinbergas and was somewhat distorted (perhaps by the journalist).

---

* Word is illegible.

At the beginning of 1943 a group of Jews started working at the factory. Their leader was Dr Zalmanas Grinbergas. One dark November evening my wife and I went to the barbed wire fence of the ghetto and took Dr Grinbergas' two-year-old son, Imanuelis. Some months later, after the situation had become less tense, the parents decided to take the child back.

In March 1944, all of a sudden, the "children's action" was carried out in Kaunas. Some children, including Dr Grinbergas' son, were hidden. The following day, on his way to work, Dr Grinbergas brought the child back to us. In July, when I fled Lithuania, I took the child with me, pretending he was my first cousin (I had his birth certificate).

In April 1945 I found myself in Swabia, where I stayed till the end of the war. In July I learned that an UNRRA division had been set up in the town of Biberach, and went there immediately to ask them to send news about the child to his relatives in Canada and Palestine. In August, with the help of UNRRA, I managed to find the child's father, who was director of the former German military hospital where former "kacetniks" were treated. The following day we went to my place to collect the child and my family. I worked in the administration of the St Ottilien hospital until 1948. The child's mother was liberated by the Soviets in East Prussia. At the beginning of 1945, after spending some time in a convalescent home, she was allowed to return to Kaunas, where she learned that her husband was alive and had their son. At the end of 1945 she arrived in St Ottilien.

At the beginning of 1946 the mother and son left for Palestine (still under British rule) where the boy fell ill with leukaemia. The father hurried to Palestine; however, the child died soon afterwards and the father wrote to us that our name (?) was inscribed on his tombstone as people who had saved him. As far as I know, his parents are divorced and both live in the USA; however, I am not in touch with them.

That is the story in brief. I have omitted the details. If you are interested, I could describe everything in detail; however, I doubt it is necessary for the book.

Also, it should be mentioned that Dr Grinbergas was head (president) of the Jewish Society of Liberated Former Political and

*"Uncle" Matas and
"Aunt" Tamara see off
Imanuelis Grinbergas
on his way to Palestine
(1946)*

Racial Prisoners. In 1945 he was flown by US military plane to the
USA and made a great career there, but this is also another issue.

I am enclosing three photos; however, I kindly ask you to return
them to me.

Doctor S. Atlasas moved to New York, and you can find out
about him through the Jewish Institute of Religion.

I have lost Dr Z. Grinbergas' official letter of thanks and other
documents. If you are not able to obtain them I shall make a copy of
the material available.

As for your enquiries and conclusions, I can say the following:
the former inhabitants of Kybartai who lived in the camp for displaced
persons near Augsburg told me about the fate of Dr Kaganskis in
1948. They mentioned the names of Jews that I knew; however,
Dr Kaganskis' fate made the deepest impression on me. I should also
mention that I heard it again when living in Australia. Here is another
fact: when I was in the camp for displaced persons, an inhabitant of
Kybartai, L. Ab., gave me a letter written to him by Dr Z. in which he
asked Ab. to make a "sworn declaration"* through the IRO that Dr Z.
had not participated in murdering Jews, but on the contrary, helped
them a lot. He wrote that he needed that document badly to submit it
to the local authorities, because otherwise he was going to have a lot

---

* Given in the original in English.

of trouble. When I asked Ab. what he was going to do, the latter smiled and said that he did not intend to make a false declaration, and it was better not to answer the letter at all. Since soon after that I emigrated, I know nothing more about it.

I was told about Captain Šimkus in 1951 by a certain R.S., who used to take pride in his relations with the Kaunas and Vilnius SD and the Gestapo (some people accused him of doing much harm to the Lithuanians). I do not remember him mentioning the first name of Š. or speaking about his fate. I only formed the impression that he had come to Australia under another name. I assume it is the same person about whom people in Kaunas spoke in 1941. He was an air force captain, was imprisoned by Smetona for supporting Voldemaras, and later worked as a cashier for the Bank of Lithuania. However, this is only a guess.

It seems to me that you won't be able to "bring at least one old man back to life from the grave and hear at least a word about old times", and you will not be a success because, as I mentioned before, I am somewhat distanced from the Lithuanian community and have never read the material you referred to. If it is not too much trouble, could you kindly send me *Masinės žydų žudynės Lietuvoje.** Perhaps I could add something or provide some explanations. For example, I am interested in the material about the Seventh Fort and its commandant (I do not remember his name). I have positive and negative information about him from the survivors.

Though I am retired now and my income is limited, I promise to cover all expenses.

Looking forward to hearing from you.

[Signed:] M. Janušauskas

From GRRCL archives: original, handwritten

---

* *The Massacre of the Jews in Lithuania.*

14. Letter from Matas Janušauskas to Domas Jasaitis about saving Jews, and post-war problems between Lithuanians and Jews

[...] 1 May 1977

1 May 77

Dear Doctor,

I have to apologise for not answering your letter immediately. The reason is that, quite unexpectedly, I had to stand in for the person who took over my last job in a private post office. The reason was his mother's death, and I had to take over for him for the whole week.

I am enclosing a copy of my reminiscences, published in *Naujienos*. As I mentioned earlier, I worked in the St Ottilien hospital for some time, where male survivors of the Kaunas ghetto were brought. Some of my former workers were among them. There were also several people from the Šiauliai ghetto. Later the hospital became a kind of transit point (which was kept strictly secret) for Lithuanian Jews (and others too) who had fled the country and gone to the West. I was the only employee who was not Jewish (with the exception of medical and junior staff) and was highly respected by both employees and patients. They considered it their moral duty to be sincere and to share secrets and reminiscences with me.

If you have the chance to get in touch with these people you could get more information about people who were saved: Bronius Bieliukas, and the dentist Gurvičiūtė and her brother; the former chief construction engineer Navickas, about the engineer Gudinkas and his family (currently in Melbourne); the family of the former chairman of the Bank of Lithuania, Juozas Paknys, about the former employee of the Bank of Lithuania Bermanaitė; Pranas Čepėnas, about Ona Šimaitė, who rescued Jews in Vilnius; the former cashier at the Bank of Vilnius, Mickevičius, about the dentist Baronienė and her daughter; Dr Voščinas; Dr Vidučinskas (now in the USA). Also, two more boys were saved (as far as I know 20 girls were saved by the end of the war) who were brought to Germany during the war. I cannot remember and cannot say exactly how many children were saved and stayed in Lithuania.

I worked in the hospital until the summer of 1948, when it was transferred to another place. In 1948 and 1949 I lived in a camp for people from the Baltic states near Augsburg (where behind my back I was called a Jew-boy, a communist agent and a mercenary; however, I paid no attention to this, explaining to friends in the camp that those people had tarnished their reputations over the Jewish issue).

In April 1949 I emigrated to Australia, where I have lived ever since.

I mentioned in my last letter that Eva Grinberg and her son left for Palestine (Israel) in 1946, that soon after that the son had fallen ill, and that Dr Z. Grinbergas joined them. I have never been to Israel, perhaps you misunderstood me.

Since much time has passed, in trying to recall these facts and names, I have to go over this nightmare again, remembering not only the pleasant facts but also those that really stained the good name of the Lithuanians.

If you are interested, I could write about the following:

1. The former military commandant in Kaunas (I have forgotten his name) who was commandant of the Seventh Fort after the Russians had fled, and who led the first shooting of Jews. He set free some Jews who he selected personally.

2. The account by the former military chaplain of Lithuania, Rabbi Sniegas, of Bishop Brizgys and his personality.

3. The opinion of Lithuania of Zechlin, the minister appointed by the Germans, and the facts to confirm that opinion.

4. The order issued by General Eisenhower to repatriate all the people from the Baltic states (a promise made to Marshal Zhukov), which was revoked after Jews in the USA intervened.

5. A. Smetona's property in Israel?

6. Lots of other details that are of interest, though not so important.

I look forward to hearing from you.

Yours sincerely, [Signed:] M. Janušauskas

From GRRCL archives: original, handwritten

15. Letter from Matas Janušauskas to Domas Jasaitis about the first days of the war in Lithuania, saving Jews, and problems between Lithuanians and Jews

[...] 23 May 1977

23 May 77

Dear Doctor,

As promised, I will give more facts; however, I would like to emphasise that much time has passed since these events, and some names and dates have escaped my memory already. I try to recall everything imagining that I am watching a film, and sometimes I am amazed by how vividly it all comes back, in the minutest detail. However, suddenly the film breaks off. Maybe a psychologist would find it interesting, but those unpleasant memories affect me so much that I have not felt myself for several days ... I always try to be fair, so I want to warn you that if some facts are vague, it is simply because I do not remember them clearly.

You probably remember that when the Russians were withdrawing from Kaunas, Kaunas radio addressed the people as the voice of independent Lithuania. Unfortunately, I did not believe that: I was sure that the Red occupation had turned into a crueller brown one. (You see, in 1941, from January to March, I was a member of the Commission for Soviet Repatriation in Klaipėda – the entry in my diplomatic passport said I was an official; this gave me the chance to get to know the real face of the Nazis. However, this again is another issue.)

1. One of the first decrees made on the radio was the order from the Kaunas military commandant relating to the Jews. Commandant Colonel X (I have forgotten his name, I might remember it by my next letter) was the same man who held this position in 1940 when the Soviets occupied Lithuania. You might know that during the first days of the war a so-called "cleaning the undesirable element" operation was performed in Kaunas. People (mostly Jews) were picked up on the streets and in their homes, mostly in the Old Town and the suburbs, and taken to prison. When the prison became overcrowded, the Jews were herded into the Seventh Fort in Žaliakalnis, next to Darbininkų gatvė, on the Neris. In the prison a

drunken German in (SD?) uniform selected over 100 people to be shot. The poet Montvila, whom I knew personally, was among them. (I was told about this by a mutual acquaintance who was later released from the prison.) I would like to mention that a "partisan" grabbed my mother-in-law by the arm on the pavement on Lukšio gatvė and pushed her into a column of Jews being taken to the prison; however, my wife, who was walking by her side, started to shout and berate that "partisan" who, seeing his mistake, pushed her back. I myself was stopped twice in the street by young armed boys who forced me off the pavement; but, having checked my passport, they let me go, without apologising. I heard of similar facts many times. Now I shall present some concrete facts about the Seventh Fort and its commandant.

A) Bronius Žvynys, a former non-commissioned officer in the hussars, worked at the Manas felt boot factory as a messenger. I recently found his name in the *Europos Lietuvis* newspaper among persons convicted in Lithuania. Since Žvynys' wage was very low, I allowed him time off to deal on the black market. He respected me and constantly repeated that if all officers were as fair and organised as I was, army life would be ideal. I sometimes used him as a courier for Jewish affairs (without telling him); I am sure that he served the Jews for a generous reward. I had good grounds to believe that he was won over by the Security Service (Gestapo?); however, I do not think he did me any harm; and that could have been the reason for his arrest. As he confessed, after hearing the order from the Lithuanian military commandant for all former military and police officers of Lithuania to register with the commandant's headquarters, he obeyed and was later sent with others to the former Ateitininkai Club. I listened amenably to his adventures. There were more people like him there. Some days later, volunteers were called for service in the Seventh Fort. Žvynys, not even knowing what kind of service it was, shied off. In the evening the drunken volunteers returned, showing their trophies, and boasted that they had liquidated communist Jews. Since Žvynys was brought up in a religious family in the country, he fabricated a lie at once that he had received a message saying that his village had been destroyed in the fighting and that his parents had suffered (as far as I remember it was in the Ukmergė district), and was dismissed from service.

*Zalmanas
Grinbergas
(first from right)
and his wife Eva
(centre) with their
son Imanuelis
before leaving for
Palestine (1946)*

B) When I settled in St Ottlien, Dr Grinbergas introduced me to Benjaminavičius (a relative of his wife) and his wife. He had been in a *kacet** with Dr Grinbergas near Landsberg, and his wife, together with Dr Grinbergas' sister (Techa Rapeika), had been in East Prussia, from where she was taken by boat to Mamburg in 1945. She stayed there till the end of the war. Benjaminavičius, as a young man, had been studying in Belgium. In 1939, when the war broke out, he returned to Lithuania. During the cleaning operation he was stopped on the street and taken to the Seventh Fort. His wife, on learning what had happened, went to the Seventh Fort, and was given permission to meet the commandant himself. (I must explain that she was blond, had no Semitic features, and spoke Lithuanian without an accent, so that few people would have suspected she was Jewish.) The commandant questioned her and her husband, and released them both. When I asked Benjaminavičius about his experience, he said that he, like everyone else who ended up there, had lost all hope of remaining alive. He said about the commandant: "He was very kind to me, though I did not know him at all; however, I have to admit that I saw him running about the fort with a smoking pistol in his

---

* A German prison.

hand ..." As I saw that he was deeply moved by what he recalled, I did not press him any further (you have to understand that our conversation took place in August 1945, when the memories were still fresh). Soon after that, Benjaminavičius and his wife disappeared from St Ottilien. I found out from unofficial sources that in the kacet in Germany he was liable to be arrested. Helped by Dr Grinbergas, he went back to Belgium to "complete his studies" (he was taken over the border illegally by American Jewish soldiers). He is most likely to be in Canada now, where relatives of his have a large trading house (Benjamin-Ottawa?). I think S. Atlasas will be able to provide you with some information, as his wife's maiden name was Benjaminavičiūtė.

C) The Nemenčik family was at St Ottilien too: the father, his wife (a dentist) and three children, between five and ten years of age. Nemenčik himself was perhaps a few years older than I was, had studied politics and economics in Kaunas, and worked for a private trading company. He was rather reserved, and never said anything about himself. We heard more about him from other people. He had a gift for journalism, and wrote articles for Jewish newspapers in Bavaria. An article of his, in which he went for Bishop Brizgys, written in Yiddish-Latin letters, was published in one of the newspapers (*Unsere Stimme?*) which was published in Landsberg. At the end of the article it said that he seemed to break off his conversation with Rabbi Sniegas, with the following: "I can do nothing but pray for you ..." (The statement of Rabbi Sniegas about that conversation will be presented separately.) Nemenčik was sent from the Kaunas ghetto to Estonia, from where he was taken to Germany. After the war he returned to Lithuania, found his family (I assume that his wife and children had been in hiding) and went to Germany. As I have already mentioned, he was quite reserved and spoke very little about himself. I knew that "the undesirable element", suspected communists, criminals, and so on, got on to the "Estonian" list that was compiled by the Council of Jews in the Kaunas ghetto. The Jews explained in a friendly way that he was involved in forging work certificates (*Sonderarbeitsschein*). He got on very well with me and often used to say: "You are a good man, it is a shame that such people are so scarce". He was the only one, who, on learning that I was leaving soon for Austria, came to the transit camp to say good-bye and wish me success. He himself was to go to the USA. I have digressed a little, but I am coming to the point again. On learning that he had been in the Seventh Fort, I asked him about his experiences there. He was arrested on the street, and taken straight to the fort, where he saw "the Lithuanians playing the master". There were no Germans. Looking for a chance to save himself, he noticed that the commandant personally selected certain people: former Jewish officers, Rabbi Sniegas, several educated people, and so on. Nemenčik and a small group of people who were close to him went up to the sentries who were guarding the people selected by the commandant and said that, by order of the commandant, they had come to join that group. The sentries believed them and soon they were all allowed to leave through the gate. Nemenčik mentioned the pistol in the commandant's hand, and said that to the best of his knowledge no more people were allowed to leave.

I want to add that the radio at that time announced that all people held in the Seventh Fort were taught "agricultural work". One of my acquaintances cynically commented: "They forgot to add: pushing up daisies ..."

Some days ago I bought the book *The Final Solution* by G. Reitlinger. Looking through the book, I found something that might be of interest to you. I am enclosing some extracts from the book separately. If I find something interesting again I shall send it to you later.

2. Rabbi Sniegas survived, and I met him in St Ottilien. He found me himself the day after my arrival there and thanked me for helping the Jews, with the following words: "God will not forget you". About a year later he moved to Munich, but every Friday he used to come "to spend the Sabbath among his own people", and almost every time he came to say hello to me. Sometimes he told me something from his experience in the army or something similar. Gradually, he lost his sight, and at the end he needed constant care and attention. I last saw him at the beginning of 1948. During one of his visits he mentioned an article written by Nemenčik (I didn't ask him which, on account of his age). He said something like this: I talked with Bishop Brizgys in the strictest confidence, and only God witnessed it. The result of the conversation was quite different from that described in the newspaper, but God will judge which of us is

right." When I asked him whether he had met Bishop Brizgys in Germany, Rabbi Sniegas said that he had spoken with a bishop (he did not say the name). It was agreed to ignore protocol, and that whoever found it most convenient should pay the first visit. Since, as I have mentioned, Rabbi Sniegas was nearly completely blind, I doubt he could have gone to visit Bishop Brizgys. I do not know if Bishop Brizgys visited Sniegas.

As far as I remember our conversation, I could tell from Sniegas' tone that their meeting in Kaunas was not very pleasant for him to recall.

3. I made the acquaintance of the Vilenčukas family in St Ottilien, and I think it is worth writing more; however, due to a lack of time, I cannot do it now, perhaps some other time. I made friends with the middle brother, Anatolijus (Tanchum). He was very sincere, full of common sense, highly tolerant, and a well-educated man. He could speak and write ten languages (now he can speak 11, as he lives in Norway). He told me a lot about his life; however, I found what he said about his conversation with the appointed minister, Zechlin, the most interesting. Vilenčukas was the director of the Film Rental Office, and thus had to deal with various people (by the way, he gave bribes in cash to Minister Skučas and to Bishop Brizgys). Since all the films were from abroad, the Currency Commission of the Bank of Lithuania controlled all regular settlements. The director, Grinkevičius, was chairman of the Commission, and K. Šerepeka was the secretary. There was an unwritten rule in Lithuania that the police and other officials had free "passes". Apart from Grinkevičius and Šerepeka, a few other people from the Currency Commission also had them. One day, when Vilenčukas put in an application for a regular payment to the German VFA company, Šerepeka demanded that more passes be issued in his and Grinkevičius' name. Vilenčukas was surprised, because he remembered that they had already been given passes. Šerepeka explained that they had promised some of their acquaintances passes. Vilenčukas said that the cinema owners only had a limited number of free passes and doubted if he would be able to fulfil their demand. The conversation ended there. Several days later, a negative answer came from the Currency Commission. Infuriated, Vilenčukas went straight to the German delegation and asked for an audience with

the minister. At first the secretary would not agree, but when he learned about the amount, he gave in and took Vilenčukas to the minister. Zechlin listened to Vilenčukas carefully (they spoke in German) and said: "Litauen ist ein unrecht Land. Sie müssen ein Bestechung an zu versuchen."* (I asked Vilenčukas to write these sentences down specially for me.) Vilenčukas explained to Zechlin that he gave bribes constantly; however, all his funds had been exhausted. Zechlin promised to help. Some days later, another employee of the Currency Commission telephoned and apologised "for that unpleasant misunderstanding", and asked them to come and collect the authorisation. Vilenčukas found out from private sources that a call from Zechlin to the Ministry of the Interior had done the job, and Grinkevičius had had to give an explanation to Paknys.

4. Late one evening in 1945, on his return from Munich, Dr Grinbergas came into my office very concerned about something, and said he wanted to have a word with me in private. "Like in the days of the ghetto," he added. He had been warned that Eisenhower's headquarters had issued a secret order to step up security at the entrances to all displaced persons camps which were still under the direct control of the US army. They wanted to find out the exact number of people in the camp, the distance from the railway station, etc. In brief, a mass deportation home was pending. Dr Grinbergas promised that in the event of any need, my family would go with his family straight to the Swiss border in a car that he had at his disposal. He warned that nobody in St Ottilien knew about it, except us, and asked me to tell nobody, in order to avoid a panic. At the same time, he said that attempts were being made at the White House to revoke the order. Winding up, he smiled and said: "Our people in America can do a lot." I kept it secret for a very long time, though some days later Dr Grinbergas said that the danger had passed over. Shortly after that, all military sentries were removed. I have to stress that it happened soon after Marshal Zhukov paid a visit to Eisenhower. Without going into the details, Dr Grinbergas told me later that there were lots of influential Jews in the White House. I have already mentioned that Dr Grinbergas was head (president)

---

* "Lithuania is a corrupt country. You have to give bribes."

of the association of imprisoned Jews, the former *kacetininkai*. He had a special office in Munich; however, many senior officials visited him in St Ottilien. There were other visitors too, including Ben-Gurion. I tried to keep out of it all the time, so I cannot say much about these visits.

5. As for Antanas Smetona's property in Palestine, I can only say the following: in 1945 a relative of Dr Grinbergas arrived, dressed in an English military uniform. I do not remember his rank; however, I know that he was a member of the Jewish regiment that was noted for its action in Africa against Rommel. Perhaps he was considering the possibility of going to Palestine, which was still under the British. Dr Grinbergas made a serious proposal to me, to emigrate to Palestine, since the quota for other nations had not yet been used up, so there were no obstacles. I refused, and the matter was over. It seems that somebody overheard our conversation, and one day I was addressed by Hirš Glas, a carpenter from Kaunas. He said to me, in a friendly way, that I should not be afraid of going to Palestine, as it was not a bad country, and told me more about it. I do not remember when the *makabiyada** was organised in Palestine and large construction jobs were carried out for the purpose. The contractor Ilgowski from Kaunas ("Dwie Chodokowskie i żydek Ilgowski"**) took on some of the work. He provided his own workers, Jews and Lithuanians. One day he took some of them (Jews?) to show them his orange plantation. Then he pointed to a nearby plantation and said: "I have bought this one for President Smetona". He did not say with whose money it had been bought and how large it was. That is all I know. I never heard anything about it from other people; however, I think Hirš Glas was telling the truth. Also, I would like to mention that Ilgowski had to pay large deposits to the British administration for each worker, to ensure that they would not stay in Palestine as illegal immigrants. He asked the workers not to dishonour him. They all promised; however, the last day all the Jews arrived, but not some Lithuanians. Life in Palestine seemed more alluring than in Lithuania.

---

* A sporting event.
** Polish for "the two Chodokowskis and the Jew Ilgowski."

Unfortunately, I cannot tell you anything about communist Jews who were senior officials. I did not know them personally, though their names were familiar to me. I did not get so high. In my opinion, their crimes against the Lithuanian nation are similar to those committed by Gedvilas, Šumauskas, Macijauskas* and others. I think it would not be a mistake to say that since the times of Mindaugas,** Lithuania has been an asylum to anyone fleeing the Inquisition, the Golden Horde, Ivan the Terrible and other persecutions. However, independent Lithuania was led astray by a fanatical Church and the "leaders of the December 17 People's Revolution", and the new generation "has lost its national dignity".*** (These words were said by a German engineer to a friend of mine during the first days of the war. That German was comparing the Lithuanians to the Poles, Norwegians and the Dutch.)

Starting with policemen, advisers and army officers, and ending with ministers, everybody had their eyes on the wallet of the Jew; later, their appetites grew and they wanted their gold, diamonds and their astrakhan fur coats. However, this is again a separate topic.

Looking forward to hearing from you again.

Yours sincerely,   [Signed:] M. Janušauskas

PS. My memory is getting better again ... Colonel Bobelis was the commandant of the Seventh Fort. Though I am quite sure about this , you might check it somewhere else.

From GRRCL archives: original, handwritten

---

* Prominent Communist Party leaders.

** Lithuania's 13th-century king.

*** Underlined by the author.

16. Statement by Fr Alfonsas Radzvilas about rescuing Jews in Kelmė

Šiauliai, Lithuania: 17 January 1973

Statement

One afternoon in the autumn of 1943, when I was the priest at Kelmė, some Jews were brought from the Šiauliai ghetto to load lorries with potatoes from a heap on the Kelmė estate. After the work was finished, the starving Jews were allowed by the guards to go and ask people for food. Making use of the darkness of night, all 23 people hid, and did not return to the lorries. Four of them came to the presbytery and asked for asylum. I let them stay, and after a day and a half there they were taken to a safer place. Others, also after finding shelter, hid temporarily. At that time the teacher Kazimieras Motušis was in Kelmė, he used to collect and take food to the Jews in the Vilijampolė ghetto in Kaunas. He was asked to find a safer and more permanent place for them. He found a place in the village of Paliepšiai, with the forester J. Demskis. The Jews were safe there until the arrival of the Soviet army. In this way, thanks to the teacher Kazimieras Motušis, 23 Jews were saved from death. Kazimieras Motušis often took care of and helped the Jews, who were in a terrible situation and suffered from German persecution.

Šiauliai, 17 January 1973

[Signed:] Rev. Alfonsas Radzvilas
Parish priest at St George's Church

From GRRCL archives: original, typed

17. Letter from Ksavera Žilinskienė* to Fr Juozas Prunskis about saving two girls

Hollywood, Florida, USA: 13 February 1977

13 February 1977

Dear Father,

I have received your letter about the issue of saving Jews. I am glad to know that at last this matter is being dealt with. Unfortunately, we are late. Complacency is the fatal mistake of our past actions. The planned book will be a useful weapon to defend the Lithuanian nation.

After receiving your letter, I contacted many people, hoping to get more information about rescued Jews; however, it was not a success. Many people are either dead or have left for other places.

My late husband, Professor J. Žilinskas, and I contributed to the rescue of Jews. We managed to save two girls who we brought to America at great risk and with a lot of trouble. We brought them up, sent them to school and helped them to settle. We adopted them, and they are an inseparable part of our family.

We do not boast about it to anybody, and expect no gratitude. One or two close friends of ours know they are adopted orphans and about their origin. Even when we came here, we had to be very careful, because we had some trouble with a group of Orthodox Jews and others.

1. One of the girls was Rita Frankaitė, a six-year-old half-Jewish girl, the daughter of Captain Jonas Frankas who lived in Šiauliai. The captain was arrested when the Russians came, was deported with others, and disappeared. Her mother was bedridden with multiple sclerosis. Thanks to some kind-hearted Lithuanians, she was not taken to the ghetto, and lived in secret with her small daughter and was looked after by a devoted Lithuanian maid and assisted by Lithuanians.

---

* KSAVERA FRANKAITĖ-ŽILINSKIENĖ (1896–?) was born in Brooklyn, USA, and studied at the Lithuanian University. From 1935 to 1940 she headed the Sisterhood of Lithuanian Girl Scouts. She was the wife of Professor Jurgis Žilinskas.

2. The other girl was Zelė Rozenfeldaitė, a 12-year-old Jewish girl. The mothers of these girls were sisters, Šapiraitės. The large and well-known Šapiras family lived on a small estate near Šiauliai and ran a market-garden. Members of the family were loyal citizens of Lithuania – doctors, lawyers, etc. As far as I know, almost all of them were killed; only one or two children were rescued, and now live in Israel.

The girls have an aunt, their mothers' sister, who lives in Argentina. We found her and corresponded with her. It turned out that since she held the attitudes of an old Orthodox Jew towards Christians, she caused a lot of trouble to us. Thus we had to break off relations with her. Last year, after 25 years of silence, through the Lithuanian consul in New York, she tried to find us. We renewed relations. She has changed, as her family has experienced a shock – her daughter married a Christian.

I enclose her address. I do not want to correspond with her. The girls write letters to her in Lithuanian. Both girls are as dear to me as real daughters. We are very close. I am a mother to them and a grandmother to their children. They love and respect me.

Rita Frankaitė graduated from Amherst College, and married a second-generation Lithuanian, Andrius Covalesky. They have a large family, ten children, and are very religious, I should say fanatical, Catholics.

Zelė, now called Lucy, graduated from St Mary's Nursing School in Waterbury, married a man called Richard Bowen, and they have six children. She was a Catholic; however, she has now become an Episcopalian. Her family is also highly religious, their children are being raised very well.

After arriving in America, we stayed with Dr P. Vileišis for several years, whose family took care of our orphans and us.

I hope this is the kind of information you want; however, if there is anything more you need, let me know.

Yours sincerely,   Ksavera Žilinskienė

From GRRCL archives: original, handwritten

18. Letter from Jackus Sondeckis* to Domas Jasaitis about saving Jews in Žemaitija**

[...] 7 February 1971

7 February 1971

Dear Domas,

[...] I am putting down whatever comes to mind. If you arrange it in your own way, perhaps you will be able to use it.

So, about saving Maša Petuchauskienė.

When did it happen? Perhaps in the summer of 1942, when I was on holiday in Šašaičiai, in the rural district of Seda. My sister Eugenija and her husband Juozas Kazlauskas had taken over our family home. One nice sunny day a woman I did not know appeared in our yard. She said she had come with Petuchauskienė, who was staying not far from there. Naturally, I asked her to bring her round at once, and we started to talk.

It turned out that the woman was Stasė Ruzgienė from Vilnius. She looked after Jews. Maša Petuchauskienė had also asked her for help.

As you know, her husband, Samuelis Petuchauskas, was deputy mayor of Šiauliai for a long time. He was also my assistant. He belonged to the Socialist Zionist Party, and was a wise, honest and loyal man, who was faithful to Lithuania, and a pleasant colleague. After the communists had come to power and Valerijonas Knyva had been appointed local commissar, Petuchauskas was asked to be director of the Department of Finance in Kaunas, and later, when the Commissariat moved to Vilnius, he went there too. When the Germans came he was one of the Jewish representatives, and was one of the first Jews to be shot.

Petuchauskienė and her son, Markas or Marijus (I don't remember exactly which, maybe he was given the Jewish name Markas and was called Marijus in Lithuanian; I think it is enough to

---

* JACKUS SONDECKIS, or SONDA, (1893–1989) was mayor of Šiauliai from 1925 to 1931. He fled to the West in 1944, and lived in Chicago from 1950.

** Samogitia, or Žemaitija, is one of the four regions of Lithuania.

Jackus (Sonda) Sondeckis

write only the initial letter of his name), lived in the ghetto. She spoke perfect Lithuanian and did not look like a typical Jew at all. She had dark hair; however, there are plenty of Lithuanian girls with dark hair. Therefore, it was not difficult for her to blend with Lithuanians. She decided to run away. Kostas Kalendra, who was chief of the Vilnius district at that time and who had been chief in Šiauliai before, and who knew the Petuchauskas very well, issued a passport in the name of Marija Petrauskienė. The question arose as to where to live. She decided to go to Šiauliai, where she had worked for a long time (she came from Šiauliai). I do not know how she managed to find Ruzgienė, but together with Ruzgienė and her son Markas, she arrived in Šiauliai and came to our house, found nobody, but learned that I was on holiday in Žemaitija. After getting the exact address, she came and asked us to let her stay there.

I understood her situation very well and, of course, was ready to do anything I could to save her from the Germans. I asked my sister to let her and her son stay in Šašaičiai. My sister agreed without hesitation. Petuchauskienė and her son stayed there, and Ruzgienė returned to Vilnius feeling very happy.

Doctors Mirjam and Mauša Blatas, who were rescued from the Telšiai ghetto
by Juozas Straupis

My sister's farm was quite large, several people worked on it, neighbours visited often, and it was therefore difficult for a stranger to go unnoticed. Petuchauskienė was no trouble, because she did not look like a Jew and spoke perfect Lithuanian. My sister used to say to everybody that she was a relative's wife whose husband had been killed. It was her son that was difficult to cope with. The nine or ten-year-old boy looked like a real Jew, and his Lithuanian was awful. Everything interested him, he made a real nuisance of himself, poked his nose into everything, spoke with the workers ...

Some time later, my sister heard in a roundabout way that the farm labourers were talking about the boy, calling him a Jewish toad, saying that their masters were telling lies by calling the boy's mother their relative, and that they were going to report it to the Germans.

My sister began to worry very seriously. She knew what would happen to both parties. She found some people, Šimkus by name, poor peasants who lived near a forest in the direction of Plungė. They agreed to take Petuchauskienė in. However, after staying there for some time, she returned to Šašaičiai. The trouble was the same – danger. Soon the fighting arrived. Petuchauskienė and her son stayed in Šašaičiai while the place was taken over by the Russians. Then she went to Vilnius. Her son received an education, and now he often writes articles about the theatre. The mother is also alive.

It is not often that people repay kindness. They usually even forget to thank. Markas Petuchauskas is an exception from this point of view. He went to Šašaičiai and thanked my sister on his and his mother's behalf for saving them from death.

I would like to take this opportunity to add what I know about other people there who saved Jews.

Samuelis Saukotas, a doctor from Seda, was taken in by the Dominicans. Over ten Jews were saved by the farmer Juozas Kerpauskas: the Faktoras family from Alsėdžiai, Dr Blatas and his wife from Telšiai, Dr Kaplanas, and others. Kerpauskas' neighbour Juozas Straupis sheltered more than one Jew on his farm.

I am finishing. Now I shall be free. I do not know how much of this "story" will be of use to you. You are free to use it as you find necessary, or throw it away.

If I were as hard as you are I would not stop asking whether it was time to terminate the activity of the Council of American Lithuanians and to concentrate everything in the hands of the Community. I don't think it is a good idea, it will only lead to greater discord and conflicts.

I wish you both all the best.

Love,   [Signed:] Jackus

From GRRCL archives: original, typed

19. The story of how Bronius Gotautas saved Jews, recorded by Fr Konstantinas Gulbinas

[...]

Descendant of a Samogitian* noble family saves Jews: The illiterate Lithuanian son who did not lose his head in the confusion of invasions

The harm that the invaders have done and are still doing emphasises painfully the importance of independence to the life of the nation. This harm includes not only physical terror, which is directly violating freedom and the rights of the people affected by the occupation, but also emotional damage, where the invaders, by using either a carrot or a stick, have turned people into spies, traitors and murderers of their brothers. During the first Bolshevik occupation (1940 to 1941) the Russians cleverly made use of the services not only of a handful of Lithuanian communists but also of some Lithuanian Jews, to suit their own ends, by compiling lists of "enemies of the people" doomed to deportation and imprisonment. And when the Red invader from the East was replaced by the brown invader from the West, the German Gestapo directed the anti-communist or anti-Semitic attitudes of many an immature Lithuanian towards the cruel mechanism of human annihilation. The most painful thing here, perhaps, is that the evil service that the invaders forced their assistants to render cast the whole nation and its history in a negative light. Therefore, the deeds of the people who did not lose their head in the confusion caused by the invasions deserve serious attention. They did not give in to the tricks of the invaders and were not put off by their threats. Putting their lives and their freedom at risk, they rescued people close to them from the hands of butchers without distinguishing between religion, race, class or party. With the passing of time, many of the heroes of

---

* Žemaitijan.

Bronius Gotautas

the unarmed struggle have passed away. Therefore, the duty of every literate Lithuanian is to record the deeds of those who are still with us. We want to introduce the descendant of an old family of Samogitian noblemen, Bronius Gotautas, to the readers of *Tėviškės žiburiai*, and tell them about his experience in rescuing Jews at the time of the German occupation of Lithuania.

1. Indirect preparation. An old Lithuanian proverb goes "Speckled is the woodpecker, but human life is even more multicoloured." The life of Bronius Gotautas did not lack variety either. Though he himself was illiterate, when the Capuchin journal *Lourdes* was founded in 1936, he became one of the most active distributors of it. He also distributed the Jesuits' *Žvaigždė*, the Marian *Šaltinis, Pranciškonų pasaulį* and religious books. He used to distribute this literature not only in one area but throughout independent Lithuania. For an illiterate man, this work was especially difficult: he could not tell anybody what the newspapers and books were about, as he himself could not read. He had to ask kind people to read the more important articles in the newspapers and more specific extracts from the books aloud to him. Gotautas was able to select, make a summary of the ideas he heard, and recount them in the most vivid way himself.

In travelling around Lithuania, he happened to meet many different people and experience many things, both good and bad. He also met comedians who liked to mock a Catholic press apostle.

One such wag tried to make a fool of him. In the presence of others he made Gotautas an offer: "You could get a litas if you sold *Laisvoji mintis*".

Gotautas was rarely at a loss for words in such cases. He found an answer that time immediately, too.

"Go to a kiosk, and get it yourself for twenty cents."

Gotautas' trips far and wide in Lithuania brought him into contact with many people, and made it possible for him to memorise geographical details of places and areas. Under the German occupation, these things were of paramount importance in the work of saving Jews.

2. Unsuccessful first meeting. Urbonas-Urbonavičius, who spent his last years quietly in Plungė, drew the attention of the Catholic churchgoer Bronius Gotautas to the fate of professors of the Old Testament. He had been a major in the tsar's army in Russia, and had experienced himself the cruelty of the Bolshevik Revolution towards people of different classes and convictions. Therefore, when National Socialism took hold of Germany, which started occupying the neighbouring countries and parts of them, one after another, he saw a similarity between what had happened in Russia and what could happen soon in the countries occupied by Germany. In the autumn of 1938, on *Kristallnacht*, that similarity was shown by the Jewish synagogues set on fire by the Nazis in many small towns and cities of Germany.

It was in his work distributing Catholic literature that Bronius Gotautas found Urbonavičius, in a small room on the top floor of the Oginskis mansion. They both had a similar background: both had grown up in the time of the tsars, and both were single, therefore their casual acquaintance soon grew into a deep friendship. Urbonavičius tried to explain that everyone had an immortal soul, no matter whether he was Catholic, Jewish, Lutheran or Orthodox. The Jews were being subjected to an especially cruel fate by the Germans. They did not seem to understand the threat or consider how to avoid it. It was necessary to warn the Jews and prepare them to rescue themselves. Urbonavičius wanted to urge the Jews to be baptised. As it was in the time of the tsars, so it had to be now: whoever converted to Christianity was no longer a Jew. And then, even if the Germans occupied Lithuania, all the Jews who were Christians would be spared their racist policies. By means of this and similar arguments, Urbonavičius talked Gotautas into going to the synagogue in Plungė and warning them publicly about the impending danger.

It seems that they both discussed all the details of the visit. Bronius Gotautas did his best to make a lasting impression on the Israelites by his appearance and behaviour. Recalling an old anecdote that he had heard about Diogenes, the Greek philosopher, Gotautas repeated it in the synagogue in Plungė one Saturday in the summer of 1939. Following the example of the Capuchins, he had a long beard, went barefoot in summer and without a cap, and wore patched trousers and a jacket which had served him for seven years, on holiday and on working days, during his all trips. That is how he appeared at the service in the synagogue. In addition, he lit a candle, held it in his right hand and slowly approached the Tablets of the Law. You can imagine the surprise and indignation of the pious Jews. Their reaction broke the deep silence. One hit Gotautas on his right hand, in which he was holding the candle, another told him indignantly to put on his cap, and all the Jews standing around made a fuss.

Gotautas took the candle in his left hand, with his right hand he gathered up the flaps of his jacket, and said: "Take hold of me in this way!"

The Jews stopped hitting him and fell silent. Gotautas asked who the rabbi was; however, the Jews would not tell him. Then Gotautas solemnly took a step towards the Tablets of the Law and went around them three times, each time repeating the words of Diogenes: "I am looking for an honest man, I cannot find an honest man".

This strange ceremony infuriated the rabbi. He stepped forward, went up to Gotautas and told him to go to the church and say these things there rather than in the synagogue. Gotautas respected the elders and priests of all creeds, so he left the synagogue quietly and told Urbonas-Urbonavičius everything.

He had probably expected some results, because, greatly excited, he said: "Jesus Christ is the light of the world, but the Jews do not recognise that light."

That time the attempts of the two Christians to warn the Jews of the impending disaster and to discuss possibilities of rescuing them ended in failure. The Second World War, which broke out shortly afterwards, brought new problems to everybody.

3. Carries on the work of distributing publications. Bronius Gotautas distributed Catholic literature until the very last day of the independence of Lithuania, and even continued during the first few months of the Bolshevik occupation. Only the working conditions had changed: all of a sudden, all religious newspapers were banned; only books that were printed in the years of independence and that had not sold out remained. The publishing arm of the Society of St Casimir had plenty of these.

When the Russians came, the St Casimir bookshop was also nationalised. The superintendent, Aleksiūnaitė, an elderly lady, maintained her position; however, a Jew was appointed to replace Fr M. Vaitkus, the former director. Nobody knows why, but the new authorities of the bookshop were very well disposed towards Gotautas. If he took all the remaining copies of an issue, he was paid 40 to 50 cents for each copy. Gotautas could not help boasting to a sister who ran the Šaričiai bookshop about this. He offered to bring her a package under the same conditions. For some unknown reason, the sister did not like his offer.

"Do you think I am a fool? I can go and fetch it myself," she said.

So she went; however, she got nothing. The director offered her only the standard 30 per cent discount and nothing more.

"Why do you give Bronius Gotautas a much higher discount?" she demanded.

The director cut her short. "It's none of your business."

Nothing was left for the nun but to ask Gotautas to supply the books. However, when Gotautas went to the St Casimir bookshop, Aleksiūnaitė was very angry with him.

"Why do you tell others?!"

But still, the Šaričiai got the books at Gotautas' price ...

Aleksiūnaitė helped Bronius Gotautas in another way too: some time later she felt that Gotautas was being spied on. And she was right. On entering the bookshop, Gotautas himself saw that a young boy was standing outside the door. "What can I do? They will find out where I live and my landlord might get into trouble," thought Gotautas. He went out into the street and saw an elderly coachman. "Will you do me a favour and take this package of books to the Birutė bookshop in Panemunė and give it to Gotautas?" He asked the old man in a loud voice on purpose, so that the boy who was following him would understand. And the latter, on hearing that the books were being given to somebody else, disappeared at once. Gotautas noticed this and took the parcel of books in the opposite direction, where they were also appreciated.

4. Jewish friends in the Red prison. Suspecting that he was being spied on in Kaunas, Bronius Gotautas left for Šiauliai to hide in the Capuchin friary. However, this created a new set of problems for him. At the end of November or the beginning of December in 1940, the GPU* arrested him there, and the chief took him to his flat, which was nearby, on the same Vilniaus gatvė. A car was called immediately and Gotautas was taken to the district court and interrogated. At first they spoke to him very pleasantly: they offered him a 1,500-rouble monthly salary, promised to put him in charge of the Capuchin friary, to have as many rooms for himself as he wished, and to let the remaining rooms to whoever he chose. The NKVD wanted evidence from Gotautas that the Capuchins, 59 people in all,** had convened secret meetings to overthrow the Bolshevik authorities.

Bronius Gotautas refused all this. Then the interrogation became more serious. "How many signatures have you collected for T. Bružikas?" "About four to five hundred, a total of three pages." "Where did you get the forms from?" Gotautas did not say that students from a high school had drawn lines on a sheet of paper. He said he had collected the signatures because he thought it might help Bružikas get out of prison. Seeing that he had fallen silent, the interrogator spoke more gently. He said he would let him go on distributing publications only on condition that he inform them who bought them. The same offer was made the second and the third night.

Eventually, on the third night, the interrogator asked about the Jesuit Fr Paukštys.

"We know everything about Paukštys." The interrogator became agitated.

"If you know everything, why do you ask me?" said Gotautas.

---

* The letters NKVD are written in hand over the letters GPU.
** Written in hand.

In answer to Gotautas' question, the interrogator struck him on the chin so hard that he fell over together with the chair. Semi-conscious, he was kept and not interrogated for three days.

Gotautas was shut up in a cellar with 20 other prisoners. A Jewish rabbi, possibly from Tryškiai, was imprisoned there too. The rabbi's relatives would visit him. One evening the chief of the Šiauliai police station, who had served since the time of independence, came to look at the prisoners with a Jewish doctor. The doctor was concerned about Gotautas' health, took his hand, checked his pulse and said that he had a temperature. By order of the police chief, Gotautas was given a long coat like a sentry's, although the other prisoners were not. The police chief probably recognised him, because on leaving he said: "Don't be afraid, Gotautas, you won't die in prison, we'll send you to hospital." At night, in great pain, Gotautas screamed at the top of his voice, and the guards rushed into the cell immediately to see what had happened. At midnight a car was called, two guards took him by the arms and dragged him outside. A third guard opened the door of the car and he was taken to the city hospital. Some days later, a doctor told the Soviet officials that Gotautas' days were numbered. If they did not want him to die under guard, he should be discharged. The guards were removed from the door of his room, and soon Gotautas felt much better. Some days later he was discharged from hospital, and stayed in hiding until the German invasion on 22 June 1941.

5. Lithuanian Jews and their rescue during the German occupation. The book *Ir be ginklo kariai** recently** appeared in Lithuania, in which many pages are devoted to Gotautas' reminiscences and his activities during this period. We will not repeat here what is said in the book; however, after mentioning in brief people, institutions and enterprises related to Gotautas' activity, we shall deal with one episode which was not mentioned in the book.

As the German army was quickly marching eastwards, the creators of "the New World Order" and people to keep control, in various uniforms or without any uniform at all, soon appeared in its

---

* *Soldiers without Weapons.*

** The words "Published in 1967" are written by hand in brackets above.

rear. The people had hardly recovered from the persecutions by the Bolsheviks, from deportation and massacre, when a new terror struck them: the shooting of the Jews. For the sake of security, Gotautas did not maintain relations with Urbonas-Urbonavičius under the Bolsheviks; however, he did not entirely sever them either. The new terror reminded both of their old plans for rescuing Jews and made them act. So Gotautas went to Plungė to see Urbonas-Urbonavičius. Asked if he was ready to join in the work of rescuing Jews, Gotautas agreed without hesitation. His first deed was to have about 75 Jews baptised by the Capuchin Father B. before they were shot. I shall describe it later.

Another time, Bronius Gotautas found two more people at Urbonas-Urbonavičius' place: a secretary and a student, who was his co-worker. As the person who knew the environs and its people the best, Gotautas acted as a messenger. However, at an agreed time, when he was on his way to Urbonas-Urbanavičius, he met a child who told him that the Germans, with the help of the two co-workers of Urbonas-Urbonavičius, had arrested and shot him in the park at half past three in the afternoon. Those who sheltered Jews met the same fate as the Jews themselves. Gotautas understood that the only thing for him to do was to run away from Plungė as soon as he could. But how? He could not go far on foot. German soldiers and plain-clothes officers were patrolling the station. What could he do? Fortunately, he met a coachman and asked him to take him to another station, in Alksnėnai. There he paid the coachman and bought a ticket to Pažaislis, from where he could easily reach the Capuchin friary in Petrašiūnai, where he could spend the night.

He again took up distributing printed material, and at the same time renewed his old acquaintances and learned how the Jews had been driven into the Kaunas ghetto, and their further fate. Gotautas then became involved in the work of rescuing Jews in and around Kaunas.

A chemist in Petrašiūnai, called Pusvaškis, did a lot in this regard. The secretary at the paper factory, Jūra Mentvilytė, also contributed greatly, by procuring forms for issuing documents. Kužinskas affixed the seals. Gotautas was in constant touch with the director of the Red Cross Hospital and the assistant chief at Kaunas police station, whose names he has forgotten. He would also collect the documents of Lithuanians who had died in hospital, through priests and reliable nurses, and give them to Jews in hiding. He put old Jews in the places of deceased Lithuanians in the St Vincent de Paul old people's home. They had to live under other people's names and had documents belonging to other people. In this way, Rabbi Šternbergas was saved at Šančiai St Vincent de Paul old people's home and later emigrated to the USA, as well as three other Jewish women, one of whom lived there until the end of the war. Sister Bonita Žemgulytė helped to baptise one young Jewish girl and took care of her. A Jewish woman found refuge in the house of a famous Lithuanian artist called Adomas Varnas in Palemonas. About 200 Jews with children were hidden in 70 St Vincent de Paul orphanages all over Lithuania. A retired chemist from Telšiai called Čekys created the possibility for 1,200 Jews to leave for Austria and thus avoid extermination. Bijaikis, the pharmacist in Pakuonis, kept a Jewish girl hidden in his house. Seven convents, with whom Gotautas kept in touch, contributed greatly to hiding Jews, and in particular their children. Pusvaškis from Petrašiūnai also took part in that work.

We have only mentioned here a few people, enterprises and institutions with which Bronius Gotautas had contact when rescuing Jews in Lithuania under the German occupation from 1941 to 1944. Baltuška, the chief of the rural district of Pažaislis, also deserves a mention. He was Gotautas' irreplaceable helper in his dangerous work. No matter where Gotautas found him – in the office, staying with friends, during the day or at night – Baltuška always issued the documents needed or a note to the secretary of the rural district who also belonged to the group for rescuing Jews, and she, in her turn, prepared the documents immediately. The same people provided with documents a number of *plechavičiuks** who had evaded German military service. One example demonstrates clearly Baltuška's position. As for other Jews, Baltuška drew up Lithuanian documents for a Mindelovičienė and her daughter. Dr Steponavičienė's housekeeper hid the daughter in her village. When Gotautas gave

---

* After POVILAS PLECHAVIČIUS (1890–1973), a former army officer, who was allowed to organise a Lithuanian detachment in 1944 to defend the country against the Soviets but would not let it be integrated into the German army, for which he was imprisoned by the Nazis.

Mindelovičienė the documents, she asked how much she owed Baltuška or what she could give him in appreciation. At their next meeting Gotautas passed on to Baltuška the question and repeated it several times. Baltuška frowned at Gotautas and said firmly: "I would not even put my life at risk for a mountain of gold. If they find out they will kill me. I take risks neither for money nor for gifts." Today it is difficult to say how many Jews the chief and the secretary of that rural district rescued by falsifying documents. The number may amount to 500.

The book mentioned above does not say anything about the transfer of 29 Jews from the Vilnius region to Pravieniškiai concentration camp in Kaunas. We shall try to give a brief account of it here as the leader remembers it.

6. Gotautas' last deed. Firstly, it has to be said that this feat was only possible because some Lithuanians who worked in German security and the German police took part in rescuing Jews and put their and their families' lives at risk.

This explains how the plan was born in the flat of a Lithuanian who worked for the security organs. He was celebrating his name day, and Gotautas happened to be at the party too. The host introduced Gotautas to a uniformed guest called Juozas Jonevičius, a Lithuanian from the Vilnius region, who was chief of the guards in the Kertupis Forest work of the Pravieniškiai camp. When introducing them, he mentioned the fact that Gotautas helped to save Jews. Jonevičius was deeply affected, and said he would join Gotautas, as for some time he had been troubled by the issue.

Some time later, about 500 Polish Jews were taken to Pravieniškiai camp, and given the task of cutting wood in Kertupis Forest. The life of the new inmates was very hard. Other prisoners at least lived in bunkers, whereas these Jews had to live in shacks that they had to build with fir branches by themselves. Jonevičius was especially moved by the fate of 30 Jews who were ill and feeble and said they could do no work at all. The commandant of the camp, a German SS officer, decided to execute them, and gave Jonevičius responsibility for implementing the plan. However, he had other plans. He knew that there was a chance of sending a group of people to Vienna. The only thing to do was to provide the people with Lithuanian documents and, of course, to manage somehow to get them away from Kertupis Forest and to Kaunas. Jonevičius was looking for someone to carry out the task, and Bronius Gotautas was just the right man.

One day the commandant of the camp told the ailing and feeble people to wash and put on clean clothes, and gave an order to Jonevičius to take them to the forest to a ditch and shoot them. Gotautas had been warned about it and asked to come to the ditch in the forest that day. When the 30 Jews were brought to the ditch, Jonevičius explained to them in Polish what the commandant's order actually meant. On hearing it, one of them had a heart attack and dropped down dead. This gave Jonevičius a good opportunity to send away his assistant who had accompanied the Jews there with him: he thought up a pretext to send his assistant back to the guardroom. Left alone with the Jews and Gotautas, who had just arrived, Jonevičius told the Jews openly and clearly the order he had been given, and assured them that he was not a murderer.

"You have a chance to save yourselves. Here is a man who is ready to help you. He will take you to my flat in Kaunas, and from there we will find what to do next."

Jonevičius remembered his orders. He fired several volleys into the air to give the impression that the Jews had been shot. He put the body of the dead Jew in the ditch, covered it with branches, and set fire to it as he had been ordered by the commandant for all 30. He covered the ditch with earth and evened it over. Then he explained the plan to the remaining Jews. Gotautas could not speak Polish, so they had to communicate in signs: he would show where to go with his hand. They went in twos, keeping a distance; those who went in front had to sign to those who followed. Gotautas knew the way through the forest and fields from Kertupis to Kaunas very well, because he had covered it many times when he went to Jonevičius' office to discuss the details of the plan. When the group set off in the evening it turned out that these 29 Jews were not only ill but also half-starved. Fortunately, Gotautas knew a certain Grubliauskas, a kind farmer who lived in a remote homestead on the way to Kaunas, who, although he did not have much himself, had helped Gotautas and his wards more than once. So now, when the group of 30 people came into his yard and hid, the hostess gave them a loaf of bread and told her daughter to give each person five apples. The girl put the remaining apples on the ground and could not help noticing how those grown-up men snatched them greedily like small children. Gotautas was the only one who did not rush to collect the leftovers, even though his stomach was rumbling too. One Jew divided the loaf of bread into 30 pieces: Gotautas took his share from his hand too.

It was late spring in 1944. The Germans were retreating; therefore, Gotautas managed to get the whole group of Polish Jews to Juozas Jonevičius' flat in Vytauto prospektas in Kaunas after dark. Though exhausted and hungry, the Jews managed to cover the distance of several kilometres. The problem was how to get food for such a large group of people when everything was rationed in the towns during the war. Gotautas knew a grocery run by two sisters called Rakauskaitė. Though they were both illiterate, they were quick-witted and did very well. They had helped Jews with food more than once, through mediators, in order not to be caught themselves. Late that evening, Gotautas and Jonevičius knocked at the door of the grocery to ask for food. The sisters gave what they could: bread and vegetables. So each Jew was given potatoes mixed with vegetables and a slice of bread. They were so tired that two men fell asleep while they were eating. The documents were arranged in no time. Gotautas brought work-books from his office, in Lithuanian and German, made in Petrašiūnai paper mill, and Jonevičius turned the Polish Jews into Lithuanian Jews by making up plausible addresses. After the whole group of 29 had reached Vienna safely and found work, Jonevičius received a letter of gratitude from them in Polish, and translated it for Gotautas. It would be interesting for him to learn if at least one of that group is still alive, and whether Juozas Jonevičius managed to carry out the plan to rescue the remaining 470 Jews in Kertupis Forest. Gotautas was not able to contribute to it, as soon he himself was arrested by the Gestapo and deported to the concentration camp in Stutthof (near Danzig), where over 40 people belonging to the Lithuanian intelligentsia had already been imprisoned.

7. Signs of joy and gratitude. Today Gotautas cannot remember the number of Jews that he rescued during the German occupation. He knows only one thing, that, in the words of Tumas-Vaižgantas,* he never asked who sent him and what right they had

---

* Pen name of the writer Juozas Tumas (1869–1933).

to do so. No matter who asked him to act as a mediator in saving Jews, he was always quick to rush there, to prevent obedient and secret agents of the Gestapo from carrying out their evil deeds. In every case when people who were not suspected by the German authorities were afraid to make use of the telephone or postal services, Gotautas helped. After the end of the Second World War, lots of Jews he saved wrote letters to him, some organisations sent him money, and one organisation still sends money. However, Gotautas could not foresee such things in those days and did not expect any reward. Being not only a Catholic by upbringing, but also genuinely devout, Gotautas regarded it as the greatest reward if an Israelite decided to adopt Christianity.

Bronius Gotautas still remembers one case. He took falsified documents to an educated Jewish woman, who surprised him by expressing a desire:

"I want to be baptised!"

"Why?"

"When I was a student I read much about different religions and sects. I found that the Catholic faith was the best. Of course I married a Jew and had children, so I had to take into account the family. However, today my husband and my children have been killed and there are no obstacles to my taking up Christianity."

In tsarist times the Jews could save themselves from pogroms if they converted to the Orthodox religion. Urbonas-Urbonavičius, the former major in the tsar's army, possibly cherished such thoughts when he started to devise plans to rescue Jews in the last years of independent Lithuania. The reality of the German occupation turned out to be quite different: they exterminated all Jews, practising, lapsed and baptised. Gotautas knew that very well, so he warned the lady:

"Converting to Christianity will not save your life."

"My life is in the hands of God. I want to do what I can. Hitler is only an instrument in God's hand. God is punishing the Jews through Hitler."

Gotautas could not give an answer to this, as he felt that the words had been taken out of his own mouth. He also knew very well how to act to help a person in matters of eternal human life.

8. A loaf of bread. No doubt everyone is familiar with the quotation from the Gospel "Man shall not live by bread alone" that one

Bronius Gotautas with
Fr Juozas Končius

writer chose for the title of his book. It also indicates how difficult it is to keep alive without bread. Bronius Gotautas experienced this especially bitterly, and unforgettably joyfully, in Germany. Together with 70 other men, he was taken out from Stutthof to dig trenches. The prisoners were also sent to dig up unexploded bombs. If, in driving from one place to another, a prisoner collapsed out of exhaustion, he was immediately shot dead. Thus after several days only 25 people were left out of the original 70. And those 25 were hardly able to drag themselves along. Gotautas was among them. Once when they were going through a railway tunnel where it was dark, a young girl suddenly jumped up to him and gave him a loaf of bread. Without saying a word, she disappeared again. Gotautas was able to have a good meal, the first in a long time, and at the same time he rejoiced at the deed of the brave girl.

He had saved lots of Jews. Unfortunately, the Jews themselves had reported him. A lawyer had warned him that a Jewish girl who had been arrested by the Gestapo probably informed on him, because the Gestapo was looking for him. However, the girl who gave him the loaf of bread was also a Jew, though a different one. Though she disappeared immediately, Gotautas recognised her and remembered her story very clearly. Her parents had had a shop on the Šakiai estate. All of her family were arrested and shot by the Germans. Gotautas never found out how she had managed to avoid annihilation. She might have been out when the others were arrested, or she might have escaped from the ghetto. He had learned that she was in hiding with the family of a Lithuanian railway worker. However, the head of the family was a former communist and was arrested by the Gestapo, and the wife was afraid that the same lot might befall her ward, and turned to Gotautas for help, asking if he knew a family with whom the girl might be safer. The girl had already been baptised a Christian. Gotautas was asked to provide her with a Lithuanian baptismal certificate. When a Lithuanian security official was looking for a nurse for his children, the girl was taken to the pharmacist Pusvaškis, who introduced her to the security official. On the way to Pusvaškis' place, when they were passing the house where Finkelbrandienė was hiding, Gotautas said to the girl:

"A Jewish woman lives here; if you want I can introduce you to her."

"No," answered the girl, "I do not want to hear, see, or know anything."

"Why?" asked Gotautas in surprise.

"How do I know that the Gestapo will not catch me? If they do, they will start interrogating me, to make me tell them where other Jews are. They will torture me, and I may give in and tell. If I know nothing, I will give nothing away."

It was not difficult for the family of the Lithuanian security official to keep the girl hidden, because there was not too much to hide. Her features and the colour of her eyes were more Lithuanian than Semitic. Living in a small town and playing with Lithuanian children, she learned to speak Lithuanian so well that everybody admired her perfect Suvalkijan* accent.

---

* Suvalkija is one of the four regions of Lithuania.

During the three years of the German occupation, Gotautas experienced a lot and forgot a lot. Not all of his experience was pleasant, especially the last, for which he was arrested and deported from Lithuania. However, even today it seems to him that all those great and untold sufferings are counterbalanced by the pleasant memories of that brave girl, who, without fearing the guards, gave him, a starving prisoner, a loaf of bread. If she is still alive, she must be a mature woman now. Perhaps she herself has a daughter of the age that she was when Gotautas took her from place to place in Lithuania and then met by chance in Germany.

From GRRCL archives: copy, typewritten

20. Letter from Veronika Sirutytė-Effertienė to Domas Jasaitis about rescued Jews

[...] 7 January 1977

7 January 1977

Dear Doctor,

About two years ago I sent Mr Audėnas* a photocopy of the letter of gratitude received from Tamara Lazersonaitė (Professor Lazerson's daughter, who escaped from the ghetto) for the care she received during the German occupation. As I do not know whether that photocopy was given to you, I am sending it to you now. Tamara, at that time she was 14 years old, I believe, had documents made out in the name of Elenutė Savickaitė. When people started asking who she was, I used to say that she was my daughter, who had come back due to the difficult food situation in Kaunas. "Ah, that's why she looks like you," said one woman. In the hope of finding her parents alive, she did not flee Lithuania with us. Unfortunately, her hopes

---

* JUOZAS AUDĖNAS (1898–1982), minister of agriculture in 1939 and 1940, who participated in the anti-Nazi resistance and, after emigrating to the USA, helped to organise the VLIK.

were not fulfilled. She left for Israel several years ago, and sometimes writes to me. There she published her diary, called *Under the Burning Sky*, and sent us a copy. Unfortunately, the book is written in Hebrew and we have not been able to decipher it yet.

There is a plan to publish the book in English too. I assume it is about her escape and life on our farm, because she wrote that the first part of her diary was taken away from her in Moscow. I do not know if they gave it back to her. Our farm was in Pakamačiai, near Saločiai, in the Biržai district. For some time on our farm we looked after Vytautas Lastauskas, the pharmacist's son, whose mother was a Jew. He was of a rather nervous disposition, so he went to live with a ranger who lived in the forest.

I would not like to take up too much of your precious time with a long letter; however, some more things from that period come to mind.

When the Russians came and our farm was nationalised, we had to leave it. As my husband was an agronomist, he managed to get a job as an administrator on the farm at Staniūnai (formerly belonging to Graf Kaiserling, later Chodakauskas) about one kilometre from Panevėžys. When the Germans came to Panevėžys, Gebietscommissar Neumas claimed it. He would come to Staniūnai quite often with guests, senior officials, to show them "his" estate. Everything had to be in perfect order on the farm. Apart from the permanent workers, a group of Jews from the ghetto would be brought to weed sugar beet every day. Usually about ten people would come; however, each day they asked my husband to let some more come. The miserable people from the ghetto got the chance to get some milk, vegetables and any other food on the farm to take back. In about three weeks the group expanded to over a hundred people. The Germans probably disliked it, and one day they took all the workers from the ghetto away, saying that they were being taken to work in a peat bog. However, other people said different things. Russian prisoners of war were brought to take their place. The prisoners participated in shooting Jews in Panevėžys. Every morning a prisoner would take me to work in Panevėžys. Once he said to me: "It is good that they shot those Jews, now I am properly dressed and I have a watch …" I did not want to listen to the story, so I do not know what part he played in it.

When we returned to Pakamačiai as tenants, since there was no hotel in Saločiai passing German officials were billeted at our place. I once told one of these "guests" that the farm had suffered greatly under the communists.

He reassured me by saying: "Don't worry about it. You won't stay here anyway. First we shall do away with the Jews, then the Poles, etc. They don't give anything to mankind. The Lithuanians will not be exterminated; however, they will be moved to other places."

He was surprised at the brutality and cruelty of the extermination of the Jews there. I asked him what they had done to the German Jews, and he said:

"We took them all to ..." (I am afraid I have forgotten the name of the place – Lizmanstatt?) ... "and as they got very tired and hungry on the journey, we treated them to some nice things, and the problem was solved."

I am afraid I am taking up your time by telling you what you already know very well. The Nazis made a film "The Cruellest Nation in the World" about shooting Jews in Lithuania. The Germans themselves appeared not to participate in it, but I happened to hear from witnesses that their military uniforms and boots betrayed them, although they were only in shirts and stood with their backs to the public. I should substantiate my statement by giving the names; however, I have either forgotten them or did not record them in the first place.

There may be a chance to find a set of *Lietuvos aidas* (1937, 1938 or 1939). Just before the war it published several lines announcing that a Jewish commission (Zionists?) that had travelled through Europe and investigated the condition of the Jews admitted that the Jews had the best conditions in Lithuania. I kept that issue of *Lietuvos aidas*. But it was left behind when we fled.

I heard from an acquaintance, Antanina Rimkienė (from Vilkija), that the doctor at Gelgaudiškis (I do not remember his name) hid three families of Jews under his roof; but after it was found out, not only the Jews but also he, his wife and three or four children were shot in his own yard. They had to dig their grave themselves.

She said she knew Statkevičienė in Germany, who was from Marijampolė, who had brought a Jewish girl with her, but her mother found her and she had to give the girl back to her mother.

To get back to Lazersonaitė: having escaped from the ghetto, as her parents had advised her, she went to Professor Pranas Mažylis. However, as the Mažylis flat was next to their clinic where there were always lots of people, through my sister Petronėlė Lastienė, Tamara was sent to our place, because it was too dangerous to keep her there.

I apologise once again for my rambling information. I would be happy if you find something in it of use.

Let God help you in your important work.

V. Effertienė

PS. Two Germans who were the first to come to Saločiai, stripped the local photographer, the Jewish girl Chataitė, of all her clothes, placed her naked in a shop window and burned her hair. She was a nice girl whom everyone respected.

PPS. My brother Jonas Sirutis, an agronomist in the Lazdijai district, was deported to Siberia in 1941 with his wife and two-year-old son because he refused to move out of his flat and let a Jewish communist occupy it (there was a shortage of good flats in Lazdijai). I still mourn my beloved brother, as he was killed in Siberia some months after he had been deported. I do not blame the whole Jewish nation for it. I blame all the Jewish communists …

From GRRCL archives: original, handwritten

21. Reminiscences of Fr J. Kardauskas about Vilkaviškis Jews and those who saved them

Chicago, USA [...]

During the first years of the Russian and then the German occupation I lived in Vilkaviškis and headed the Vilkaviškis Roman Catholic parish. During the German occupation I baptised Lapidusas, the son of the owner of the Vilkaviškis shoe shop. He was put in prison. The Lithuanian warders of the prison tried to help the arrested people. Jonas Svobonas (he is now dead) prepared Lapidusas for his baptism. With the warders' knowledge, he was taken to the church, and I christened him Jonas.* Jonas Svobonas was his godfather. The baptism itself was not the most important thing, the important thing was to receive the baptismal certificate, backdated as far as possible. I issued a certificate backdated ten years, I believe. Thanks to that certificate, he was released from prison and avoided execution. To the best of my knowledge, he now lives in Canada.

I cannot remember the names (of husband and wife) of the owners of the Olimpija publishing company in Vilkaviškis, who, having escaped being shot, hid on one of the farms in the parish of Alvitas. A hideout was made for them in hay in the barn, which they would leave when the coast was clear. I was asked to baptise them. I rode there by bicycle. I baptised them both, and issued certificates with a previous date. The wife died soon after that. He stayed in hiding with a farmer in the parish of Vilkaviškis, not far from the chapel at Paežeriai. The farmer's daughter (I do not remember her name) prepared him for confession and for receiving the Eucharist. One evening, as had been agreed, I went to Paežeriai chapel, where he made his confession (I was surprised at the way he did it, with thoroughness and a perfect understanding of the sins) and piously received Holy Communion. I heard that he hid on farms during the whole German occupation.

As I was asked by one of my parishioners, and having received permission from His Excellency Bishop Karosas, I baptised a Jewish girl, a dentist, in my small room, who had lived with a Catholic

---

* John.

agronomist for some time already (I do not remember his name). Right there, after the baptism, with the parishioner acting as a witness, I married them and issued a marriage certificate backdated by ten years, with her parents' names changed into Lithuanian ones. Soon they moved to Zypliai, near Šakiai, because he got a job as a teacher at Zypliai school. To the best of my knowledge they survived; however, I never found out what became of them.

On the day the Vilkaviškis Jews were taken out of the town, after the barracks, a Jewish girl, who had been baptised, somehow lagged behind the group. Lithuanian guards followed the group to keep order. They found the girl sitting by a tree with a Lithuanian Bible in her hands, and asked who she was waiting for. She told them that she was a Jew; however, she had not been able to keep up with the others. Seeing the Bible in her hand, they asked why she had it with her, and she explained that she had been baptised and that now she was a Catholic. The Lithuanian guards secretly took her to the other side of the town and told her to go to a safer place. Father Pijus Karalius (he died here, in Cicero) took her into the presbytery in Lankeliškiai. There she received the other sacraments, and Bishop Podolskis confirmed her. I heard she now lives in Canada.

The Vilkaviškis bailiff, Pališkis, sheltered a Jewish woman in his small barn in Vilkaviškis. Nobody knew about it for a long time. Finally, the German authorities found out, arrested her and sent the Pališkis family to Marijampolė prison. With the Bishop of Vilkaviškis, priests and influential residents of the town interceding for them, the Pališkis were released after six months. I never heard what happened to the Jewish woman. (Kazys Povilaitis, who lives in Chicago, could provide more detailed information.)

The Tabariškis family had an oil press next to the orchard of the Vilkaviškis presbytery. Before the Germans came, the Russians deported the Tabariškis to Russia. Their daughter, a small girl, was somehow left behind. A Lithuanian maid who had worked in the Tabariškis house took care of her. When the Germans came, she was afraid to keep the girl. Matilda, the former housekeeper of Bishop Adomas Povilaitis, became her new guardian. The bishop christened her Teresė. She survived, and as far as I know, she lives in Leningrad. When her guardian and godmother Matilda Dobilaitė was still alive she used to go and visit her.

I did more good turns to the Jewish people; however, I cannot remember everything now.

Rev. J. Kardauskas
Formerly of Vilkaviškis Catholic Church (from May 1940 to 31 July 1944).

Addendum

Fr Justinas Steponaitis, the present priest at Athol, could add some information. He was also at Vilkaviškis during the first Russian and German occupations.

My sister Marytė was godmother to a Jewish girl, and Pranė Kamantauskienė, another of my sisters, was also godmother to a Jewish girl.

I think Fr Steponaitis baptised much more Jews, I just used to issue falsified baptismal certificates.

Also, Kazys Povilaitis, currently residing here in Chicago (he lived then in Vilkaviškis) could provide a lot of useful information.

Rev. J.K.

From GRRCL archives: original, typed; addendum written by hand

לאות
הוקרה על הצלת יהודים בתקופת השואה תוך הסתכנות והקרבה:
בהתאם לחוק זכרון השואה והגבורה - יד ושם (תיקון) התשמ"ה - 1985

מוענקת בזה **אזרחות כבוד** של מדינת ישראל

ל **יוזאס ו-ברוניה סטראופיס**

כביטוי לרגשי כבוד ותודה שרוחש עם ישראל לחסידי אומות העולם
אצילי הנפש אשר במעלם האירו את השבת תקופת הנאציזם באירופה.

In recognition of the rescue of Jews during the Holocaust, fully
aware of the dangers and severe risks to

And in accordance with the resolution of the Knesset
of March Twenty Fifth, Nineteen Hundred and Eighty Five

Honorary Citizenship
of the State of Israel is hereby awarded

To Juozas & Bronie Straupis

This recognition is an expression of the esteem and thanks harboured by the
People of Israel for those Righteous Among the Nations who, through their
noble deeds, rekindled the light of humanity during the darkness of the Nazi
era in Europe.

Jerusalem, Israel
November 5, 1991

ניתן היום בירושלים, ישראל
כז חשון התשנ"ב

Dr. Yitzhak Arad
הנהלת יד ושם
Yad Vashem Directorate

הועדה לציון חסידי אומות העולם
The Commission for the Righteous

RESCUED PEOPLE WRITING ABOUT THOSE WHO SAVED THEM

22. Article by Liucė Pomerancienė "I Marvel at her Noble Heart"

Canada: 23 September 1976

> Editor's note: After much effort, Liucė Pomerancienė and Danielius Pomerancas managed to leave occupied Lithuania. Both Jewish, they went through the horrible nightmare of the German occupation, and, thanks to some Lithuanians, their entire family survived. Their daughter, Danutė Pomerancaitė-Mazurkevičienė, is a well-known violinist. Danielius Pomerancas used to be a famous violinist, and his wife, Liucė Pomerancienė, was a teacher of German. We publish here her account of their sufferings during the German occupation of Lithuania.

I marvel at her noble heart: How Elena Petrauskienė saved a violinist born in the Kaunas ghetto

On 22 June 1941 the radio announced that war had broken out. When the German army came, all the Jews of Kaunas were herded into the ghetto in Vilijampolė. Every morning we were taken from the ghetto to work, and in the evening we were brought back to the ghetto. My daughter Danutė was born in the ghetto. We were young, hungry and constantly persecuted. I gave birth in a cellar, without any medical help. Soon the first "action" started: all the inmates of the ghetto were gathered together, lined up, and old, ailing and feeble people who were incapable of working were singled out. I could hardly stand (I was so weak after the birth) and had a baby in my arms. The Germans lined the people up, making some go to the right, and others to the left. Old and ailing people were sent to the right, whereas people capable of working were sent to the left. Those who found themselves on the right were taken to the Ninth Fort to die, and those on the left were sent to work. My husband and I were sent to the left. Perhaps in their hurry the sorters made a mistake, I do not know. I nearly suffocated my baby out of happiness.

One day the news went round the Vilijampolė ghetto that all Jewish children and old people had been taken away from Vilnius and other towns. Danutė was a year and eight months at the time. We had to think about her future: what should we do if the Germans started taking children and old people out of our ghetto? My sister was married to a Dr Karlinskas. She was a friend of Elena Žalinkevičaitė-Petrauskienė, the singer Kipras Petrauskas' wife. When we were taken to the town to work I telephoned her. We agreed to meet. I told her about my problem, and said that I had a baby daughter who I wanted to save because the Germans had started taking children from the ghettos in other towns. Elena Petrauskienė kindly agreed to help and promised to think about procuring documents.

We worked in the Lapė fur workshop. One day the director of the factory, Juozas Simonavičius, became very agitated and announced that the Germans were taking all the children and old people away from the ghetto. I was shocked by the news. I was convinced I would not find my daughter when I returned home ... We women working in the Lapė factory cried, we could not hold back our tears. After work, we were all taken back to the ghetto. I went along dragging my feet, because I was sure that I would not find my girl. I could not believe my eyes when, on entering our house, I saw my husband hiding her under a pillow. He motioned to me to keep silent, and said that the Germans were still looking for children. What could I do? I saw a kitchen knife on the table and I thought that if the Germans came, I would seize the knife and kill my family: it would be better to perish immediately than to fall into the hands of the butchers ...

My husband, having stayed at home, had managed to save our daughter. On learning that the Germans had arrived in the ghetto, he hid in a cellar with our daughter and some other children. When the children there started to cry, he went to another place.

Through the window we could see the Germans going into a neighbouring house and taking away the children. We waited scared stiff, for our turn ... What a surprise, the Germans did not come to our house! Thus our Danutė stayed with us.

Unfortunately, our troubles did not end there: we had to find a way to get Danutė out of the ghetto. I decided to give her sleeping pills, so that we could carry her out, that is, so that she would not cry on the way. I did; however, Danutė would not fall asleep. The following day I gave her sleeping pills again. This time it worked, she fell asleep. I put her into a potato sack and handed it to the director of the Lapė workshop, Simonavičius, over the wall, as had been agreed. Danutė started to cry, as if understanding that we were separating. Fortunately, she soon became quiet again, and nobody noticed.

Shortly after that, Danutė found herself at Elena Petrauskienė's house. Our message to her was: "If we parents do not survive, let Danutė stay with you."

Danutė's new guardian sent her with her own children to their farm. My husband and I did not see Danutė for many years. Our hearts were full of pain and longing ...

One summer's day I went to work as usual. My husband was not allowed to go, he had to stay in the ghetto. We heard terrible news at the workshop – the ghetto was on fire. Our brigade leader, Spiegelglazovas, confirmed the news and advised us to hide wherever we could, since the Germans were picking up Jews in the ghetto and taking them away. They came to the factory too. Whoever could, hid. I hid in a corner behind some boards. The Germans went everywhere, but they did not find me. When everything had calmed down, I crawled out and went home. I was so afraid and confused that I could not even remember where the house of Kipras Petrauskas was. I asked a Lithuanian woman on the street the address. She took me to the house where Petrauskas lived. On my way I thought the Germans would catch me and take me to Dachau concentration camp ...

I found Elena Petrauskienė, who was about to leave for her farm, to take the children, and go with them to Palanga. She left, and I stayed in her house. My heart was full of fear: if someone were to call, find me and report me ... I cried, and could not calm down. I was so miserable without my husband and our daughter.

My husband was taken to Dachau with other Jews from the ghetto. He stayed there till the end of the war.

Half a year after the war, Kipras Petrauskas returned from his farm; however, neither Elena Petrauskienė nor the children came with him. It turned out that at the end of the war she had stayed with the children in Palanga and, to avoid being caught up in the fighting, she went to Germany. We heard nothing about her for four years. We did not know whether she was alive or dead.

During that time, my husband returned from Dachau. He was half-alive, exhausted, tortured and starved. He weighed only 30 kilograms.

One day, quite unexpectedly, I received a letter and a photograph of the children from Elena Petrauskienė. My Danutė was among them (marked). I was overjoyed, and thought that perhaps the time would come when we would all see one another again. The news that they were alive set my mind at rest. I felt a heavy weight being lifted from my heart.

I started corresponding with Elena Petrauskienė. One day I received a letter from the American zone in Germany in which an organisation asked me to agree to take Danutė back. I answered that I wanted to take the child back from the hands of the people to whom I had entrusted her.

Suddenly I received a telegram informing me that Elena Petrauskienė and the children were returning to Lithuania. That was a day of special joy for me: the child who had been sentenced to death was born for a second time!

When I reached the Petrauskas' house in Kaunas I stopped at the door and could not move. I could hardly bring myself to ring the doorbell. A small girl opened the door, and ran up to me, but she did not know that I was her mother. Thus, the first meeting was both joyful and sad, because an invisible wall had been put up between Danutė and me. More time was needed for Danutė to understand that we were her parents, because she was only six and a half years old. She could not understand what suffering we had gone through.

When Danutė was seven we moved to Vilnius. The Petrauskas family went to live in Vilnius too, since the Opera House moved there. Danutė lived both with us and with the Petrauskas.

Since she showed exceptional musical talent she went to study at Vilnius Conservatoire, and later in Moscow to study in the class of the famous Professor David Oistrakh. Having graduated from the

Conservatoire and post-graduate studies, she married the violinist Yuri Mazurkevičius. They were both professors at Kiev Conservatoire and soloists with the Vilnius Philharmonic Society.

Finally, in 1975, our family found ourselves in the free world, and we settled in Canada. We revelled in the freedom we had craved so much and could never have.

Though I live far from Elena Petrauskienė, I feel that she is dearer to me than anyone else in the world. I cannot help wondering at her noble heart, civilised ways and kindness, which she showed Danutė, despite the great danger which threatened her. Today we are both happy mothers.

Tėviškės žiburiai (Canada): 23 September 1976, No. 39 (1390)

23. Article by Dr Olga Horwitz "A Lithuanian who Rescued Jews" on the occasion of the funeral of Professor Antanas Starkus*

Chicago: August 1975

Editor's note: When the former Stutthof prisoner Dr Antanas Starkus died last year, Dr Olga Horwitz (Gurvičiūtė), a Jewish dentist currently working in Chicago, made a speech at his grave. The Nazis had put her in the ghetto, from which she managed to escape with the help of a decent guard (a German). The speech of Dr Olga Horwitz, which was published in the journal *Medicina*, is printed here.

A Lithuanian who rescued Jews

I have also come to bid my farewell and say my last "thank you" to Dr Antanas Starkus. His body has died, but his spirit will live eternally in the hearts of his family, his friends and those who were close to him.

---

* ANTANAS STARKUS (1901–1975) taught at Vilnius and Vytautas Magnus universities. During the war he helped to hide Jews. In 1943 he was sent to Stutthof; in 1948 he emigrated to the USA.

As long as my heart beats I shall never forget the determination of Dr Starkus and his family in rescuing me. I lived with the Starkus family during the war for one and a half years. It was a long and horrible existence, teetering between life and death, not only for me but also for Professor Starkus and his family, including his little son and daughter.

I remember as if it had happened only yesterday when one Sunday, returning from church, the children ran up to me and said: "Quick, hide, guests are coming!" The children sensed the danger, but they never questioned it; they kept silent, took care of me and shared their last piece of bread with me. The children were brought up in the spirit of their parents.

Many of us who have come here to bid Dr Starkus farewell knew him as a volunteer, an active member of Catholic societies, and a physician. I knew Dr Antanas Starkus as a true person. I can confirm Father Yla's* words, who said that without Dr Starkus' kindness and attention he would not have survived Stutthof. The same is true for me.

Many of those who have spoken mentioned the Kingdom of God. If there is one, Dr Starkus is sure to be among its residents. He tried to set up the Kingdom of God here, on Earth, by his deeds, his sacrifice. He was generous and noble. He was honest and a man of worldly wisdom. He sold his soul neither to Stalin nor to Hitler. Instead of hatred, revenge and greed, he gave love, understanding and self-sacrifice to subjugated people. Even at moments when I almost despaired and did not expect to live to see another day, he managed to kindle hope in me again and show that not all of mankind had turned into beasts. He was a pure and bright drop in an ocean of blood.

Thank you Doctor! Let your noble spirit set an example to your countrymen, mankind and the next generation.

Naujienos (Canada): August 1975

---

* Fr Stasys Yla was sent to Stutthof in 1943. His book *Žmonės ir žvėrys* (Men and Beasts) came out in English in 1971 as *A Priest in Stutthof.*

Ką Tamsta žinai apie žydu globą Lietuvoje naciu okupacijos laikais?

1. Pavardė, vardas ir gyv. vieta Lietuvoje asmens, kuris Tamstos žiniomis yra globojęs žydų tautybės asmenis.

Marija Lakevičienė ir jos duktė Jadvyga Lakevičiutė - Jablonuskienė Trakų g-vė 10, Kaunas

2. Jei žinoma, tiksliai nurodyti globotųjų žydų tautybės asmenų pavardes ir jų gyv. vietas prieš naciams okupuojant Lietuvą.

Dalia - Salomė Vilenčikaitė, senvis Vilenčiullu Jokūbo duktė 3 metų gyv. Kaunas, Venario 16 g-vė

3. Iš kurio getho, kalėjimo ar kurios kitos vietovės minėtasis žydų tautybės asmuo buvo globojamas)

paimta augmti, nuogta iš Kauno getho.

4. Kokia parama buvo teikiama minėtam globotajam (buvo slepiamas, parūpinti fiktyvūs dokumentai, globojami nepilnamečiai vaikai, teikiamas maistas, slėptos ir saugotos žydų kultūrinės vertybės.

auginta, kaip įsūnytas vaikas, nurlepus tilvg ją tautų cų ir parūpinus fiktyrus metrilag.

5. Kurie asmens ir kokiu būdu yra nukentėję nuo nacių už globą bei paramą žydų tautybės asmenims Lietuvoje. (Buvo sušaudyti, areštuoti, kalinti ir pan.) Nurodyti nukentėjusių asmenų pavardes bei jų gyv. vietoves Lietuvoje

6. Ar Tamstai nėra žinoma daugiau panašių atsitikimų, o jei žinoma, prašome nurodyti globojusių ar globotųjų asmenų pavardes ir gyv. vietas Lietuvoje, o taip pat ir dabartiniu metu Vokietijoje.

7. Gal dar kas nors žinoma, kas nepaminėta šioje anketoje? Jei žinoma, prašome visa tai nurodyti.

Lrukiešak, 1947 XII.

vieta ir data

Pastaba: Ši anketa privalo būti kiek galima tiksliau ir skubiau užpildyta. Parašu anketa netvirtinama. Reikalui esant, vi-as šiuo klausimu informacijas teikia Liet. Antinacinės Rezis. buv. Politinių Kalinių S-gos Centro Valdyba.

The questionnaire circulated in displaced persons camps in Germany in 1947 and 1948

24. Article by Šeina Gertnerienė
"A Letter to American Lithuanians"

Canada: January 1977

Editor's note: This article was written at the beginning of 1977, to be published in *Tėviškės Žiburiai*. However, due to an incorrectly written address, it reached the magazine only on 6 April 1977. Its author lives in Tel Aviv and keeps in touch with several Lithuanians currently living in Lithuania.

A letter to American Lithuanians

I am of Jewish nationality, a citizen of Israel, and a teacher by profession. I arrived here from Lithuania five years ago. My husband, also a teacher, and two sons, both engineers, arrived together with me. When I lived in Lithuania, I was a teacher at one of the largest Lithuanian secondary schools in Kaunas (No. 4).

The article about Jewish and Lithuanian hatred "What is such a Farewell Worth?", published in *Tėviškės Žiburiai* in Canada on 22 July 1976, encouraged me to write and share my thoughts with the author and other Lithuanians who are interested in the fate of their nation.

I ask everyone in advance to understand me correctly: I am asking them to understand my goodwill and intentions, though among the pleasant experiences, I am going to mention some sad facts, which disconcert us, people of Jewish nationality, and you, Lithuanians. My hope is that presenting many different facts will direct the young people of today (no matter what nationality they are) to a better and more positive choice in their philosophy of life.

A chance occurrence on New Year's Eve prompted me to write now. At one o'clock in the morning I was woken up by the sounds of the Lithuanian song "Ilgiausių metų"* coming from a neighbouring house in which a Jewish family lived that had come from Lithuania. On other occasions too Lithuanian songs can be heard coming from flats in which live Jews of Lithuanian origin.

Here is another fact. Last year a congress of Lithuanian Jewish Youth took place in the hall of Lithuanian Jews in Tel Aviv. Many

---

* "Wishing you a long life."

young people gave speeches in Lithuanian. When asked if they knew Hebrew, they answered that they did; however, they liked to recover the past.

So where is that hatred that the article writes about? Don't such facts prove the opposite?!

It is true that the author of the article criticises the speech given by Oleiskis, the chairman of the Organisation of Lithuanian Jews in Israel. My aim is not to speak in favour of or to blame somebody; however, having lived about 50 years in Lithuania, I cannot remain indifferent and let the idea that all Lithuanians hate Jews, and vice versa, prevail. This is not the case. Oleiskis said in his speech: "Jewish Lithuania is a concept with a wide range of meanings including spiritual and cultural life. The soul of the Lithuanian Jew soared in a purely Jewish world" (*Gachelet*, page 1, April 1976, Tel Aviv). Speaking about fascist murderers, perhaps he should have mentioned their number or the percentage of them. Then the reader would have treated the matter differently. Similarly, the author of the article published in *Tėviškės Žiburiai* exaggerates the atrocities that young Jewish people committed against Lithuanians when the Russians came to Lithuania. One cannot draw conclusions about a whole nation on the basis of a small number of young people intoxicated by an idea.

Generally and objectively speaking, when looking at relations between the Lithuanians and the Jews, it would not be a mistake to say that those of us who left for Israel maintain friendly relations with Lithuanians. We exchange letters with our Lithuanian friends, neighbours, and people who were kind to us, etc. I enclose here a copy of some letters that we receive even now, five years after we left. We exchange ideas, gifts, and so on. Clearly our parting was not as simple and as easy as the writer in *Tėviškės Žiburiai* thinks. I do not want to speak on behalf of other people and say what they felt at parting. In my letter I will say how I bade farewell to Lithuania and its people. Believe me, it was especially painful for me to part with my past. It was a feeling of love for my historic motherland, Israel, and a deep desire to live and work in my historic motherland, my strong wish to become equal with other nations who have a motherland, that made me leave. When we left Lithuania we took with us a lot of values, for which I am especially grateful to my sons' and my own teachers and lecturers. I cherish most pleasant memories about the teachers and staff with whom I worked at one school for 20 years. The teachers were really wonderful. There were talented teachers, writers, readers, workers, dancers and artists among them. How can anyone forget such things?

Some people ask me if they let me feel that I was a Jew. No, never. In the post-war years, when I started to work in school, perhaps I myself was too sensitive when looking at Lithuanians; however, with time I saw that all my colleagues were sincere, they did not begrudge me a kind word, me, a teacher of Jewish nationality. We were friends both at work and after work. When thinking about my past, I often remember those pleasant and educated people with whom I mixed.

Besides, I feel deep a gratitude to a large group of Lithuanian country people who helped me during the German occupation. It is thanks to them that I am alive today. I often remember those industrious people who could work from morning till night. They could do any kind of work, from labouring and joinery, to sewing, knitting and embroidery. On Saturday evenings they would sing and dance. It is difficult to list all these wonderful things that have been committed to my memory and enriched my experience. I shall always be grateful to them.

***

Now I will go on to more painful and sadder reminiscences. I must admit that I cannot forget those awful years of the German occupation. I find it difficult to forgive the murderers of innocent children. I do not desire revenge, not at all. Revenge depends on the character of an individual person, no matter what his nationality. There are people who say: "Forgive them, Father! They know not what they do." There are people who want to teach those bad people a lesson in order to prevent others from repeating their evil. Unfortunately, we do not know such facts. In this respect, I would like to agree with the author B.R. in *Tėviškės Žiburiai* who says that "the wounds which were inflicted on the crossroads of fate should perhaps be cured and understood". I agree with others who find it difficult that the crimes of the murderers should be forgotten. To conceal everything bad means to contribute to the law of the jungle all over the world – kill and live! If we parents, of whatever nationality, are concerned about the future of our children, we have to oppose what is evil, mean and ugly to our children, with good. We have to show that revenge is evil. By learning the facts and their results, young people will be able to choose a more humane way of living. By seeing what the enthusiasm of murderers resulted in, young people will make more correct choices. It goes without saying that only then will they desire to behave in such a way as not to disgrace their people or bring unbearable suffering on them.

I would like to give some facts here. I am a living coffin now. I was in Lithuania during the German occupation, and I witnessed many events. I saw what went on before the Second World War, during the war and in the post-war years. The governing bodies changed several times in Lithuania. Some people rose, others fell, and vice versa. The results were always the same: in the end brother killed and abused brother.

1. In 1938 I was a student at Klaipėda Teacher Training College. When the Nazis came to Klaipėda, I saw them with my own eyes come to the college and throw away training equipment like expensive microscopes. As they did it they yelled: "Klumpen und Juden heraus!"* Both Lithuanians and Jews experienced the same tragedy.

2. When the Russians came to Lithuania in 1940, some young people, zealous communists, got to work. Communists of Jewish nationality joined them, and together they abused and harmed their own people. Many Lithuanians and Jews were deported to Siberia. This was the second time that both Jews and Lithuanians shared the same fate.

3. In 1941 the Germans came to Lithuania. Former fighters for communism fled to Russia. Another wave of young people rose and encouraged young people to help the Nazis. They said that they were going to save their motherland. These contributed greatly to the slaughter of innocent people of Jewish nationality.

It is important to mention the fact that I witnessed it myself. Buses full of Ukrainians and Latvians arrived in Lithuania to assist

---

* "Away, miserable creatures and Jews!"

in killing Jews in small Lithuanian towns. Intoxicated with Nazi ideas, they killed innocent old people and babies. However, their enthusiasm died down quite quickly.

4. In 1943 and 1944, in Kupiškis, I saw with my own eyes how these young fascists ran to hide from Germans who were catching Lithuanians and taking them to German concentration camps. If anybody resisted, blood was shed again. My fate and that of many other Jews hiding in villages was the same as the fate of those Lithuanian fascists. The Germans were our mutual enemies; however, the bloodshed was not over yet.

5. With the war drawing to a close, the Russians returned to Lithuania again. The young Lithuanians and the Jews who had fled to Russia also returned. Revenge was sought. The blood of a Lithuanian was shed by his Lithuanian brother. Untold harm was done in restructuring the countryside. Parents cried after losing their sons; the whole Lithuanian earth quivered, permeated with the blood of its own people. This is the saddest page in our history, the saddest for Jews and Lithuanians alike.

I would like to mention here that people of Jewish nationality suffered again in 1946 and 1947. They were committed communists, and died at the hands of other communists. The writers Kvitko, Fefer and others were killed in prison in this way. And all for what?

This slaughter was obscured by the veil of a crazy idea.

Aren't similar atrocities, similar massacres, being committed nowadays? Brother still kills brother. Aren't the events in Ireland and the Lebanon clear evidence that the world is heading for an abyss?

We live in a time when people can fly to the Moon, and when modern nuclear weapons can destroy mankind. Has not the time come yet for the younger generation to say "enough": enough of pitting man against man, nation against nation? An end must be sought to revenge; enough of the law of the jungle! The time has come for young people to find an idea to help man tie the hands of the murderer, an idea which would teach man to love other men and to extend his hand to the weak. Unfortunately, neither communism nor Christianity managed to do this during the Second World War. So let us, parents, whatever our nationality, look for an idea for the future of our young people, to help create a world in which our children can feel safe and secure, and not tremble at the sight of a beast in the shape of man.

Only then will we be able to hope that the time that the ancient Jewish prophet Joshua spoke about is coming: "The time will come when man will love man, a wolf and a lamb will live together and a small child will shepherd them".

January 1977   Šeina Gertnerienė

Editor's note: The author of this article, wishing to show her good relations with the Lithuanians, enclosed copies of extracts from letters received from Lithuania, and one card, a New Year's greeting. The greeting was sent by the daughter of the Lithuanian parents who had looked after Šeina Gertnerienė's family. She writes: "My dearest, a Happy New Year to all of you. Let success accompany everything you do and let the fire of your hearth and home burn brightly. Let your everyday toil bring good to the people. Teresė, Panevėžys. 15 December 1976."

Tėviškės žiburiai (Canada): April 1977

25. Letter from Tamara Lazersonaitė to Petras Effertas

Haifa, Israel: 20 February 1975

Haifa
20 February 1975

My Dear Mr Effertas,
    Many years have passed since I last wrote to you. It is rather difficult for me to get down to writing; however, I think about you very often, wondering how you are and whether you are in good health. Vera wrote to me several very nice letters, and I still have them.
    In about half a year my diary will be published in Israel, the story of the Pakamačiai estate, *Under the Burning Sky*, a part of which I sent to you before and which will be included in it. So the world will learn about the noble Lithuanian landowners from Pakamačiai …
    I also gave the photograph that you sent me to the publishers (on the St Lawrence River), but it was too amateur. Could you send me a better one, it would make things easier for the publishers. The first issue of the book in Israel will be published in Hebrew. The

publisher has asked me to give permission to publish it in English. However, I suppose it would be better to publish the book in English in America. I think American Lithuanians could help me, because the material was written in the Lithuanian language. I shall be able to apply to Jewish organisations only after it has been published in Hebrew.

Some words about my life. I live in Haifa. It is a very nice city on the coast. I work in one of the oldest cities in Israel, Akko, in a school laboratory. I am responsible for all practical work in the natural sciences. My husband works in a laboratory at a factory. Our eldest daughter is studying pharmacy at Jerusalem University. She married some months ago. Our younger daughter is taking her final school examinations in summer, and in autumn she will go to serve in the army for two years.

I am enclosing a letter of gratitude to you, which has been written by some of our famous writers (perhaps you have read something by Meras?).

In the meantime, I have nothing to send you in return for your noble deed during the war.

If ever you make up your mind to visit our sacred land, which has been so amply sprinkled with blood, you will always be most welcome.

With gratitude and love
Yours,   Tamara

From GRRCL archives: original, handwritten

26. Letter written in gratitude to Petras Effertas for saving Tamara Lazersonaitė

Israel: February 1975

Dear Mr Effertas,
Thirty years have passed since the Nazi occupation was brought to an end in Lithuania, during which you displayed a profound humanity and heroism in saving Tamara Lazersonaitė.

We Jews, now citizens of Israel, who experienced the barbaric years of the German occupation in Lithuania, value tremendously

Gerb. p _Efertai_

Praėjo 30 metų nuo to laiko, kai Lietuvoje buvo likviduota nacistinė okupacija, kurios metu Jūs parodėte gilų humaniškumą ir didvyriškumą, gelbėjant _Tamara Lazersonaitė_

Mes, žydai, dabartiniai Izraelio piliečiai, pergyvenę klaikius okupacijos metus Lietuvoje, aukštai vertiname Jūsų pasiaukojimą, kai teikėte pagalbą persekiojamam žydui, statydami mirtinam pavojui ne tik savo, bet ir savo artimųjų gyvybę.

Žydų tautos istorija ilga, besitęsianti tūkstančius metų. Bet mes visuomet minime ir nešiojame savo širdyse vardus tų, kurie sunkiausiais laikais parodė esą tikri žmonės, – neišblėsta jų istorinis atminimas, pagal mūsų tautinę tradiciją jie vadinami "Pasaulio Teisuoliais, ant kurių laikosi pasaulis".

Ir Jūsų vardas nebus užmirštas.

Su gilia pagarba,

Išgelbėtųjų Lietuvos žydų vardu:

Dr.
Gyd. F. Gurvičienė

M. Jelinas
Rašytojas

J. Meras
Rašytojas

1975-II

A fascimile of an acknowledgement

your self-sacrifice in providing help to a persecuted Jew, by putting your life and the lives of your family at risk.

The history of the Jewish nation is long, lasting thousands of years. However, we always remember and keep in our hearts the names of those people who retained and displayed noble human traits during difficult times – history will always remember them. According to our national tradition, they will be honoured with the title of Righteous Gentile, on whom the world rests.

Your name shall not be forgotten.

Sincerely yours,
On behalf of rescued Lithuanian Jews:

[Signed:] Dr. F. Gurvičienė, M. Jelinas, writer, J. Meras writer,
February 1975

From GRRCL archives: original, typed

27. Letter written in gratitude to Aldutė Audėjutė-Krutulis for saving Ben Epraim

Israel: February 1975

Dear Aldutė Audėjutė-Krutulis,

Thirty years have passed since the Nazi occupation was brought to an end in Lithuania, during which you displayed a profound humanity and heroism in saving Rachilė and Abelis Foimčik, currently Ben Epraim.

We Jews, now citizens of Israel, who experienced the barbaric years of the German occupation in Lithuania, value tremendously your self-sacrifice in providing help to a persecuted Jew, by putting your life and the lives of your family at risk.

The history of the Jewish nation is long, lasting thousands of years. However, we always remember and keep in our hearts the names of those people who retained and displayed noble human traits during difficult times – history will always remember them. According to our national tradition, they will be honoured with the title of Righteous Gentile, on whom the world rests.

Your name shall not be forgotten.

Sincerely yours,
On behalf of rescued Lithuanian Jews:

[Signed:] Dr. F. Gurvičienė, M. Jelinas, writer, J. Meras,
writer, 1975

From GRRCL archives: original, typed

28. Testimony by Chaim and P. Finkelstein about those who saved their children and other Jews

New York: 15 June 1950

To Whom it May Concern,

We hereby testify that Vincas Tercijonas, a doctor of medicine who worked as a paediatrician in Kaunas (Lithuania), and his wife, in cooperating with the Lithuanian underground from 1942 to 1944, rescued the lives of our children: our son Simon (seven years old) and our daughter Helen (16 years old) when we were in the Kaunas ghetto and later in Stutthof concentration camp. Our children were kept on a farm, where they lived till the end of the war.

The Tercijonas also helped to save other Jews who were persecuted by the Nazis and put in the Kaunas ghetto. One of them was Sara Oleiskienė, a physician, who escaped and was hidden (under a false name) in an orphanage in Vilnius, where she worked till the end of the war.

Tercijonas lived in Lithuania until August 1944. Then he and his family fled the second Russian occupation and escaped to Germany. Twelve of his close relatives were deported to Siberia in June 1941.

We declare that we are honoured to be able to express our gratitude and respect to Tercijonas and his wife for their noble deeds.

15 June 1950   [Signed:] Chaim Finkelstein, Dr. P. Finkelstein

From GRRCL archives: original, typed

29. Letter from Ruvenas Levitanas to Bronius Gotautas

Boston, USA: 3 December 1963

Boston
3 December 1963

Dear Mr Gotautas,

My father wrote to me that you, most Honoured Father, are alive and well and living in Germany.

I was very happy to hear about you. We thank our Lord for saving you.

If I can be of any help to you, I would be glad. I want to know that you are in good health and happy. We live near Boston. I have a wife and three sons.

If it is not too much trouble, write some words to me, please.

Best wishes,

Ruvenas Levitanas (formerly Juozas Gintautas)

From GRRCL archives: original, typed

30. Testimony by Samuel Atlas about Matas Janušauskas, who rescued Jews during the war

Cincinnati, USA: 29 June 1949

Cincinnati
29 June 1949

United Hebrew College
Institute of Jewish Religion

To Whom it May Concern,

I wish hereby to testify to the character and personality of Matas Janušauskas from Kaunas in Lithuania, who arrived with his family in Australia recently from Germany. Mr Janušauskas is of very good character, an exceptionally noble personality. He and his family were noted for their self-sacrifice and help during the German occupation in Lithuania, to Jews who were persecuted by the Nazis. He helped a lot of Jews who were in trouble by putting his and his family's lives at risk. Such personalities are rarely found among people of other than Jewish nationality.

Out of the many especially humane deeds of his, I shall only mention some that relate to my family. He took into his home the child of my nephew, Zalman Grinberg, thus saving him from certain death. Now Dr Grinberg lives in Israel and occupies a leading position: he is director of Beilinson Hospital, not far from Tel Aviv. Mr Janušauskas also helped my brother, Jacob Atlas, and his family who currently live in Montreal, Canada. Mr Janušauskas was director of a Kaunas factory. He employed a great many Jews from the Kaunas ghetto in the factory and did a lot of good for them. The Jewish nation is deeply and everlastingly grateful to him for his great and noble deeds during that tragic period.

Now that he and his family have arrived in Australia, a foreign country where nobody knows him, I, in my turn, can testify to his impeccable reputation. I hope that the Australian Jewish community will help him in every possible way. Without doubt, he deserves the complete trust and attention both of the Jewish community as a whole and of each of its members separately.

I sincerely hope that this testimony contributes at least modestly to repaying the enormous debt that all Jews and I feel towards people such as Mr Janušauskas.

Sincerely yours,   Dr Samuel Atlas,
                              Professor of Philosophy and Talmud

From GRRCL archives: original, typed

ŽŪVANČIŲJŲ GELBĖJIMO KRYŽIUS

LIETUVOS RESPUBLIKOS
PREZIDENTO
DEKRETU

Galina Petrašiūnienė

UŽ YPATINGĄ PASIŽYMĖJIMĄ
GELBĖJANT ŽŪVANTĮ ŽMOGŲ
APDOVANOTA ŽŪVANČIŲJŲ GELBĖJIMO KRYŽIUMI

ORDINŲ KANCLERIS

p. Mikkauskas

VILNIUS,
1994 m. *liepos* mėn 14 d.
DEKRETAS Nr. 357

THEY CONSIDERED IT THEIR DUTY

In 1953, by a special act of the Knesset, Yad Vashem, the Holocaust Martyrs' and Heroes' Remembrance Authority, was established in Israel. The institute pursues three goals: perpetuation, research and education. It is a monument to the nation's sorrow. It reviews documents submitted by Holocaust survivors, and grants rescuers the title of Righteous Gentile. Rescuers are awarded a medal and a certificate, and a tree is planted in their honour on the Boulevard of Remembrance. The title has been conferred on 497 people from Lithuania.

On 23 September 1992, the Lithuanian president awarded for the first time a group of rescuers with the Cross for Saving People under Threat of Death. This medal has been presented to 455 people, from Lithuania, the USA and Canada.

The Rescuers' Section at the Vilna Gaon Jewish State Museum has compiled a list of the names of more than 3,000 people who rescued Jews in Lithuania. This list holds the names of rescuers, where they lived at the time, their occupation, their family details, and the names and number of Jews they rescued. If a Jewish family or individual did not survive, their fate and that of those who tried to rescue them is also described.

Various factors motivated people to rescue someone. Farmers who were devout Catholics could not simply stand by and watch the massacre of their neighbours. They considered rescuing someone they knew to be their duty. Educated people would hide Jews with whom they had gone to school or studied or worked.

When a human's heart is full of kindness, there is enough bread for everyone.

Viktorija Sakaitė

Righteous Gentiles*

SURNAME, FIRST NAME	YEAR OF AWARD
1. ADOLF KRISTINA	1996
2. ADOMYNAS ANTANAS	1998
3. ADOMYNIENĖ ONA	1998
4. ADOMYNAITĖ NATALIJA	1998
5. ALEKSANDRAVIČIENĖ PAULINA	1980
6. ANDRAITIS ANTANAS	1994
7. ANTANAITIS VINCAS	1979
8. ANTANAITIS JONAS	1979
9. ANTANAITYTĖ STASĖ	1979
10. ANUŽIS ČESLOVAS	2000
11. ANUŽIENĖ ELENA	2000
12. ANUŽIS IGNAS	2000
13. ANUŽIENĖ ELENA	2000
14. AUDIEJUS JUOZAS	1970
15. AUDIEJIENĖ ONA	1970
16. AUGUSTINOVIČ ONA	1998
17. AUGUSTINOVIČ JUOZAS	1998
18. BABARSKIS ALFONSAS	2000
19. BABARSKIENĖ JADVYGA	2000
20. BAGDONAVIČIUS PRANAS	1992
21. BAJORINAS PRANAS	1982
22. BALČIKONIS ANTANAS	1994
23. BALČIKONIENĖ AGOTA	1994
24. BALČINAS JONAS	1995
25. BALČINIENĖ BARBORA	1995
26. BALČINAITĖ STEFANIJA	1995
27. BALČINAITĖ PETRONĖLĖ	1995
28. BALKIENĖ NINA	1994
29. BALTUTIS VYTAS	1980
30. BARTKEVIČIUS JUOZAS	1980
31. BARTKEVIČIENĖ STASĖ	1980
32. BAUBLYS PETRAS	1977
33. BAUBLYS SERGEJUS	1977
34. BAUBLIENĖ JADVYGA	1977
35. BEINARAVIČIENĖ URŠULĖ	1992
36. BEINARAVIČIUS VLADAS	1992
37. BELECKIENĖ MORTA	2000
38. BERČIŪNAS JURGIS	1996
39. BERČIŪNAITĖ BIRUTĖ	1996
40. BERNIKIENĖ PETRĖ	1996
41. BIELSKYTĖ- AKUCKIENĖ ONA	1998
42. BYLA VINCAS	1996
43. BILECKIENĖ PETRĖ	1982
44. BINKIENĖ SOFIJA	1967
45. BINKIS KAZYS	1988
46. BINKIS GERDAS	1988
47. BINKYTĖ ELEONORA	1988
48. BOGUSLAUSKAS ANTANAS	1992
49. BRAŽĖNIENĖ KONSTANCIJA	1970
50. BRUŽAS STANISLOVAS	2000
51. BRUŽIENĖ VALERIJA	2000
52. BUIVYDAITĖ- KUTORGIENĖ ELENA	1982
53. BUKONTAS JERONIMAS	1995
54. BUKONTIENĖ MARIJA	1995
55. BUTKIENĖ PETRONĖ	1981
56. BUTKEVIČIENĖ MARIJA	1998
57. BUTKEVIČIŪTĖ ONA	1998
58. BUTKEVIČIUS JONAS	1998
59. BUTKEVIČIENĖ TEKLĖ	1998
60. BUTKEVIČIUS KAROLIS	1998
61. BUTKEVIČIENĖ JUOZAPOTA	1998
62. ČERNIAUSKAS BRONISLAVAS	1993
63. ČERNIAUSKIENĖ ONA	1993
64. ČERNIAUSKAITĖ GENOVAITĖ	1993
65. ČESNAVIČIUS ANTANAS	1995
66. ČESNAVIČIENĖ MARIJA	1995
67. CHLOPINAITĖ ELENA	1974
68. ČIURLIONIENĖ SOFIJA	1991
69. ČIŽINAUSKAS JONAS	1992
70. ČIŽINAUSKIENĖ ONA	1992
71. ČIŽINAUSKAITĖ BIRUTĖ	1992
72. DAILIDAVIČIUS VINCAS	1996
73. DAILIDAVIČIENĖ URŠULĖ	1996
74. DAUGUVIETIENĖ OLGA	1985
75. DAUGUVIETYTĖ NELĖ	1985
76. DRUPAS VLADAS	1981
77. DUBROVSKI ANASTASIJA	1985
78. DUŽINSKAITĖ ELŽBIETA	1997

---

* Figures (as of 1 March 2002) provided by Viktorija Sakaitė.

79.	EIGELYTĖ STEFANIJA	1997	128.	IVANAUSKAITĖ GIEDRUTĖ	1984
80.	ELIJOŠAITIS PRANAS	1994	129.	JABLONSKIENĖ JADVYGA	2000
81.	ELIJOŠAITIENĖ ONA	1994	130.	JAKIENĖ ONA	1992
82.	ELIJOŠAITIS BRONIUS	1994	131.	JAKAS LEOPOLDAS	1992
83.	ESERTAS ARTŪRAS	1995	132.	JAKAITĖ ALDONA	1992
84.	GADEIKIS PRANAS	1997	133.	JANKAUSKIENĖ-	
85.	GADEIKYTĖ JULIJA	1997		ŠIMKUTĖ ONA	1996
86.	GADLEVSKIS JUZEFAS	1983	134.	JANKUS AUGUSTINAS	1991
87.	GADLEVSKA HELENA	1983	135.	JANKIENĖ STASĖ	1991
88.	GAIGALIENĖ JUZEFA	2000	136.	JASELSKIS VLADAS	1977
89.	GAIGALAITĖ STEFANIJA	2000	137.	JASELSKIENĖ ELENA	1977
90.	GALVONAITĖ MARCELĖ	1996	138.	JASELSKYTĖ HELENA	1977
91.	GASIŪNAS JUOZAS	1997	139.	JASULAITIENĖ ELENA	2000
92.	GAVELIENĖ JADVYGA	2002	140.	JEMELJANOVA ANASTASIJA	2000
93.	GAVELIS STASYS	2002	141.	JOCIENĖ-BASIENĖ MARIJA	1998
94.	GECEVIČIENĖ BRONĖ	1991	142.	JOKUBAUSKIS STANISLOVAS	1999
95.	GECEVIČIUS ADOMAS	1991	143.	JONAITIS HENRIKA	1980
96.	GEDAIKA PETRAS	1998	144.	JONUŠIENĖ-	
97.	GEDAIKIENĖ LIUDVIKA	1998		PREMENECKAITĖ GENĖ	2000
98.	GEDEIKIS JUOZAS	1999	145.	JUCEVIČIUS STASYS	1980
99.	GEDEIKIENĖ BRONĖ	1999	146.	JUODGALVYTĖ-	
100.	GEDMANTIENĖ MICHALINA	1993		KISIELIENĖ MARIJA	1997
101.	GILYS LEONAS	1983	147.	JUREVIČIUS JONAS	1997
102.	GILIENĖ ALEKSANDRA	1983	148.	JUREVIČIENĖ JUZĖ	1997
103.	GINTALAS IGNAS	1998	149.	JUREVIČIŪTĖ LIONĖ	1997
104.	GINTALIENĖ KRISTINA	1998	150.	JUREVIČIENĖ ADELĖ	1979
105.	GINTALAS JUOZAS	1998	151.	JUREVIČIUS PETRAS	1979
106.	GOBIS ANTANAS	1979	152.	JURGILIENĖ BRONĖ	1998
107.	GOTAUTAS BRONIUS	1974	153.	JURKŠAITIS JUOZAS	1990
108.	GLAVECKIENĖ ANELĖ	1998	154.	JURKŠAITIENĖ MARIJONA	1990
109.	GRAŽEVIČIUS JONAS	1995	155.	JUŠKEVIČIUS MYKOLAS	1980
110.	GRAŽEVIČIENĖ		156.	JUŠKEVIČIENĖ ANASTASIJA	1980
	VANDA-MARIJA	1995	157.	KANCEVIČIUS PRANAS	2000
111.	GRAŽEVIČIŪTĖ VANDA	1995	158.	KANCEVIČIENĖ ZOSĖ	2000
112.	GRYBAUSKAS ANDRIUS	1996	159.	KANCEVIČIŪTĖ-	
113.	GRIGAITIS ZENONAS			JASULAITIENĖ ELENA	2000
	(son of Žiužnys)	1994	160.	KALINKIENĖ VERONIKA	2000
114.	GRIGALAITIS PRANAS	1991	161.	KAREIVA PRANAS	1997
115.	GRIGALAITIENĖ BRONĖ	1991	162.	KARPAVIČIUS POVILAS	1995
116.	GRIGONIS JUOZAS	1996	163.	KARPAVIČIENĖ ALEFTINA	1995
117.	GRIGONIENĖ FELICIJA	1996	164.	KASPERAITIS PRANAS	1991
118.	GUDAITIENĖ JUZĖ	1978	165.	KASPERAITIENĖ ZOSĖ	1991
119.	GULBINOVIČ ALEKSANDR	1983	166.	KAŠINSKAS PIJUS	1978
120.	GULBINOVIČ VERONIKA	1983	167.	KAŠINSKIENĖ MAGDA	1978
121.	HANFMAN DORA	1985	168.	KAUŠINIS KLEMENSAS	1996
122.	HANFMAN ANDREJ	1985	169.	KAVALIAUSKAS KAZYS	2000
123.	IBENSKIS JUOZAS	1980	170.	KAZLAUSKAITĖ TEOFILĖ	1985
124.	IBENSKIENĖ ONA	1980	171.	KAZLAUSKAS JUOZAS	1996
125.	INKRATAS JUOZAS	1985	172.	KAZLAUSKIENĖ EUGENIJA	1996
126.	IVANAUSKAS GINTAUTAS	1992	173.	KERPAUSKAS JUOZAS	1981
127.	IVANAUSKIENĖ ELENA	1984	174.	KERPAUSKIENĖ ADOLFINA	1981

175. KERYS POVILAS	1994	
176. KERIENĖ MANIA	1994	
177. KIBELAITĖ JUOZAPA	1997	
178. KILIKEVIČIUS PIJUS	1978	
179. KISLAUSKIENĖ-		
DAMBRAUSKAITĖ REGINA	1993	
180. KLEIBA ADOLFAS	1996	
181. KLIMAS PETRAS	1993	
182. KLIMIENĖ JADVYGA	1993	
183. KLIMAITĖ FELICIJA	1993	
184. KRIVIČIUS STANISLOVAS	1998	
185. KRULICKAS JONAS	1993	
186. KRULICKIENĖ VIKTORIJA	1993	
187. KRULICKAS VIKTORAS	1993	
188. KRUŠINSKAS VLADAS	1969	
189. KORSAKAS VITAS	1990	
190. KUDŽMA ANDRIUS	1993	
191. KUNCAITIS ANTANAS	1996	
192. KUPRAITIS ANTANAS	1980	
193. KUPRAITIS JUOZAS	1980	
194. KUPRAITIS JONAS	1980	
195. KUPRĖNAS KAZYS	1980	
196. KURPAUSKAS PRANAS	1981	
197. KURPAUSKIENĖ MARYTĖ	1981	
198. KUTORGA VIKTORAS	1982	
199. LABUL BRONISLAVA	2001	
200. LADYGIENĖ STEFANIJA	1992	
201. LANDSBERGIENĖ ONA	1995	
202. LASTIENĖ PETRONĖLĖ	2000	
203. LAŠIENĖ URŠULĖ	1997	
204. LEONAVIČIUS EDUARDAS	2000	
205. LEONAVIČIENĖ ONA	2000	
206. LEŠČINSKIENĖ MARIJA	1995	
207. LIKEVIČIUS VYTAUTAS	1996	
208. LIKEVIČIENĖ NATALIJA	1996	
209. LIUTKEVIČIUS IGNACIJUS	1983	
210. LIUTKEVIČIENĖ JANTINA	1983	
211. MACENAVIČIUS ANTANAS	1976	
212. MACENAVIČIENĖ MARIJA	1976	
213. MALADAUSKAS PETRAS	1979	
214. MALADAUSKIENĖ URŠULĖ	1979	
215. MALIŠAUSKAS HENRIKAS	1996	
216. MALIŠAUSKIENĖ MARIJA	1996	
217. MARGAITIS ANTANAS	1991	
218. MARGAITIENĖ LIONĖ	1991	
219. MARKEVIČIUS JUOZAS	1991	
220. MARKEVIČIUS JONAS	1991	
221. MARKEVIČIUS ROMAS	1991	
222. MARKEVIČIŪTĖ VALERIJA	1991	
223. MARKOVSKIS CHARITONAS	1992	
224. MARKOVSKAJA ALEKSANDRA	1992	

225. MARKOVSKIS IVANAS	1992	
226. MARKOVSKIS MITROFANAS	1992	
227. MARKOVSKAJA ANA	1992	
228. MARKOVSKAJA MAVRA	1992	
229. MARTINKUS VACLOVAS	1995	
230. MARTUL JUZEFA	1993	
231. MARTUL-BUDRIKIENĖ LIUCIJA	1993	
232. MASEVIČIUS JUSTINAS	1983	
233. MASEVIČIENĖ		
(first name unknown)	1983	
234. MATORA ANA	2001	
235. MATULEVIČ ONA	1991	
236. MATUZEVIČIUS ANTANAS	1981	
237. MATUZEVIČIENĖ ELENA	1981	
238. MATUZEVIČIŪTĖ ANTONINA	1981	
239. MAZURAITIS JONAS	1976	
240. MAZURAITIS ALFONSAS	1976	
241. MAZURAITIENĖ ONA	1976	
242. MAZURAITYTĖ SUZANA	1976	
243. MAZURAITIS ZENONAS	1976	
244. MAZURAITYTĖ MEFODIJA	1976	
245. MEŠKĖNIENĖ ANA	2001	
246. MICHAILOVAS ALEKSEJUS	1992	
247. MICHAILOVA ELIZAVETA	1992	
248. MIKALAUSKAS ANTANAS	1994	
249. MIKALAUSKIENĖ STASĖ	1994	
250. MIKLAŠEVIČIUS PETRAS	1996	
251. MIKLAŠEVIČIENĖ MARIJA	1996	
252. MIKULIČIUS PETRAS	1995	
253. MIKULIČIENĖ ONA	1995	
254. MINIOTAS LEONARTAS	1996	
255. MINIOTIENĖ ONA	1996	
256. MINKEVIČIENĖ KOTRYNA	1990	
257. MINKEVIČIUS SERGEJUS	1990	
258. MINIOTIENĖ ELZĖ	1982	
259. MITKA STANISLAVAS	1995	
260. MITKIENĖ LEOKADIJA	1995	
261. MOCKAITYTĖ ELENA	1996	
262. MORDOSAS BRONISLAVAS	1995	
263. MORDOSIENĖ MARIJONA	1995	
264. MORKŪNAS VACLOVAS	1995	
265. MORKŪNIENĖ BRONISLAVA	1995	
266. MORKŪNAS EDVARDAS	1995	
267. MORKŪNAS MEČISLOVAS	1995	
268. MORKŪNAITĖ ČESLAVA	1995	
269. MOŠINSKIS HALINA	1982	
270. MOZURIŪNIENĖ-		
BINKYTĖ LILIJANA	1988	
271. MURALIENĖ JADVYGA	1997	
272. NACEVIČIŪTĖ-		
BINKYTĖ IRENA	1988	

273. NAGYS-VAITKŪNAITĖ BIRUTĖ 1994
274. NAGINĖ VYTAUTAS 2000
275. NAGINIENĖ STASĖ 2000
276. NAVICKIENĖ ONA 2000
277. NAVICKAITĖ STASĖ 2000
278. NAVIENĖ STASĖ 1997
279. NAVYS (first name unknown) 1997
280. NORVAIŠAITĖ ALDONA 2002
281. NORVAIŠAITIENĖ URŠULĖ 2002
282. NORVAIŠAITIS JUOZAS 2002
283. OLŠVANG-OSOVSKY JUZEFA 1974
284. PAJEDAITĖ BRONĖ 2001
285. PALKAUSKAS KAZYS 1996
286. PALKAUSKIENĖ MARYTĖ 1996
287. PALKAUSKAS VLADAS 1996
288. PAŠKEVIČ MARIJA 2000
289. PAŠKEVIČ-
     TOMAŠEVSKAJA ELŽBIETA 2000
290. PAŠKOVSKIS VACLAVAS 1998
291. PAŠKOVSKAJA ONA 1998
292. PAUKŠTYS BRONIUS 1977
293. PAUKŠTYS JUOZAS 1977
294. PAULAUSKIENĖ BRONISLAVA 1982
295. PAULAVIČIUS JONAS 1983
296. PAULAVIČIENĖ ANTONINA 1983
297. PAULAVIČIUS KĘSTUTIS 1983
298. PAULAVIČIŪTĖ DANUTĖ 1983
299. PEKARSKIS VIKTORAS 2000
300. PEKARSKIENĖ EUGENIJA 2000
301. PEKARSKYTĖ NEONILA 2000
302. PETKEVIČIENĖ JULIJA 2002
303. PETKEVIČIUS TADAS 2002
304. PETRAUSKAS KIPRAS 2000
305. PETRAUSKIENĖ ELENA 2000
306. PETRAUSKIENĖ LIDIJA 1994
307. PETRULAITIENĖ VERONIKA 1979
308. PETRULIS JUOZAS 1980
309. PETRIK ANTONINA 1990
310. PIKČIŪNAS ANTANAS 1995
311. PLOKŠTO VLADISLAV 1994
312. PLOKŠTO URŠULĖ 1994
313. POCIENĖ STEFA 1981
314. POŠKA ANTANAS 2001
315. POŽĖLA VLADAS 1980
316. PROKOPOVIČ ZOFIJA 2001
317. PŪKAITĖ GĖNĖ 1967
318. PUPŠYTĖ-
     LAURINAITIENĖ GĖNĖ 1997
319. RAČINSKAS KAZIMIERAS 2000
320. RADAVIČIUS DANIELIUS 1997
321. RADAVIČIENĖ JUZEFA 1997

322. RADLINSKAS JONAS 2001
323. RADLINSKIENĖ FELICIJA 2001
324. RAGAIŠIENĖ ALEKSANDRA 1998
325. RAGAUSKAS ANTANAS 1991
326. RAGAUSKIENĖ ONA 1991
327. RAKEVIČIUS ČESLOVAS 1993
328. RAKEVIČIUS JUOZAS 1993
329. RAKEVIČIUS JAROSLAVAS 1976
330. RAKEVIČIUS ZENONAS 1994
331. RAKEVIČIUS ALGIMANTAS 1994
332. RAMANAUSKAS JUOZAS 1983
333. RAMANAUSKIENĖ SOFIJA 1983
334. RAUBA GENRIK 1983
335. RAUBA ADOLFINA 1983
336. RAUBA VLADISLAV 1983
337. RAUBA JOHANA 1983
338. REKAŠIUS VINCAS 1994
339. REKAŠIENĖ STANISLAVA 1994
340. RENČINAUSKIENĖ NATALIJA 1995
341. RIAUKAITĖ ALFONSA 2002
342. RIAUKIENĖ JUSTINA 2002
343. RINKEVIČIUS VYTAUTAS 1976
344. RINKEVIČIENĖ ELĖ 1976
345. RINKEVIČ JAN 1983
346. RINKEVIČ JADVYGA 1983
347. RIMAVIČIENĖ JUZEFA 1998
348. RUDZEVIČIŪTĖ-
     AUKŠTAKIENĖ PETRUTĖ 1996
349. RUSTEIKAITĖ MARIJA 1996
350. RUTKAUSKAS JUOZAS 1996
351. RUZGYS JONAS 1979
352. RUZGIENĖ STASĖ 1979
353. SALENEKAS JUOZAS 2001
354. SALENEKIENĖ MATILDA 2001
355. SAMBORAS ANTANAS 1980
356. SAMBORIENĖ VANDA 1980
357. SANKIENĖ ZOFIJA 1994
358. SANKUTĖ TERESA 1994
359. SANKUTĖ JANINA 1994
360. SARPALIS VLADAS 1978
361. SARPALIENĖ ANELĖ 1978
362. SAUNORIS JONAS 1994
363. SAVICKIENĖ KASTULĖ 1978
364. SAVICKAS VINCAS 1978
365. SAVICKIENĖ MARIJA 1982
366. SAVICKAS JONAS 1982
367. SIMOKAITIS JUOZAS 1992
368. SIMOKAITIENĖ ZOSĖ 1992
369. SKAČKAUSKAITĖ-
     VAIČIŪNIENĖ ANTONINA 1993
370. SKIRVAINYTĖ ANELĖ 1980

371. SONDECKIS JACKUS 1996
372. SONGAILA ALFONSAS 1992
373. SINKEVIČ HELENA 2001
374. STAKAUSKAS JUOZAS 1974
375. STANEVIČIUS VINCAS 1993
376. STANEVIČIENĖ JULIJA 1993
377. STANEVIČIŪTĖ BIRUTĖ 1993
378. STANEVIČIUS VYTAUTAS 1993
379. STANILKO JULIJA 1995
380. STANKEVIČIENĖ URŠULĖ 1978
381. STANKEVIČ JAN 1983
382. STANKEVIČ
    (first name unknown) 1983
383. STANKEVIČ VERONIKA 1995
384. STASIŪNAITIS JUOZAS 1995
385. STASKEVIČIENĖ PAULINA 1994
386. STASKEVIČIUS JUOZAS 1994
387. STASKEVIČIŪTĖ ZOSĖ 1994
388. STASKEVIČIŪTĖ ANICETA 1994
389. STATAUSKAS JONAS 1996
390. STATAUSKIENĖ STASĖ 1996
391. STATKEVIČIŪTĖ ELENA 1984
392. STEPONAVIČIUS JONAS 1995
393. STEPONAVIČIENĖ
    MICHALINA 1995
394. STRAUPIS JUOZAS 1981
395. STRAUPIENĖ BRONĖ 1981
396. STRIMAITIS JUOZAS 1992
397. STRIMAITIENĖ ONA 1992
398. STRIMAITIS STASYS 1994
399. STRIMAITIENĖ VERONIKA 1994
400. STRIMAITYTĖ MILDA 1994
401. STULPINAS BOLESLOVAS 1993
402. STULPINIENĖ ONA 1993
403. SVEITYS PRANAS 1982
404. SVIDERSKIS ALFONSAS 1980
405. SVIDERSKIS STASYS 1997
406. ŠALAVĖJIENĖ IEVA 2000
407. ŠATŪNAS STASYS 2000
408. ŠATŪNIENĖ ONA 2000
409. ŠAUDVYTIS PRANAS 2000
410. ŠAUDVYTIENĖ GENOVAITĖ 2000
411. ŠIMAITĖ ONA 1966
412. ŠIMELIS MYKOLAS 1983
413. ŠIMELIENĖ JADVYGA 1983
414. ŠLEŽEVIČIUS VLADAS 1994
415. ŠLEŽEVIČIENĖ URŠULĖ 1994
416. ŠNEIDERIS JUOZAS 1979
417. ŠNEIDERIENĖ ANTONINA 1979
418. TALAČKA MYKOLAS 1994
419. TALAČKA JUOZAPAS 1994

420. TALAČKA SIMONAS 1994
421. TALAČKIENĖ ONA 1994
422. TALLAT-KELPŠIENĖ AGOTA 1997
423. TALLAT-KELPŠA
    STANISLOVAS 1997
424. TALLAT-KELPŠIENĖ
    ANTANINA 1997
425. TALAT-KELPŠA JURGIS 1997
426. TAMAŠAUSKAS KAZYS 2001
427. TAMAŠAUSKIENĖ JADVYGA 2001
428. TARAPIENĖ ANELĖ 1983
429. TARAPAS STASYS 1983
430. TARAPAITĖ ELENA 1983
431. TARAPAITĖ MONIKA 1983
432. TARVAINYTĖ ROZALIJA 1996
433. TEIŠERSKIS JONAS 2000
434. TENIUKAS JUOZAS 2001
435. TENIUKIENĖ ONA 2001
436. TENIUKAS PETRAS 2001
437. TENIUKAS JUOZAS 2000
438. TENIUKIENĖ VALERIJA 2000
439. TOLIUŠIS DOMINYKAS 1996
440. TOLIUŠIENĖ PETRUTĖ 1996
441. TČARKOVSKIS JUZEFAS 1983
442. TČARKOVSKAJA
    (first name unknown) 1983
443. TRINKŪNAS JUOZAS 2000
444. TRINKŪNIENĖ ELENA 2000
445. TVERJONAITĖ ROZALIJA 1998
446. UBOREVIČ ELENA 1995
447. URBANOVIČ MARIJA 2002
448. URBANOVIČ VIKENTIJUS 2002
449. URBONAS ANDRIUS 1997
450. URBONIENĖ MARIJA 1997
451. URBONAITĖ ONA 1997
452. URBONAS JUOZAS 1997
453. UŽEMECKAS ANTANAS 1996
454. UŽEMECKIENĖ VERONIKA 1996
455. VAICEKAUSKAS JONAS 1995
456. VAICEKAUSKIENĖ
    VLADISLAVA 1995
457. VAICEKAUSKAITĖ JANĖ 1995
458. VAINAUSKAS ALEKSANDRAS 1995
459. VAINAUSKIENĖ ONA 1995
460. VAIŠNORAS ADOLFAS 1990
461. VAIŠNORIENĖ BRONĖ 1990
462. VALIONIS VINCAS 1996
463. VALIONIENĖ TEOFILĖ 1996
464. VARČIKAS VLADAS 1988
465. VASILIAUSKAS VLADAS 1997
466. VASILIAUSKAITĖ STASĖ 1997

467. VASILIAUSKAITĖ VERONIKA 1997
468. VASILIAUSKAS IGNAS 2000
469. VASILIAUSKIENĖ MARIJA 2000
470. VASILJEVA USTINJA 2000
471. VENCLAUSKIENĖ
STANISLAVA 1995
472. VENCLAUSKAITĖ DANUTĖ 1995
473. VENCLAUSKAITĖ GRAŽBYLĖ 1995
474. VYŠNIAUSKAS STANISLOVAS 1995
475. VYŠNIAUSKIENĖ ROŽĖ 1995
476. VITKAUSKIENĖ JULIJA 1966
477. VITKAUSKAS ARĖJAS 1966
478. VITKENCAS KAZYS 1997
479. VITKENCIENĖ EMILIJA 1997
480. VOJEVODSKIJ VLADISLAV 2000
481. VOJEVODSKA MICHALINA 2000
482. VOKIETAITIS ANTANAS 2001
483. VOKIETAITIENĖ ONA 2001
484. VOKIETAITYTĖ-
PAŠKEVIČIENĖ STANISLAVA 2001
485. VORONECKIJ VIKTOR 2001
486. ZADARNOVSKIJ STEFAN 1964

487. ZARONAS JONAS 1982
488. ZASIMAUSKAS STASYS 1992
489. ZASIMAUSKIENĖ PETRUTA 1992
490. ZELBA JONAS 1997
491. ZELBIENĖ ALEKSANDRA 1997
492. ZUBOVAS VLADYS 1991
493. ZUBOVIENĖ DANUTĖ 1991
494. ŽEMAITAITIENĖ NATALIJA 1979
495. ŽEMAITAITIS PETRAS 1979
496. ŽEMAITIS VLADAS 1974
497. ŽEMECKIENĖ ANTANINA 1996
498. ŽILĖNAS KAZIMIERAS 2000
499. ŽILĖNIENĖ APOLONIJA 2000
500. ŽILEVIČIUS ADOMAS 1994
501. ŽILEVIČIUS STASYS 1994
502. ŽILEVIČIUS JONAS 1995
503. ŽILEVIČIENĖ ONA 1995
504. ŽIUŽNYS JERONIMAS 1994
505. ŽIUŽNIENĖ ADELĖ 1994
506. ŽUKAUSKAS STASYS 1991
507. ŽVIRONAITĖ VERONIKA 2000
508. ŽVANSKA ELENA-HELENA 1993

People Awarded the Cross for Saving People under Threat of Death*

SURNAME, FIRST NAME	YEAR OF AWARD
1. ADOMAVIČIENĖ MARIJA	2001
2. ADOMAVIČIUS JONAS	2001
3. ADOMAVIČIŪTĖ-POVILAITIENĖ LIUDMILA	2001
4. ANDRAITIS ANTANAS	1993
5. ANDRIŪNIENĖ STEFANIJA	2000
6. ANDRIUŠKEVIČIENĖ JOANA	2001
7. ANDRIUŠKEVIČIUS PETRAS	2001
8. ANDRIUŠKEVIČIŪTĖ-ŽEMAITIENĖ EUGENIJA	2001
9. ALAUNIENĖ ONA	1999
10. ALEKNAVIČIENĖ SOFIJA	2001
11. ALEKNAVIČIŪTĖ-MILIENĖ BRONĖ	2001
12. ALEKSANDRAVIČIENĖ PAULINA	2000
13. ANDRIUŠKA ALEKSAS	1999
14. ANTANAVIČIUS POVILAS	1999
15. ANTONOVIČ JADVYGA	2001
16. ANTONOVIČ VINCENTAS	2001
17. ANTONOVIČ-BAUER LIUCINA	2001
18. ARLAUSKAS KAZYS	1999
19. ARLAUSKIENĖ VERONIKA	1999
20. AUDĖJIENĖ ONA	2000
21. AUDĖJUS JUOZAS	2000
22. AUDĖJUTĖ-KRATULIS ALDONA ONA	2000
23. BABARSKIS ALFONSAS	1999
24. BABARSKIENĖ JADVYGA	1999
25. BAJERČIUS KONSTANTINAS	1998
26. BAJORINAS PRANAS	2000
27. BAJORINIENĖ ANTANINA	2000
28. BAKŠYS FELIKSAS	1992
29. BALČIŪNAS ADOMAS	1999
30. BALČIKONIENĖ AGOTA	1995
31. BALČIŪNIENĖ ANELĖ	1999
32. BALKIENĖ NINA	2000
33. BALIUKEVIČ ZOFIJA	1998
34. BANAITYTĖ-PALUCKIENĖ LIUDOVIKA	2000
35. BARČIENĖ MARIJONA	1997
36. BARTKEVIČIENĖ STASĖ	2000
37. BARTKEVIČIUS JUOZAS	2000
38. BARTNIKAITĖ ONA	2000
39. BAUBLIENĖ JADVYGA	1995
40. BAUŽIENĖ JADVYGA	1995
41. BEILES JUDEL OŠER	2001
42. BELECKIENĖ MORTA	2001
43. BELEROVIČIENĖ ŠEINA	1993
44. BERČIŪNAS JURGIS	1998
45. BERNOTAITĖ JULIJA	1999
46. BERŽINSKAS ANTANAS	2000
47. BERŽINSKIENĖ VIKTORIJA	2000
48. BINKIENĖ SOFIJA	1993
49. BIŽIENĖ JANINA	2000
50. BIŽYS JUOZAS	2000
51. BORUTA KAZYS	1997
52. BLAŽAITIS ANTANAS	1995
53. BRAZAUSKIENĖ STASĖ	1995
54. BRAZIENĖ ADELĖ	1998
55. BRAZIENĖ JADVYGA	1999
56. BRAŽĖNAS MINDAUGAS	2001
57. BRAŽĖNIENĖ KONSTANCIJA	2000
58. BUKAUSKIENĖ STEFANIJA	1997
59. BUKONTAS JERONIMAS	1992
60. BUTKEVIČIENĖ MARIJA	2001
61. CHLOPINAITĖ ELENA	2000
62. ČIŽINAUSKIENĖ ONA	1994
63. ČIURLIONIENĖ SOFIJA	1999
64. DAGILIENĖ MARIJA	1993
65. DAGILIS ANTANAS	1993
66. DAILIDAVIČIENĖ URŠULĖ	1999
67. DAILIDAVIČIUS ALGIMANTAS	2001
68. DAILIDAVIČIUS VINCAS	1999
69. DALUNGAUSKIENĖ BRONĖ	1999
70. DAVIDONIS EUGENIJUS	1999
71. DAUGIRDIENĖ ZOFIJA	1993

---

* Figures (as of 1 March 2002) provided by Viktorija Sakaitė.

Index of Biographical Names

Photographs from Sofija and Domas Jasaitis' family,
Saulius Sondeckis' and Liudvikas Šmulkštys' personal archives
and Domas Jasaitis' archives

Published by GARNELIS, Klaipėdos g. 6, 2600 Vilnius, Lithuania.
Printed by AB VILSPA, Viršuliškių skg. 80, 2600 Vilnius, Lithuania.